Feminism, Bakhtin, and the Dialogic

SUNY Series in Feminist Criticism and Theory
Michelle A. Massé, Editor

Feminism, Bakhtin, and the Dialogic

Edited by
Dale M. Bauer
and
Susan Jaret McKinstry

State University of New York Press

Published by
State University of New York Press, Albany

© 1991 State University of New York

For information, address State University of New York
Press, State University Plaza, Albany, N.Y. 12246

Production by Diane Ganeles
Marketing by Fran Keneston

Library of Congress Cataloging-in-Publication Data

Feminism, Bakhtin, and the dialogic/edited by Dale M. Bauer
  and Susan Jaret McKinstry.
      p.   cm. — (SUNY series in feminist criticism and theory)
    Includes bibliographical references and index.
    ISBN 0-7914-0769-1 (acid-free). — ISBN 0-7914-0770-5 (pbk. : acid
-free)
    1. Feminist literary criticism. 2. Bakhtin, M. M. (Mikhail
Mikhailovich), 1895 – 1975. 3. Women in literature. 4. English
fiction — 20th century — History and criticism. 5. American
fiction — 20th century — History and criticism. I. Bauer, Dale M.,
1956 –   II. McKinstry, S. Jaret (Susan Jaret), 1953 –
III. Series.
PN98.W64F36   1991
820.9′9287 — dc20

                                                                90-47263
                                                                CIP

10   9   8   7   6   5   4   3   2   1

Contents

Introduction
Dale M. Bauer and Susan Jaret McKinstry   1

1. The Dilemmas of a Feminine Dialogic
   Diane Price Herndl   7

2. Voices from the Margin: Bag Ladies and Others
   Suzanne Kehde   25

3. Prolegomenon for an Ecofeminist Dialogics
   Patrick D. Murphy   39

4. Irigarayan Dialogism: Play and Powerplay
   Gail M. Schwab   57

5. Critical Imperialism and Renaissance Drama:
   The Case of *The Roaring Girl*
   Deborah Jacobs   73

6. Style and Power
   Josephine Donovan   85

7. Radical Writing
   Peter Hitchcock   95

8. A Quote of Many Colors: Women and Masquerade in
   Donald Barthelme's Postmodern Parody Novels
   Jaye Berman   123

9. "Witness [to] the Suffering of Women": Poverty and Sexual Transgression in Meridel Le Sueur's *Women on the Breadlines*
    Susan Sipple   135

10. The Central Nervous System of America: The Writer As/In the Crowd of Joyce Carol Oates's *Wonderland*
    Brenda O. Daly   155

11. Language and Gender In Transit: Feminist Extensions of Bakhtin
    Sheryl Stevenson   181

12. Subject, Voice, and Women in Some Contemporary Black American Women's Writing
    Mary O'Connor   199

13. Problems of Gordimer's Poetics: Dialogue in *Burger's Daughter*
    Louise Yelin   219

Afterword
    Patricia Yaeger   239

Contributors   247

Index   251

Introduction

Dale M. Bauer and Susan Jaret McKinstry

On December 6, 1989, Marc Lepine shot fourteen women at the Ecole Polytechnique of the University of Montreal, accusing his victims of being "feminists." Refused admission into the Ecole Polytechnique, he sought to destroy the women admitted into the competitive engineering school. Taking individuality and rationalization to its extreme, Lepine murdered those "feminists" who represented for him a challenge to masculine control. The gender polarity that Lepine constructed destroyed him; he committed suicide after his rampage because he could not imagine recognition of the "other" — women, feminists — in his fantasy of autonomy and power.

Lepine's anti-feminism took the most radical form possible — assassination — but we would argue that a new and violent backlash against feminism takes place in linguistic as well as psychotic forms. This anti-feminist backlash is addressed in the following chapters, which deal with the various stances feminist critics take in arguing for *and* with a feminist dialogics. No ahistorical or singular method, feminist dialogics challenges the assumption in contemporary culture of a monolithic or univocal feminism.

Moreover, feminist dialogics — as the authors conceive of it here — overcomes the public-private split which has become part of the rationalization of daily life. As Jessica Benjamin argues, "The public world is conceived as a place in which direct recognition and care for others' needs is impossible — and this is tolerable as long as the private world 'cooperates'" (Bonds of Love 197). The public sphere becomes alienated, atomized; the private sphere, a compensatory, but inadequate sphere. Feminists turn to Bakhtin's notion of the word and dialogue in order to break down this separation of public rationality and private intersubjectivity. In using Bakhtin's theories to address this split, feminist critics advocate taking on rhetorical or dialogic authority

1

(see Bizzell, Spivak) that would reinvent a shared ethics within intersecting public and private worlds. Although we live in the midst of critical skepticism, where our focus on difference has dominated discussion, we might turn now to feminist dialogism to make a case for egalitarian values, values which might heal a rationalized world which buttresses male domination. As Benjamin has it, "the underlying structure of male domination is so depersonalized and has so little, apparently, to do with individual men" (215). Feminist dialogics, thus, works to uncover not just masculine bias but a more subtle and seemingly neutral rationality, an impersonality that pervades all social life, depriving both males and females of recognition from each other. The loss of recognition — erroneously blamed on feminists leaving the private sphere and entering the public space of the engineering school — led Marc Lepine to murder. The larger issue is the failure of a masculinized or rationalized public language (what Bakhtin would call the authoritative voice) that is split off in cultural representations from the private voice (Bakhtin's internally persuasive language). A feminist dialogics would bring these two languages together in dialogue.

The conjunction of feminist and Bakhtinian theory leads us to an investigation of the ways in which dominant culture has incorporated feminism as a threat. That perception of threat speaks to the authority feminism has claimed in critical and popular culture. The violent example of the killer in Montreal is not merely a sensational or random event. Rather, we can draw from it to see how feminism has been incorporated in contemporary discourse — from *Die Hard* to Supreme Court appointments. The chapters in this book show how to resist that cooptation and insist on an empowerment of feminist voices. Violence is not the only response to feminism, but its intensity testifies to the fear that feminism might indeed change the status quo, as various feminisms already have.

The following chapters show the process by which feminism has changed the way we envision the world and point to ways in which changes might still occur. We find that feminist dialogics takes into account both recent critical work on standpoint theory and dialogic criticism. Standpoint theory argues that we must acknowledge our positionality — our identity politics — as the beginning of critical agency and action. Dialogism, Bakhtin's theory about encountering otherness through the potential of dialogue, is central to feminist practice because it invites new possibilities for activism and change. Dialogism — like standpoint theory — has as its base the understanding that people's responses are conditional, human circumstances are irreducible and contingent. Dialogic consciousness or standpoint depends neither on essentialism nor truth, but on context and condition. A feminist dialogics is not just agonistic or oppositional; it also suggests an identity in dialectic response, always open and ongoing.

Why a feminist dialogics? Why now? One of the questions plaguing feminism has been the interrelation of theory and practice, especially in the light of violent attacks and critical offenses. And in arguing for a feminist dialogics, we have been careful to address this problem in order to work toward a theoretical practice and a practical theory that allow feminists to intervene in the transmission of the status quo. The models advocated here allow us to consider agency and resistance in the process of cultural formation and critique. These chapters hold the view that resistance is determined by positionality and that the factors of race, class, and gender affect the form resistance takes in language. Resistance is not always voiced in authoritative or public ways; what is crucial to a feminist dialogics is the idea that resistance can begin as private when women negotiate, manipulate, and often subvert systems of domination they encounter. Both private and public discourses are means of cultural resistance and intervention. As many of the chapters in this collection show, speech is not always a sign of power, or silence a sign of weakness. Rather, the contexts of silence and speech determine gendered relations. Resistance to dominant ideologies can potentially lead us to rethink human agency and lived experience.

This book is devoted to a pedagogical as well as a political imperative. In seeing the connection between the material conditions in which feminist literary critics work and the subjects they study (gendered objects and subjects themselves), feminist dialogicians make a case for a critical subjectivity that shows genders, classes, and races in dialogue rather than in opposition. But even in opposition, the authors of these chapters do not see dialogue as shut off or shut down, but in process, in flux. That is, the feminist dialogic analysis of these works all point to a way of reading that recognizes dialogue's political and social force.

Feminism, Bakhtin, and the Dialogic takes as its starting point a critical theory and practice that show the dialogic authority of gendered voices. For feminists, Bakhtin's theories of the social nature of the utterance — of both the inner and outer words — provide a critical language that allows us to pinpoint and foreground the moments when the patriarchal work and the persuasive resistance to it come into conflict. By highlighting these contradictions, a feminist dialogics produces occasions for the disruption and critique of dominant and oppressive ideologies. The conflict of discourses in a novel, the inevitable polyvocality of a genre that reproduces language as a web of communications between narrator and narratee, speaker and listener, character and character, and even (implied) author and (implied) reader, does reveal the dominant discourse. For example, we expect the "inevitable" happy ending of marriage in nineteenth-century fiction as the voice of that discourse. At the same time, however, the novel's polyvocality can indicate potential resistances to oppressive conventions in interpretive or discourse communities — such as an individual character's response to that social dictate, or a disapproving narrative tone.

A feminist dialogics is, above all, an example of the cultural resistance that Teresa de Lauretis argues is a necessary strategy for feminist political practice. For the object is not, ultimately, to produce a feminist monologic voice, a dominant voice that is a reversal of the patriarchal voice (even if such a project were conceivable), but to create a feminist dialogics that recognizes power and discourse as indivisible, monologism as a model of ideological dominance, and narrative as inherently multivocal, as a form of cultural resistance that celebrates the dialogic voice that speaks with many tongues, which incorporates multiple voices of the cultural web.

This collection of thirteen chapters on Bakhtin and feminism combines theoretical definition with the praxis of a feminist dialogics. The first four chapters explore the conjunctions of feminist theory, Bakhtin's notion of dialogism, and the social dimensions of language, providing theoretical models for the practical criticism to follow. Diane Price Herndl's argument for a feminine dialogic poses the question, "Does the novel use a feminine language, or is the feminine a novelized language?" Price Herndl sets up a dialogue between Bakhtin's theory of novelistic discourse and feminist criticism's own dialogic, suggesting that the intersection of feminism and Bakhtin reveals the politics of both literary history and academic discourse. Taking up Price Herndl's call, Suzanne Kehde's and Patrick Murphy's works argue for the social and political importance of uniting Bakhtin and feminism. Kehde sees Bakhtin's theory of parody as a way to "empower the feminist critic at least to listen to marginalized voices," and she applies her theory to Henry James, arguing that "the context of parody may free submerged voices" in "novels where we may suspect the parodic effect is not part of the authorial intention." In the same vein, Patrick Murphy argues that "pluralistic humanism has run its course," and he responds by combining "ecology and feministics" to "break dialogics out of the anthropocentrism in which Bakhtin performs it." He claims that "ecofeminist dialogics," "a liveable critical theory" that emphasizes recognition of the "other," the non-human subject, can reform our self-centered conceptions of nature and ecology. Gail Schwab's essay disputes the common critique of Luce Irigaray's theories — particularly her theory of *l'ecriture feminine* — as "apolitical and essentialist." Arguing for the "dynamic political potential of dialogism," Schwab details the connection between Irigaray's politics, her dialectic style, and feminist dialogism, and concludes that "no other feminist writer is so profoundly dialogic."

The next chapters explore a range of English and American texts to demonstrate the intersection of feminism, Bakhtin, and literary history. Deborah Jacobs' essay on Dekker and Middleton's *The Roaring Girl* demonstrates how the ahistorical, "novelized" reading of pre-novelistic texts transposes "historically specific values onto representations of the pre-bourgeois subject," thus "mass-reproducing the transhistorical thematizing of the world" that limits texts — and voices — to essentialist, gendered meanings. Josephine Donovan defines literary style as "resistance to subordination," claiming that "paratactic, non-subordinating sensitivity" in the style of early women writers like Margaret Cavendish illustrated the difference between authoritative or public discourse and private, internally persuasive language without privileging either voice, and thus contributed to the creation of the novel as a "dialogic, counterhegemonic" genre. Peter Hitchcock defines dialogism as "nothing if not the concretization of text and context," arguing that "without a specific socio-historical context," dialogism "simply has no meaning." He studies Pat Barker's radical dialogism in order to explain her attack on the economic failure in Britain and its effects on working women's lives, thereby linking fictional and political praxis. Jaye Berman cites the active role of women in postmodern comedy and parody as a sign of the contemporary failure of authority. She claims that the female characters in Donald Barthelme's parodic fiction engage in carnivalesque dialogism and masquerade as a means of critiquing the dominant, patriarchal culture through speech, through "polylogues" that are neither patriarchal monologues nor feminist discourse. Susan Sipple's essay combines historical research on pre-Depression female hobos and Depression-era female transients, with a focus on Meridel Le Sueur's social fictions about Depression-era female transients whose "bodies stand as signs of the failure of capitalism and patriarchal control." Their "grotesque" behavior subverts the cultural expectations of the female — and maternal — body. Brenda Daly analyzes Joyce Carol Oates's dialogic exploration of the "social aspects of homeostasis" through the male voice in *Wonderland,* a novel with two versions: the first ends with monologic triumph, while the revised edition "replaces univocal closure with the ambivalence of dialogue." Sheryl Stevenson extends Bakhtin's theories of language as "the constituting element of a radically social psyche" into modernist fiction and feminist issues. Brigid Brophy's novel *In Transit*, according to Stevenson, questions the monologic construction of gender in a language that is always "in transit," resulting in "linguistic leprosy" and "gender-amnesia."

The last two chapters — by Mary O'Connor on black women writers and Louise Yelin on Nadine Gordimer and apartheid — are the most explicitly political, arguing (as Schwab does) for the feminist dialogic as the most radical political feminist strategy today. O'Connor asks how we can define female solidarity and female self-definition in a culture that silences both, using Bakhtin's model of the self as an intersection of conflicting voices to explain the multivocal empowering of black women through "dialogized evaluation" in works by Alice Walker, Ntozake Shange and Gloria Naylor. Yelin, focusing on the intersection of monologism and dialogism, European "center" and colonial "margins," illustrates how Nadine Gordimer's *Burger's Daughter* allows us to revise Bakhtinian concepts to include race and gender as central elements of the social heteroglossia, and thus enable the "dismantling of apartheid" through "vocal and collective opposition."

Patricia Yaeger's "Afterword" returns the collection to its opening, to the question of the political implications of feminist speech, as she celebrates the "noise and nuisance of the dialogic." Discussing the place of a transsexual in definitions of "woman," and the relation of disabled (differently-abled) women and conventional romantic fiction that demands an idealized sexual body, Yaegar recognizes the necessary dialogue among feminists. Feminist dialogics becomes a way of recognizing competing voices without making any single voice normative. Resisting and subverting the monologic speech that produces silence, these chapters celebrate the personal and social power of feminist dialogics.

Works Cited

Benjamin, Jessica. *The Bonds of Love*. New York: Pantheon, 1988.

Bizzell, Patricia. "Beyond Anti-Foundationalism to Rhetorical Authority: Problems Defining 'Cultural Literacy'" in *College English* 52, 6 (October 1990): 661 – 675.

Spivak, Gayatri. *In Other Worlds*. New York: Methuen, 1988.

1

The Dilemmas of a Feminine Dialogic

Diane Price Herndl

"Novelistic" discourse, as defined by Bakhtin, and "feminine language," as elaborated by many French and American feminist theorists, often seem like very similar uses of language, despite the fact that the novelistic language Bakhtin described has nothing to do with either women or the feminine, and feminine language is not necessarily tied to the novel. Bakhtin's theory of dialogism seems quite similar to what feminist critics describe as the "feminine language" of women's writing. For this reason the relationship between the "dialogic" and that non-patriarchal, feminine logic that some feminist theorists find in women's novels needs to be examined, as does the relation between "novelistic discourse" and "feminine language." A dialogue between Bakhtin and feminist critics may help to illuminate the relationship between dia-logic and feminine logic. Such a dialogue is, true to most of the dialogue that Bakhtin describes, important to the extent that it is political and raises questions of power by asking whose voice is dominant in "feminine language": woman's "true" voice or a voice she has learned from the novel?[1]

In "Freedom of Interpretation: Bakhtin and the Challenge of Feminist Criticism," Wayne Booth claims that if Bakhtin had lived today, he would have come to accept feminist criticism. But the fact remains that Bakhtin, like almost all literary critics in the first half of this century, did not include women — as authors or speakers — in his discussion of literature. Even though he covers the "developments in the European novel" from its beginnings through the end of the Victorian period, the index to *The Dialogic Imagination* lists the names of only three women authors (Ann Radcliffe, Mme. de Lafayette, and Mme. de Scudery), all of whom get only parenthetical references in the text. He did not consider Fanny Burney, Jane Austen, the Brontë

7

sisters, George Eliot or George Sand even though he does mention
Fielding, Stern, Dickens, Thackeray, Balzac, Flaubert, and even Tobias
Smollett. Such exclusions seem too systematic to be overlooked or easily
excused; as early as the First World War, most critics allowed at least
"two and one half women" (as Terry Eagleton puts it) into the canon
of British literature. One, then, is likely to wonder why Bakhtin, the
revolutionary thinker, was so conservative in his evaluation of the novel's development. Setting aside any thoughts that women writers did
not merit his attention, one is led to ask whether women writers were excluded because they did not fit his pattern. Or did they fit it too well?

Like Bakhtin's theory of novelistic discourse, theories of feminine
language describe a multivoiced or polyphonic resistance to hierarchies and laughter at authority. Furthermore, in the hierarchies Bakhtin mentions, the novel always takes the woman's structural place as the
excluded other: masculine/feminine, epic/novel, poetry/novel. If both
Bakhtin and feminism are right (and for the moment, at least, I must
beg this question), then feminine and novelistic discourses must use
the same kind of language. So the question becomes: Is the novel a
feminine genre, or is woman's language novelized? Does the novel use
a feminine language, or is the feminine a novelized language? The
answers to these questions make a great deal of difference in our understanding of literary history and feminism.

This chapter is itself an exercise in dialogism, presenting first an
overview of the points at which Bakhtin and feminist criticism share
similar ideas and then putting these similarities to the test. Rather than
simply asserting that the two theories support one another, this chapter questions whether that seeming agreement does not actually undercut both. Only in the dialogue between the two can we find a useful,
productive agreement.

In *The Dialogic Imagination,* Mikhail Bakhtin sets out the funda-
mentals of his theory of novelistic discourse. Because of the novel's
position as an "unofficial" genre when compared to the epic or to poetry, Bakhtin holds that theories of "poetics" are inappropriate for discussing the language of the novel because it "does not fit within the
frame provided by the concept of poetic discourse" (269). The novel,
he claims, resists the authority of official genres. The epic and poetry
are "defined" genres which abide by rules; they are hierarchical, ahistorical, and canonical. "Poetics," whether Aristotelian, Augustinian, or
philosophical, "serve one and the same project of centralizing and unifying the European languages" (271). As David Carroll has pointed
out, Bakhtin's challenge to "poetics" is directed at "poetic ideology"

rather than the "practice of poetry," because the study of poetics "consists in the idealization of literary or poetic language" and therefore pays homage to authority and ideology by creating a "sacralized" language (78). The novel resists such hierarchies, authority, and "sacralization" because it is an unstable, undefinable, historical genre; it "is associated with the eternally living element of unofficial language and unofficial thought (holiday forms, familiar speech, profanation)" (20).

This association with the unofficial and resistance to authority means that the novel is able to participate in the "carnival" of laughter. This "ambivalent laughter" is dialogic because it is "at the same time cheerful and annihilating" (21). It is both festive and mocking; it is directed at everyone — those in power and those subjected to it. Bakhtin calls it *carnival* laughter because it is opposed to the "official." In *Rabelais and His World,* he explains that the carnival "celebrated temporary liberation from the prevailing truth and from the established order; it marked the suspension of all hierarchical rank, privileges, norms and prohibitions ... the feast of becoming, change" (10). The novel, for Bakhtin, is the extension into our age of this festival.

The novel is able to resist hierarchy and achieve carnival laughter because of its "double-voicedness," its "dialogism." Ordinary language, Bakhtin argues, is always used in context; it always expects an answer. Meaning is created not through a single voice, but in the interaction of voices — that is, in dialogue. "Discourse lives, as it were, on the boundary between its own context and another, alien, context" (284).

The novel, because it records ordinary speech (or at least attempts to do so), also participates in the interaction of voices. This may be done through many means, but as long as there is conflict in the novel between characters' voices or between the narrator's voice and the characters', there will be "heteroglossia," multiple voices expressing multiple ideologies from different strata of language-in-use. This always leaves the novel speaking more than one language.

Such heteroglossia occurs in official discourse, which is closed and sanctioned, like rhetorical discourse, but "remaining as it does within the boundaries of a single language system[,] it is not fertilized by a deep-rooted connection with the forces of historical becoming that serve to stratify language" (325). Therefore, even though characters have different voices in the epic or poetry, their voices come from the same ideological strata of society, are informed by the same idealized literary language, and serve to express the author's "individual polemic." In the novel, though, discourse is always open, always changing, always discourse-in-process. For this reason, the novel will achieve

a dominance among the other, closed and dead, genre. Bakhtin pre-
dicts a "novelization" of all genres because the novel's very resistance
to authority would cause it to become a "super-genre," one impossible
to define and therefore impossible to limit.

This representation of different voices from different strata of
society means, Bakhtin claims, that "Any stylistics capable of dealing
with the distinctiveness of the novel as a genre must be a *sociological
stylistics*" (300, author's emphasis). If women represent a different
strata of society, if they use a particular language because of educa-
tional, professional, and class differences, then a *sociological* analysis of
their language-in-use should be valuable in Bakhtin's project. In fact,
many feminist theorists argue that this is precisely what the task of
feminist criticism should be.[2]

Feminist criticism assumes that women represent a different strata
of society, an oppressed one. It also assumes that women's exclusion
from the dominant society has made a systematic and fundamental
difference in the kind of art women make, the ways women think, and
the ways women use language. But to speak of a "woman's" art,
thought, or language, one must have a workable definition of "woman."
Biology is, of course, one method, but a reductive one. Many feminist
critics, influenced by the post-Saussurean critique of defining by opposition, suggest that a more useful method of defining "woman" is
not merely to look at her "material, social, and psychological condition" but also to examine the *exclusion* that has defined that condition,
the "status of womanhood in Western theoretical discourse" (Felman,
3). This discourse is one that works by opposition: in such a system of
thought (a phallogocentric, male-dominated system), woman is placed
in the inferior position: Man/Woman. "Theoretically subordinated to
the concept of masculinity, the woman is viewed by the man as *his*
opposite, that is to say, as *his* other, the negative of the positive, and
not, in her own right, different, other, Otherness itself" (Felman, 3).
When woman is in a position analogous to Silence, Absence, and Madness in the paradigm of Western thought (Speech/Silence, Presence/
Absence, Logic/Madness), these critics ask, what happens to her language? If her language is something other than silence, it must either
be a usurped language (the language/logic of men used by women), or
it must be something fundamentally "other" itself. Thus, a central
question for feminist criticism has been what happens to language if it
is used "other-wise."

Not surprisingly, theorists have said that "speaking from the place
of the Other" makes a marked difference in the way women use language; this feminine language is said to be contralogic, "not conform-

ing to solid male rules of logic, clarity, consistency" (Gallop "Snatches," 274). In resisting the "official" language of logic, women's language can become "depersonalized" and "pluralized" (Furman, 50), and "de-centered," "polyphonic or dialogic" (Jardine, 230). Because it is spoken by "no one," that is, because it comes from the "place of absence," a feminine language does not assume the authority of logical discourse and, therefore, escapes the hierarchy of the official language. Luce Irigaray argues, in fact, that it is the very nature of woman to be "not One"; she argues that because her "sexuality, always at least double, is in fact *plural,*" her language is also plural: "[in] her language ... 'she' goes off in all directions and ... 'he' is unable to discern the coherence of any meaning. Contradictory words seem a little crazy to the logic of reason" ("This Sex," 103, author's emphasis). Feminine language, then, is marked by process and change, by absence and shifting, by multivoicedness. Meaning in feminine language is always "elsewhere," between voices or between discourses, marked by a mistrust of the "signified."

Thus, when faced with critical questions of authority, the feminine author is never there. When the feminine text is asked, "What does it matter who is speaking?" it answers "Nothing, everything." It matters not at all because "no one" is speaking. It matters everything because no "one" is. In the feminine text, there is a plurality of voices, put together by someone who is "not one." The feminine writer has no name of her own. The woman's name is the name of the Father; she is "Other," not her real name, not her "proper" name. Therefore, the feminine voice cannot be identified as "one" because it cannot be named and because every time she speaks, she is aware of all the other silenced feminine voices.

In feminine texts it is never clear who speaks, where the speaking is coming from, but it is clear that there is always more than one speaker, more than one language because it is always "an-other's" speech, serving "an-other's" language. A feminine language lives on the boundary. A feminine text overthrows the hierarchies. It is ab-sence-silence-madness present-speaking-sane. It proves the hierarchies mistaken. Like the voices Bakhtin hears in the novel's carnival, the female voice laughs in the face of authority.

Women and the novel have been closely associated since the mod-ern genre's beginnings (despite the fact that Bakhtin was able to ig-nore women in his history of the novel).[3] Ian Watt's *The Rise of the Novel* sees a close parallel between the increase in women readers and the increase in the novel's popularity. In the eighteenth century, he claims, literature was "primarily a feminine pursuit" (43), and women, the largest group with enough leisure time to enjoy reading, pursued the novel. Not only were most readers of the novel women, but the "majority of eighteenth-century novels were actually written by women" (298).[4] Josephine Donovan, in "The Silence is Broken," argues that women writers were attracted to the novel because they could write prose narrative despite their relative lack of education; because it was a new form, "there were really no classical models nor critical rules that one would have to know in order to practice its writing" (209). Watt suggests that "the feminine sensibility was in some ways better equipped to reveal the intricacies of personal relationships and was therefore at a real advantage in the realm of the novel" (298). Watt's conventional view of "feminine sensibility" nevertheless leaves ambiguous the question of whether women became the subject matter of the novel because they were the primary writers/readers, or whether women became interested in the novel because it took women's lives as its subject matter. It also leaves open the question of the relation between "feminine language" and "novelistic discourse," of whether there is a separate "feminine sensibility" which is expressed differently to "masculine sensibility," or whether "feminine sensibility," and the "feminine language" in which it is expressed, is a modern notion, an adaptation of "novelistic discourse." These questions of origin are important because they can be restated: Was the novel the way women began writing about their lives or were they first shown how to write that way? Again, is the novel a "feminine" genre or is "feminine language" novelistic?

If the Novel is a Feminine Genre

As we have already seen, the novel and the woman share the same paradigmatic "place" in phallogocentric thought. If the novel is still considered the "thinking man's television" today, it was certainly not much esteemed at its beginnings in the early eighteenth century. Terry Eagleton notes that the "eighteenth century was in grave doubt about whether the new upstart form of the novel was literature at all" (17). Ian Watt maintains that it was not until Jane Austen wrote *Pride and Prejudice* (1813) that the novel came to its "full maturity" (296). Robert Scholes maintains that it only reached its "classic form in the nineteenth century when it was poised between realistic and naturalistic modes" (*Structuralism,* 137). The novel may have risen to heights of popularity by the early eighteenth century, but it did not become a critically acknowledged genre until much later.

Eagleton shows that English literature — and with it the novel — became a suitable subject for men to study sometime in the early twentieth century. Poetry was still valued more highly, however, and when critics did stoop to study the novel, it was often with an eye to revealing its "true" classical origins. Bakhtin notes that it was not until the early twentieth century that "interest began to grow in the concrete problems of artistic craftsmanship in prose" and complains that even then,

> as before, the peculiarities of the stylistic life of discourse in the novel (...) lacked an approach that was both principled and at the same time concrete (...); the same arbitrary judgmental observations about language — in the spirit of traditional stylistics — continued to reign supreme, and they totally overlooked the authentic nature of artistic prose. (260)

The coincidence of the "classic form" of the novel and the rise of the study of English had many causes. Eagleton attributes it largely to the rising nationalism brought on by World War I. One could also easily argue that when the novel finally achieved greatness, people wanted to study it. But if we look at the novel as a distinctly *feminine* genre, if we take its femininity to be its most characteristic feature (in both subject matter and language style), then such a coincidence looks very different.

Novelistic discourse achieves a state of non-definability, of otherness, of freedom from hierarchy. Literary criticism, on the contrary, is a very different kind of discourse. Its nature is to define, to hierarchize, and to find similarity (to make a canon). Further, as Nelly Furman has pointed out, "Literary criticism, whatever its methodology or focus of interest, is an exercise in and of power; its speaker moves into a traditionally masculine role" (51). And the literary criticism of the early twentieth century, especially, had power as its goal; it looked for *the* meaning in the text, sought closure, attempted definition. If novelistic discourse is a specifically feminine discourse, then "masculine" criticism may well be an attempt to control and to silence a feminine threat. Insofar as criticism is "logical" and the novel is "emotional" or "dialogical," criticism seeks to dominate it, to bring it under control. If criticism can name, limit or define the novel, it can tame, control and appropriate it. Seen this way, literary criticism of the novel becomes a method of appropriating the "feminine" through "power" and "denial": it uses its power to control the "proliferation of meaning" to deny the status of the novel.

One way that criticism attempts to control literature is through assigning what Michel Foucault calls an "author-function" to the writers of novels. Foucault describes the power of the author-function, of naming a text by its author's name (an Austen novel, a Brontë novel), as an act of limiting, and, if the feminine writer has no "real" name, no "proper" name, such an assignment has to be doubly so.

> How can one reduce the great peril, the great danger with which fiction threatens our world? The answer is: One can reduce it with the author. The author allows a limitation of the cancerous and dangerous proliferation of significations within a world where one is thrifty not only with one's resources and riches, but also with one's discourses and their significations. The author is the principle of thrift in the proliferation of meaning. (158–9)

Altering Foucault's metaphor, from cancer to sexuality, we can see that the feminine text, with its open, plural, multiple discourse, threatens the "reproduction" of meaning. Feminine control over reproduction, of course, has always been threatening. Thus, criticism can name a text a "woman's book" and deny it the full range of its meanings; it can name a text "feminine writing" in a canon in which "masculine writing" is valorized, compare the two and find the feminine writer *lacking;* this is what Nancy Miller calls "a politics of benign neglect that reads difference, not to say popularity, as inferiority" ("Emphasis Added," 37). Indeed, Annette Kolodny asserts that this is exactly what happened in the first half of this century. She argues that many feminine texts did not lack merit, but lacked a critical readership that could understand them. These literary critics did not question their ability to read; instead, they criticized the feminine writers' ability to write and accorded the feminine text a lesser status. Kolodny asserts that it was the lack of an author-function, a "proper" name for these texts, that led to this diminished position:

> The problem, then, is as circular as it is hermeneutical: the individual text could not be appreciated because the whole in which it was embedded was not known (or appreciated); and no appreciation of the larger whole could be generated when its individual components proved intractable to male interpretation. ("Reply," 590)

The feminine text was caught in the phallogocentric double-bind of criticism: without an author-function, it would not be read; but with an author-function, it could not be read. The author's name was a pose, a facade, a means to limit the reproduction, proliferation of meaning and to deny that (false) meaning any important position.[5]

Much of the work of feminist criticism has been to rediscover and on occasion to establish this "author-function," creating a context in which feminine texts can and will be read. Nancy Miller speaks for many feminist critics when she states, "it matters who writes and *signs* woman" ("The Text's Heroine," 49). Nonetheless, assigning an "author-function," establishing the "authority" of a text, may be precisely the kind of limiting and controlling of meaning which the feminist critic, anxious to avoid definition and hierarchy, would seek to avoid. If criticism is necessarily appropriative and an exercise in and of power, then one may not be able to have a "feminist" criticism that is also a "feminine" criticism. One solution that has been offered to this dilemma is that in the very idea of a "feminine" criticism, one allows a feminine writer to assume her "natural" position; one allows her to speak other-wise and proclaims oneself the subjective reader, reading other-wise.[6] But in explaining her use of language, one must pin it down, explain it, approach it "logically." One cannot even speak non-logically about the other, because to speak at all is to assume authority, to attempt to explain. "Being Atopic, the other makes language inde-cisive: one cannot speak *of* the other, *about* the other; every attribute is false, painful, erroneous, awkward: the other is *unqualifiable* ... " (Barthes, *Lover's Discourse*, 35). Further, claiming that one's own dis-course is subjectively marked has the paradoxical effect of increasing one's authority: One must assert the authority of experience or posi-tion to persuade others to pay attention to merely "subjective" state-ments about a text. If the novel is a feminine genre, there may be no way to speak of it without appropriating its feminine position.

If Feminine Language is Novelistic

As we have already seen from Ian Watt and Josephine Donovan, the primary readers of novels have always been women, and, for the most part, the writers have been women, too. But from whom did these women writers learn to write? Ian Watt assures us that the men who wrote novels in the eighteenth century chose their feminine, do-mestic topics not necessarily because of their own interest in those sub-jects, but because they were aware of their market. Reclaiming the novel's classical heritage (whether in epic, poetry, Menippean satire, or Ovidian love letters), those origins are masculine. Further, insofar as all language works by opposition, and that opposition is the basis of masculine, phallogocentric thought, who *really* speaks in the novel? Christiane Rochefort describes the woman writer's dilemma this way:

Are you [the woman writer] free?

First, ... you are swimming in a terrible soup of values — for, to be
safe, you had to refuse the so-called female values, which are not
female but a social scheme, and to identify with male values, which
are not male but an appropriation by men — or attribution to men —
of all human values, mixed up with the anti-values of domination-
violence-oppression and the like. In this mixture, where is your real
identity? (185)

The woman is likely to be at a loss to know whether she's using her
own language or the language *ascribed* to her by culture. The feminine
writer must confront the question of whether speaking the language
of the other is really her *own* language, or if it is merely assuming her
place in the phallogocentric paradigm. If we use Bakhtin's definition
of dialogism, *"another's speech in another's language,* serving to express
authorial intentions but in a refracted way" (*DI*, 324), we can see that
feminine language could be described as "a woman speaking man's
language, expressing her intentions, but in a refracted, masculine-de-
fined way." Thus, what is valued by feminist criticism as "woman's language" is not woman's language at all, but women speaking as cultural
stereotypes. The woman writing as a woman, then, gets her idea of
what it is to write *as* a woman from a *masculine* definition. Looking at
that definition, then, may help to understand what it would mean to
the woman writing, and to the woman reading, to assume that cultural
place.

Jacques Lacan has explained that the woman's position, because it
is assumed within the system of language, which is ruled by phallic-
dominated oppositions, is assumed as a masquerade, or a fiction.[7] This
does not mean, of course, that women do not exist, but that the idea of
something *in essence* not-man, is a (male) fantasy, a (male) fictional construct. In assuming "her" place in the phallogocentric paradigm, then,
the woman comes to occupy a fictional position. In writing as "Other,"
in using the "Other's" language, she writes and speaks for the man,
reinforcing *his* idea of her. She does not write "as a woman," but as
"not-man." She speaks a fictional language, the language ascribed to
her, but not her own language. What she can desire, know, and, therefore, say is determined within the system of language by the logic of
which she is presumed to be outside. It is her taking up this position
"outside" logic that puts her squarely "inside" it.

Thus, the assumption that feminine language is novelistic presents
even larger problems for the feminist critic than does treating the

novel as a feminine genre. "Writing as a woman" gets caught in a much more insidious tautological circle than the one described by Peggy Kamuf in "Reading Women Writing." Instead of "a woman writing as a woman writing as a ... " it means "women write as women have been taught women write as women have been taught ... " It removes the possibility of a truly "feminine" language; using language at all means to work within a system whose terms are masculine. Then to practice feminist criticism is either to ignore the system or to participate in it; any claims that women's writing is "different" would then mean upholding woman's "place." Any call on the "authority" of women's experience is, not only to usurp the masculine position (as we saw in the last section), but is to claim the authority, the truth, of a (male) fiction.

A Logical Conclusion

Although we can always discount one or the other position to make our own more tenable, if both Bakhtin and feminist critics are right, then feminist criticism is highly problematic, whether we assume that the novel is a feminine genre or feminine language is novelistic. If the novel is a feminine genre, the role of the critic is to control and appropriate a meaning which was feminine to begin with, thus making the critic's position always a masculine one, an unfortunate stance for a feminist. If feminine language is novelistic, then the feminist critic can never speak outside a language which is defined by the masculine; the very idea of anything that is "feminist" is based squarely within the phallogocentric paradigm.

But just as feminist criticism is thrown into question when one considers the two positions together, so is Bakhtin's writing about the novel. If the novel is, indeed, a feminine genre, then Bakhtin's overlooking women writers is not as easily glossed over as Wayne Booth claims. If multivoicedness is a feminine characteristic, if dialogism is largely a gender-, rather than genre-, marked trait, then Bakhtin was not merely culturally backwards, but was ignorant about the very nature of the genre. On the other hand, if feminine language is novelistic, has been novelized, then novelization is much more monologic than Bakhtin claims. If it has the power to control women's language, and therefore women's thinking, then it is authoritarian—Bakhtin just did not see this because it was *he*, as a man, who wielded the authority.

A Dialogical Conclusion

If we do not want to accept the idea that either Bakhtin or feminist criticism is wrong, and we do not want to accept either's ultimate impossibility, then an exercise in dialogism is necessary to find a way to have both and use them, too. Because only through dialogism can we assert that it is on the boundary between the two discourses — in the illumination of their conflict — that we can find a way to use both.

To use both, one would have to accept both the ideas that the novel is a feminine genre and that feminine language is novelistic. In accepting both, instead of arguing for one position or the other, one acknowledges the history of the novel and its relation to women but with an important difference: giving up the search for a definitive conclusion as to whether women defined the novel or vice versa. At some point, one simply has to accept the fact that we do not know and cannot find out which came first, which has priority in the hierarchy. The novel and the feminine writer use the same kind of language without discarding either masculine novels or feminine criticism, because it would mean that all novelists simultaneously assert and subvert their own language as they record it. We (male and female, writer and reader) are always taking part in a dialogue not entirely under our control. The masculine writer, just by working in a feminine-dialogic genre, would be subverting the masculine-monologic language of oppositions. The feminine writer, by writing in a masculine-monologic language, would be subverting the feminine-dialogic genre. The result of all this subversion would be, ultimately, to laugh in the face of the hierarchy's authority.

Such a position would mean that the critic would then look for places where the language of the novel is subversive. She would look for points where disagreeing discourses do not cohere and examine what those points of contradiction can tell about the boundaries themselves. This kind of criticism would resist offering "a reading" and offer, instead, "readings." It would therefore resist the masculine-monologic place of asserting any one meaning, because the meaning would always be "not one." This dialogic feminine criticism would not just pay lip-service to two readings while clearly privileging one (which is what many post-structuralist writings tend to do); it would, instead, emphasize the plural meanings — even contradictory meanings — in the text. In doing this, the critic would run, almost inevitably, into problems of her own authority. But by offering readings that themselves contradict, or even cancel each other out, that authority is more thoroughly undercut than it is by just proclaiming that other readings are equally valid, or announcing one's own subjectivity. By resisting an impulse to privilege one reading over the other, the critic relinquishes power.

The Dilemma of a Dialogic Feminism

Unfortunately, this dialogical conclusion, suggesting that the critic place her own authority in question, raises yet another dilemma for the larger project of feminist criticism: How much power does the feminist critic — or any social critic — really want to relinquish? The move toward non-hierarchical, "feminine" criticism has obvious positive political import, but at some point the political need for strategic readings may well outweigh the desire to escape monological, hierarchical ways of thinking and writing.

One of the strengths of feminist criticism has been and continues to be its diversity. The polyphony within the discourse of feminism — between formalist, reader-response, psychoanalytic, socialist, post-structuralist, lesbian, black, chicana, third-world, and working-class feminists, to name a few — represents an important space in contemporary criticism where dissident and marginal voices can find a genuine forum.

On the other hand, the polyphony of the oppressed, like the carnival voices Bakhtin describes, is not composed of voices with political power, but of voices reacting to oppressive institutional power, united only in their opposition to that power. They are defined by negation — opposition to power — not by positive political purpose. David Carroll acknowledges this problem in Bakhtinian theory:

> The carnivalesque could, however, be challenged on political grounds not only for being a naive, utopic, aesthetic ideal, an idealistic model for social relations that is unrealizable outside of momentary, exceptional, predetermined conditions — that is, when the authorities allow it — but also for acquiescing to the power of the authorities and accepting the socio-political status quo and the few moments of freedom it parcels out. (80–1)

Carroll argues that one can escape this dilemma by recognizing that the carnival questions the "normalcy" of monolithic, hierarchical social relations and exposes them as themselves momentary and arbitrary. But one must remember that Bakhtin's carnival, however much it exposed the arbitrariness of the social relations of power, remained an event allowed (if not sanctioned) by institutional authority, which

served that institution by providing an outlet for the oppressed to pre-
vent any *real* insurrection. It was an artificial subversion of hierarchies
which prevented any organized question of them. That is, carnival
represents an event staged by those with power to subvert any potential power which might be developed by the oppressed.[8]

Given this understanding of carnival and the polyphony it allows,
one must examine the recent trend in feminist criticism toward relent-
less attack (in the guise of "critique") on other feminist criticisms with
a different point of view.[9] Female feminist critics distrust male feminist
critics; materialist feminists disagree with psychoanalytic ones, and
vice versa; textual feminist scholars eschew post-structuralist feminists; American feminists criticize French and British feminists, as Europeans, in turn, criticize the Americans.[10] The points of agreement—
if indeed any remain—are lost among the points of disagreement. In
this climate, one must face the possibility at some point that the space
which has been opened for feminist criticism may be merely a carnival
provided by institutional authority—an event staged to allow feminists
to drown out their own voices and thereby return to silence. The polyphony may well succeed in producing only cacaphony, with every
sound getting lost among the other, competing sounds. Feminist critics
should address themselves to the issue of with whom they are in dialogue and what sort of dialogue it is. We need to examine our own
authority within the academic carnival.

Notes

1. In discussing "feminine writing," I do not necessarily mean to discuss
a biological distinction. There are women whose writing is masculine, men
whose writing is feminine. When referring to the biological differences, I'll use
"women" or "men"; when referring to a non-bio-logical difference, I'll use
"feminine" and "masculine."

2. Many feminist critics argue that women's place in society and their
experiences of domesticity, lack of education, and oppression — their "sociological" differences — create a distinctly different feminine sensibility, use of
language, and attitude toward narrative. Just a few examples: Josephine Donovan, in "Toward a Women's Poetics," argues that "traditional women's experience and practice in the past and in nearly all cultures" — epistemology,
poetics, and narrative techniques — are shaped by interruptibility and circu-
larity. Jane Tompkins' work on domestic fiction, *Sensational Designs*, suggests
that a study of the feminine culture of the nineteenth century is necessary to
be able to read and understand nineteenth-century women's fiction. Nancy
Miller, in "Emphasis Added: Plots and Plausibilities in Women's Fiction," ar-

gues that historically, women's experiences have led them to a different sense of what counts as "plausible." The essays in *Discovering Reality: Feminist Perspectives on Epistemology, Metaphysics, Methodology, and Philosophy of Science*, edited by Sandra Harding and Merrill B. Hintikka, explore in various ways the question of the relation between women's sociological place and epistemology.

3. I am not considering here any discussions of the forms called novelistic in classical literature. For the purposes of this part of my discussion, the novel as a genre began and "rose" (i.e., assumed a relatively stable place in the society) in or around the early eighteenth century.

4. Although Watt's discussion is limited to Britain, the same is true for the United States. For more on the history of the American novel and its relation to women writers, see Nina Baym, *Woman's Fiction: A Guide to Novels by and about Women, 1820–1870*. Ithaca: Cornell University Press, 1978.

5. We should note here that nineteenth-century women authors' frequent choice of masculine pennames may have been an attempt to avoid this particular limiting function. The measure of how well it worked may well be that, with the exception of Jane Austen, the most canonical women novelists are those who wrote under masculine signifiers, at least initially (George Eliot, George Sand, and the Brontë sisters, or Bell brothers).

6. This is the suggestion put forward by Nelly Furman.

7. Mary Russo, in "Female Grotesques: Carnival and Theory," discusses the relation between feminine masquerade and carnival.

8. This understanding of the limited space that carnival makes for real subversion of the structures of power is influenced by Clifford Geertz's and Mary Douglas's work on "rituals of status reversal."

9. Mary Russo points to other dangers for feminist criticism in the theory of carnival: the "ambivalent redeployment of taboos around the female body" and the threat of violence toward women during carnival. She also considers the "carnival" of post-structuralist theory.

10. I deliberately refrain from "naming names" here in an attempt to avoid participating in this carnival assault myself. For a perspective on the act of *not* noting sources here, see Shari Benstock's "On the Margins of Discourse."

Works Cited

Bakhtin, Mikhail. *The Dialogic Imagination*. trans. Caryl Emerson and Michael Holquist. Austin: University of Texas Press, 1981.

_____. *Rabelais and His World*. trans. Helen Iswolsky. Cambridge: MIT Press, 1968.

Barthes, Roland. *A Lover's Discourse: Fragments.* Trans. Richard Howard. New York: Hill and Wang, 1978.

———. *S/Z.* trans. Richard Miller. New York: Hill and Wang, 1974.

Benstock, Shari. "On the Margins of Discourse." *PMLA* 98 (1983): 204–25.

Booth, Wayne. "Freedom of Interpretation: Bakhtin and the Challenge of Feminist Criticism." *Critical Inquiry* 9 (1982): 45–76.

Carroll, David. "The Alterity of Discourse: Form, History, and the Question of the Politic in M. M. Bakhtin." *Diacritics* (Summer 1983): 65–83.

Cixous, Hélène. "The Laugh of the Medusa." in *New French Feminisms.* ed. Elaine Marks and Isabelle de Courtivron. New York: Schocken Books, 1981. pp. 245–264.

Donovan, Josephine. "The Silence is Broken." in *Women and Language in Literature and Society.* ed. Sally McConnell-Ginet, Ruth Borker, and Nelly Furman. New York: Praeger, 1980. pp. 205–218.

———. "Toward a Women's Poetics." *Tulsa Studies in Women's Literature* 3. 1–2 (1984): 99–110.

Eagleton, Terry. *Literary Theory: An Introduction.* Minneapolis: University of Minnesota Press, 1983.

Felman, Shoshana. "Women and Madness: The Critical Phallacy." *Diacritics* 5.4 (1975): 2–10.

Furman, Nelly. "Textual Feminism." in *Women and Language in Literature and Society.* ed. Sally McConnell-Ginet, Ruth Borker, and Nelly Furman. New York: Praeger, 1980. pp. 45–54.

Foucault, Michel. "What is an Author?" in *Textual Strategies.* ed. Josue V. Harari. Ithaca: Cornell University Press, 1979. pp. 141–160.

Gallop, Jane. *The Daughter's Seduction.* Ithaca: Cornell University Press, 1982.

———. "Snatches of Conversation." in *Women and Language in Literature and Society.* ed. Sally McConnell-Ginet, Ruth Borker, and Nelly Furman. New York: Praeger, 1980. pp. 274–283.

Gauthier, Xaviere. "Is There Such a Thing as Women's Writing?" in *New French Feminisms.* ed. Elaine Marks and Isabelle de Courtivron. New York: Schocken Books, 1981. pp. 161–164.

Harding, Sandra, and Merill B. Hintikka, eds. *Discovering Reality: Feminist Perspectives on Epistemology, Metaphysics, Methodology, and Philosophy of Science.* Dordrecht, Holland: D. Reidel Pub. Co., 1983.

Irigaray, Luce. "This Sex Which is Not One." in *New French Feminisms.* ed. Elaine Marks and Isabelle de Courtivron. New York: Schocken Books, 1981. pp. 99–106.

_____. "When Our Lips Speak Together." *Signs* 6.1 (1980): 66–79.

Jardine, Alice. "Pre-Texts for the Transatlantic Feminist." *Yale French Studies* 62 (1981): 220–236.

Kamuf, Peggy. "Writing Like a Woman." in *Women and Language in Literature and Society.* ed. Sally McConnell-Ginet, Ruth Borker, and Nelly Furman. New York: Praeger, 1980. pp. 284–299.

Kolodny, Annette. "Dancing Through the Minefield: Some Observations on the Theory and Practice of a Feminist Literary Criticism." *Feminist Studies* 6.1 (1980): 1–25.

_____. "A Map for Rereading: Or, Gender and the Interpretation of Literary Texts." *New Literary History* 11 (1980): 451–67.

_____. "Reply to Commentaries: Women Writers, Literary Historians, and Martian Readers." *New Literary History* 11 (1980): 587–592.

Kristeva, Julia. "Oscillation between Power and Denial." in *New French Feminisms.* ed. Elaine Marks and Isabelle de Courtivron. New York: Schocken Books, 1981. pp. 165–167.

Lacan, Jacques. "God and the *Jouissance* of The Woman" in *Feminine Sexuality.* ed. Juliet Mitchell and Jacqueline Rose. New York: Norton, 1982.

_____. "A Love Letter." in *Feminine Sexuality.* ed. Juliet Mitchell and Jacqueline Rose. New York: Norton, 1982.

Marcus, Jane. "Still Practice, A/Wrested Alphabet: Toward a Feminist Aesthetic." *Tulsa Studies in Women's Literature* 3.1–2 (1984): 79–97.

Miller, Nancy K. "Changing the Subject: Authorship, Writing, and the Reader." *Feminist Studies/Critical Studies.* ed. Teresa de Lauretis. Bloomington: Indiana University Press, 1986.

_____. "Emphasis Added: Plots and Plausibilities in Women's Fiction." *PMLA* 96 (Jan., 1981): 36–48.

_____. "The Text's Heroine: A Feminist Critic and Her Fictions." *Diacritics* 12 (1982): 48–53.

Russo, Mary. "Female Grotesques: Carnival and Theory." *Feminist Studies/Critical Studies.* ed. Teresa de Lauretis. Bloomington: Indiana University Press, 1986.

Rochefort, Christiane. "Are Women Writers Still Monsters?" in *New French Feminisms.* ed. Elaine Marks and Isabelle de Courtivron. New York: Schocken Books, 1981. pp. 183–186.

Scholes, Robert. *Structuralism in Literature.* New Haven: Yale University Press, 1974.

Tompkins, Jane. *Sensational Designs: The Cultural Work of American Fiction.* New York: Oxford University Press, 1985.

Watt, Ian. *The Rise of the Novel.* Berkeley, CA: University of California Press, 1957.

2

Voices from the Margin: Bag Ladies and Others

Suzanne Kehde

Every morning and evening as I shuttle from my apartment in Hollywood, through Watts, to Taper Hall and back, I see an old woman who lives on the corner of Western and Beverly. She keeps her possessions in a grocery cart, talking to herself as she rearranges them. Sometimes when I drive by early, she's so still under her blankets I worry she's dead. On this particular Friday, the day I intend to put the final touches to my paper on feminist literary criticism, thirty-five thousand people in San Francisco and seventy-five thousand in Washington, D.C. are demonstrating against governmental policies on welfare, South America, and South Africa.

Terry Eagleton's *Literary Theory: An Introduction* suggests that all schools of literary criticism subscribe to the ruling ideology and thus serve to maintain the current power structure. Does feminist criticism, I wonder as I clamp my anti-theft device onto my steering wheel, serve to keep that crazy old woman on the corner, where no one hears whatever it is she has to say?

The work of Gayatri Chakravorty Spivak both implicitly and explicitly addresses this issue. In "Explanation and Culture: Marginalia," she has discussed "a certain program at least implicit in all feminist activity: the deconstruction of the opposition between the private and the public" (201). The public — the masculine — consisting of "the political, social, economic, [and] intellectual," is at the center; the private — the feminine — consisting of "the emotional, sexual, and domestic," is on the margin. Because Spivak has become aware of the "ideological victimage" attendant upon her "privileged" status as a "'westernized Easterner'" ("French Feminism," 155), she realizes that the center welcomes "selective inhabitants of the margin in order better to exclude the margin" ("Marginalia," 206); thus the feminist must reject the invitation to join the center.

In a review of Jacques Derrida's *Limited Inc: a b c* (1977), Spivak speaks of the "change of mind-set" necessary for "revolutionary 'programs'" as though both are in the realm of the possible (38). By 1985, however, having considered the relations between the technocracy and the ex-colonial society, between men and women, between privileged races and unprivileged races, between privileged classes and unprivileged classes, between privileged women and unprivileged women, between First and Third World women, as well as the place of the university in the technocracy and of the humanists in the university — in short, all manifestations of "the center" and their attendant "margins" — she has come to "think less easily of 'changing the world' than in the past" ("Feminism and Critical Theory," 139). This observation comes at the end of an essay tracing "the itinerary of [her] thinking . . . about the relationships among feminism, Marxism, psychoanalysis and deconstruction" (119), the configurations of which fields have continued to change while she has been considering them. Thus, while she is reflecting "upon the way these developments have been inscribed" in her own work, she offers her "itinerary" both as an individual case and as an example of a general move within the historical moment. In a talk given several years previous, she had voiced the hope of finding a way to "infiltrate the male academy and redo the terms of our understanding of the context and substance of literature as part of the human enterprise" (125). In this earlier, more optimistic mood she had put forward the following suggestion:

> Part of the feminist enterprise might well be to provide "evidence" so that [the] great male texts do not become great adversaries, or models from whom we take our ideas and then revise or reassess them. These texts must be rewritten so that there is new material for the grasping of the production and determination of literature within the general production and determination of consciousness and society. After all, the people who produce literature, male and female, are also moved by general ideas of world and consciousness to which they cannot give a name. (125)

In her later reflection on this talk, Spivak extends the task of the feminist critic to include the development of "a reading method that is sensitive to gender, race, and class" (125). By the time of writing, she has narrowed her sights to "teach[ing] a small number of the holders of the can(n)on, male or female, feminist or masculist, how to read their own texts, as best I can" (139). Her spelling of can(n)on, however, undercuts her statement, indicating as it does that she has not lost her sense of the revolutionary struggle.

Bakhtin's theory is enormously appealing because, resisting too great an emphasis on the arbitrariness of language, it perceives language as a more open sign-system than did Saussure. Caryl Emersen argues that Bakhtin and his circle "posited four *social* factors that make the understanding of speech and writing possible" (Emerson, 23), amending Saussure thus: "the sign is external, organized socially, concretely historical, and, as the Word, inseparably linked with voice and authority" (240). These amendments modify the original opposition between *langue* and *parole*. Bakhtin accepts the two poles but sees them as ends of a continuum rather than discrete entities. The psyche itself is a boundary phenomenon rather than an internal phenomenon, for it is constituted by the interactions between "lateral . . . relationships with other individuals in specific speech acts" and "internal relationships between the outer world" and itself. "Thus the word, Bakhtin affirms, 'constitutes the foundation . . . of the inner life. Were it to be deprived of the word, the psyche would shrink to an extreme degree'" (Emerson, 26). Bakhtin develops this concept of the relationship between word and psyche in opposition to — in dialogue with — Freud's theory of the unconscious, which, denying both history and society, valorizes subjectivity at the expense of community.

Vygotsky, Bakhtin's contemporary, conducted clinical investigations into the ways in which "outer words become inner speech" (Emerson, 27). Although there is no evidence that the work of either was directly influenced by the other, "the ultimate implications of their thought" intersect (27). Just as Bakhtin rejected the Freudian unconscious, so Vygotsky rejected Piaget's theories of language acquisitions based on Freudian thought. Piaget, supposing children reluctant to adjust to their environment, explained "egocentric thought" by the assumption that a child's thought was originally autistic and became realistic only under social pressure; Vygotsky, however, concluded from some ingenious clinical investigations that "egocentric speech was not, as Piaget had suggested, a compromise between primary autism and reluctant socializaton but rather the direct outgrowth (or, better, ingrowth) of speech which had been from the start socially and environmentally oriented" (29). Thus "'development in thinking . . . is not from the individual to the socialized, but from the social to the individual'" (30).

This suggests a base for an approach to the kind of reading, or re-writing, Spivak proposes. Both Bakhtin and Vygotsky have written specifically about literature, especially the novel, in ways that empower the feminist critic at least to listen for marginal voices. Bakhtin, "discovering a 'dialogic imagination' at the heart of human life in all its forms" (Booth, 150), considers the novel the highest form of literary discourse because of the inclusiveness and the continuing newness of "the most fluid of genres" ("Epic," 11). "Multiform in style and variform in speech and voice" ("Discourse," 261), presenting a "diversity of social speech types ... and a diversity of individual voices" (262), it "reflects more deeply, more essentially, more sensitively and rapidly, reality itself in the process of unfolding" ("Epic," 7):

> The novel has become the leading hero in the drama of literary development in our time because it best of all reflects the tendencies of a new world still in the making; it is, after all, the only genre born of this new world and in total affinity with it. In many respects the novel has anticipated, and continues to anticipate, the future development of literature as a whole. In the process of becoming the dominant genre, the novel sparks the renovation of all other genres, it affects them with the spirit of process and inconclusiveness. It draws them ineluctably into its orbit precisely because this orbit coincides with the basic development of literature as a whole. In this lies the exceptional importance of the novel, as an object of study for the theory as well as the history of literature. (7)

Bakhtin sees the novel as deprivileging the monologic authorial voice because a new relationship appears between "the underlying original formal author" and the world he represents, for "the 'depicting' authorial language now lies on the same plane as the 'depicted' language of the hero" (27). In short, they share a zone of potential conversation, "a zone of *dialogic contact*" (45). The formal requirements of the novel demand dialogue, the inclusion of voices the novelist has not internalized; it is also that literary form where all the voices that have gone into the making of the collective self may be heard.

The presence of many voices in the novel is due not only to their internalization on the part of the author but also to the cultural factors surrounding the novel's long pre-history. It retains the vestiges of this struggle in its essential heteroglossia; the voices from the margins are still present and can be heard by the attentive ear.

Liberating as Bakhtin's concept of the novel's many voices may be, his idea of its historical relationship to parody may be even more useful to those who wish to rewrite the great male texts of the past. He maintains that scholarly investigation of parody has been too conceptually limited. He relates it to the tradition of carnival, by which he means the great festivals temporarily inverting the power hierarchy, such as the ancient Roman Saturnalia or the medieval European celebrations of Twelfth Night or the First of May. To the Greeks, phallus-bearers and mimers were common figures whose function was to travesty "national and local myths" (57), to provide "the corrective of laughter and criticism" (57). The history of literature is full of examples of "parodic-travestying forms" (52). Because all these forms share language, they constitute an "extra-generic or inter-generic world [that] is internally unified" (59). This unity seems to Bakhtin something like a great Ur-novel:

> multi-generic, multi-styled, mercilessly critical, soberly mocking, reflecting in all its fullness the heteroglossia and multiple voices of a given culture, people and epoch. In this huge novel — in this mirror of constantly evolving heteroglossia — any direct word and especially that of the dominant discourse — is reflected as something more or less bounded, typical and characteristic of a particular era, aging, dying, ripe for change and renewal. (60)

The novel arose out of "this huge complex of parodically reflected words and voices" (60). Thus the novel, including in itself a parody of itself, becomes Spivak's zone of deconstruction. In this view, *Tristram Shandy,* for example, rather than being a sport, is an extreme instance of the generic type.

However, if Bakhtin's concept of parody is to be useful to the reader bent on rereading texts, it must be applied to the novels where we may suspect the parodic effect is not part of the authorial intention, where the writer has recorded voices, perhaps internalized, perhaps misunderstood, speaking against the hierarchy of power. The lesser works of Ernest Hemingway could be entered in the Harry's Bar contest without any appearance of incongruity. But Hemingway's greater works respond to the same context of parody. For Jake Barnes, Robert Cohen speaks in the voice of a parodic romantic lover. What then are we to make of Jake himself? In the text murmurs the voice of another Jake, the man devoid of sexual imagination, who acts as mocking phallophor to the male hierarchical world view he pretends to speak for. Thus is freed the voice of Brett Ashley, the only healthy character in the novel, who copes with life in a ruined world, where every French and English village has its hospital sheltering the faceless, limbless maimed and its cenotaph listing the fallen.

The context of parody may free submerged voices in the fiction of writers whose authorial intentions are more ambiguous than those of Hemingway. In Henry James's *The Wings of the Dove,* for example, Merton Densher seems to be in possession of the moral yardstick by which the action is to be measured. Traditional readings suggest that Densher is the real protagonist, his moral education its true subject.

"It is a story of conversion," says Christof Wegelin (528), its theme thus encompassing Densher's redemption, Milly's triumph, and Kate's fall. This desire to make the most of Christian mythology — an extreme instance of the male hierarchical principle — even leads F. O. Matthiessen to infer that James didn't know his Old Testament: in his eagerness to establish Densher as the moral center and Kate as the dark woman tempting him to mortal sin, he maintains that "since it is certainly not Kate who is led into evil," James must have forgotten that the tree of knowledge is "inescapably [an image] of temptation" when he wrote of "Densher's having tasted of the tree and being thereby prepared to assist her to eat'" (494). J. A. Ward, Dorothea Krook, and Sallie Sears have in turn called Kate corrupt (534), morally deficient (550), and condemned (563). However, even in the second volume, which is written primarily from his point of view, Densher's is not the only voice. Bakhtin's enlarged — and enlarging — view of parody establishes a context which, freeing the voices of Kate Croy and Milly Theale, enables us to hear their dialogue with each other, muted though it is by the voice of Densher, the spokesman for the official ideology.

It is often remarked that the credibility of characters like Fanny Assingham and Fleda Vetch is undermined by the names James has chosen for them; similarly, Merton Densher, with a patronymic homophonous with *denture*, hardly seems a man to be taken at face value — which face, all things considered, seems to constitute his major attraction. Possessed of long legs, straight fair hair, and a well-shaped head (46), he is a man whose appearance is significant. In this he resembles Kate's unspeakable father, whose "plausibility" (24) as the perfect English gentleman is a parodic comment on the type in general.

Both Densher and Croy want to appropriate Kate according to the precepts of the official ideology in ways so excessive, so deaf to her individual voice, that they constitute ironic commentary. Croy wants her to acquiesce in Mrs. Lowder's plans for a brilliant, prosperous marriage so that she can support him; Densher urges her to marry him at once in spite of the fact that he earns enough to keep only himself. Although Lionel Croy's opinions in general are perhaps not to be trusted, on the principle that it takes one to know one, his comments on Densher, "the beggarly sneak," are worth attention:

> "He *must* be an ass! And how in the world can you consider it to improve him for me ... that he's also destitute and impossible? There are boobies and boobies even — the right and the wrong — and you appear to have carefully picked out one of the wrong." (33)

Croy and Densher each pressure Kate to act in a way that enhances his situation rather than hers, in accordance with his values and his consequent perception of her value. Their comments on each other, in pointing out the self-serving nature of each other's intentions, are a powerful criticism of the subordinate position of women.

In the scene in which Densher first appears, his thoughts are couched in the vocabulary of the chivalric gentleman: he wonders whether it is "more ignoble to ask a woman to take her chance with you, or to accept it from your conscience that her chance could be at best but one of the degrees of privation" (54); he describes the unspecified acts of Lionel Croy as bringing "dishonour" to Kate's family. His choice of words implies that for him the essence of manhood is control: he complains, "What can be so base as sacrificing me?" and, when Kate suggests that he ought to meet Mrs. Lowder before they decide whether to rush into an immediate registry office marriage, he querulously inquires whether Kate wants him to "grovel" (61). In short, he thinks and speaks in the official monologue of the English gentleman.

In a novel in which Lionel Croy appears to be the epitome of the perfect gentleman, and Densher (the sexual blackmailer) the spokesman for the gentleman's code, the English gentleman himself, one of the dearest of British national myths — which Bakhtin specifies as a historical target of parody — is under attack. That the most powerful figure is Mrs. Lowder, a widow, suggests that the male hierarchy, the power structure itself, is being travestied. In this view, Densher is not, as a resistant colleague suggested, "a mere ficelle," but a (mere) phallus, in Bakhtin's word a phallophor, who carries before him an exaggerated version of the nature and value of his manhood as false as the teeth his name suggests.

This is not to imply that James was as sensitive to issues of gender, race, and class as feminists may hope Spivak's envisioned readers — or rewriters — will become. However, his attention to the consciousness of women situates his concern squarely on the point where the marginal and the central meet. While James may not have been as intentionally parodic as Dickens, neither was he as sympathetic to the values of the male hierarchy as Hemingway.

Unlike Isabel Archer, who is much more controlled by the male world than she realizes (Fowler, 82), Kate clearly perceives the restrictions her gender imposes on her, reflecting as she does that "she might still pull things round if only she were a man" (22). However, the inscription of the dominant values of her consciousness causes her to seek an indirect way to express her love for Milly.

Although neither lives out of a grocery cart, both women are marginal to London society, Kate because of her dependent status, Milly because of her foreignness and her illness. Both are under attack, Milly by her knowledge of her impending death, Kate by the importunities of her needy family and of Merton Densher, who is the most interesting person in her life before she meets Milly. The similarity in their situations creates a bond between Kate and Milly, strengthened by their closeness in age, their attraction to each other, and their attraction to the same man. Their initial meeting is described in the language of love at first sight: Milly's "eyes were mainly engaged with Kate Croy ... That wonderful creature's moreover readily met them." She was "frankly conscious of the possibilities of friendship for them" (98). She tells Lord Mark: "[Kate] understands ... She's better than any of you. She's beautiful" (108). She also tells him, "She's the handsomest and cleverest and most charming creature I ever saw, and ... if I were a man I should simply adore her. In fact I do as it is" (275). Milly says, "I'd do anything ... for Kate" (232). She believes "it's in *her* that life is splendid, and part of that is even she's devoted to me" (256). Kate says to Milly, "You're superb," and always Kate's "kind, kind eyes" (138) are watching her friend. Kate's "sweetness was all for *her*" (139). From the start it is "a pretty part of the intercourse for these young ladies that each thought the other more remarkable than herself" (113). Before Densher returns from the assignment in the United States during which he has met Milly, "they were afloat together," and it is "the happiest hour they were to know" (112). Their developing affection constitutes what Bakhtin calls "a different and contradictory reality" (59) outside that of socially sanctioned categories, which is the essence of parody.

Densher's return inhibits the dialogue between the two women. Their short-lived isolation from the pressure of social expectations ends, and their attraction to each other falls into second place because of the prevalent necessity of the male connection. Susan Stringham, Aunt Maud, Sir Luke Strett — all concerned with Milly's happiness — think that the love of a man is what she needs. John Carlos Rowe has pointed out that this idea prevails in James's work, where marriage is the "primary social institution"; although James criticizes marriage, his characters are "trapped by its values" (89), which are those of the official ideology — the very ideology whose voice Kate and Milly have been internalizing all their lives.

Because of the child's long socialization, the voice of dissent is so tentative that the conflict may well be situated within the very consciousness of the marginal. Thus the dissenting voice is rarely as monologic as the voice of official ideology. Nonetheless, Kate is well aware of the social pressures operating on her and Milly. She tries to warn Milly away from the "monster" of London society, fearing that Milly might come to hate her as a member of it. But Milly cannot imagine doing so: "Why do you say such things to me?" Kate, inspired, answers, "Because you're a dove." And Milly feels herself "ever so delicately, so considerately, embraced" (171). Milly "would have something to supply, Kate something to take — each of them ... something for squaring" (167) the monster. Thus they agree to support each other, but end up submitting to the values of the male hierarchy rather than resisting them.

Such submission necessarily inhibits them, so that much of what they need to say to each other is only implied. On the one hand, Kate believes Milly likes, even loves, Densher. She knows Milly is seriously ill. One of Milly's stipulations is that she not be treated as an invalid. Kate knows that Densher, unlike herself, is not seriously affected by the illness of others. So if there is one thing she can offer Milly, it is Densher: "You're what I have most precious, and you're therefore what I use most" (214). On the other hand, Milly believes she can help Kate with Aunt Maud by diverting Densher, the unsuitable suitor. Aunt Maud, Mrs. Stringham, and Sir Luke seem taken by the idea of Milly's interest in Densher, which further reinforces the social expectation that such a relationship will constitute the culminating experience of her life.

Unlike Alice James, whose illness was a matter of great interest to her, Milly initially copes with her coming death in large part by denying its approach. Kate sees the way she clings "to the Rockies" (182), to Densher's ability to distract her. Kate repeatedly tries to make him understand: "We're doing our best for her. We're making her want to live ... It's wonderful. It's beautiful" (305). Milly seems to comply with Kate's wishes: "Oh you don't know ... how much I'm really on her hands" (233). Even Susan Stringham, seeing Milly and Densher together, feels that "there was none other [besides Kate] to be employed" (211) for what becomes *their* plan, hers and Aunt Maud's and Sir Luke's as well as Kate's. Susan tells Densher, "What we hope ... is that you'll be faithful to us" (298); Kate says, "You must simply be kind to her [and] leave the rest to *her*" (239). Milly herself inadvertently assists by being sympathetic to his status as Kate's rejected suitor and promising to behave well for him: "I will never be anything so horrid as ill for you" (229). Kate repeatedly gives him the opportunity to break off with Milly. He will neither back out nor really commit himself, although he begins to entertain the idea: "He had been the first to know her," and he was beginning to think that he was there not just "through

Kate and Kate's idea, but through Milly and Milly's own and through himself and *his* own" (286 – 7). Kate's most difficult job is to keep Densher from wavering. To do so she must step back: "Thus was a wondering, pitying sister condemned wistfully to look at [Milly] from the far side of the moat she had dug round her tower" (262). Kate's thoughts are constantly on Milly's needs: "her sincerity about her friend, through this time, was deep, her compassionate imagination strong [giving] her a virtue, a good conscience, a credibility for herself, ... that were later to be precious to her" (262). Thus Kate, succumbing to the official ideology, colludes with the power structure to provide for her friend what it considers most appropriate for female happiness.

Milly moves to the scene of her final isolation, turning, like Alice, to "the adventure of not stirring" in a foreign land (Fowler, 101). Densher's interpretation of events, structured by the English gentleman's notions of honor, overrides the women's voices. He constantly frustrates the progress of the plan to keep Milly content. Milly needs to "give and give and give" (274), and since Densher is so willing to ignore the fact that she is ill, she is able to give him her time. But Densher thinks "waiting was the game of dupes ... It was all there for him, playing on his pride of possession as a hidden master" (189). And as this master, he presses Kate: "I can go on perhaps ... with help. But I can't go on without" (293). Kate sees that Milly "recognizes her situation [with Densher] as too precious to be spoiled" (292). This is not enough for Densher, and he threatens to leave. Kate tells him it will kill Milly. He's not moved. His threat stands. "Then go," (294) Kate finally says.

Densher is the first to articulate the idea that he could marry Milly, inherit her money, and after her death marry Kate. Densher not only refuses to understand Kate's good intentions, he makes her an accessory to his mercenary play: "Since she's to die I'm to marry her?" If she is to keep Densher attending Milly, Kate must proceed: "Her lips bravely moved" (308), repeating his words. Densher remains in character; he blames Kate for his actions, makes her responsible even for his thoughts. But she will go along in order to keep him with Milly; after all, "she has [often] seen herself obliged to accept ... other people's interpretation of her conduct. She often ended by giving up to them — it seemed really the way to live — the version that met their convenience" (34). She is used to having her voice muffled. Densher considers himself the "master of the conflict" and promises to "do everything" (311 – 12) if Kate will sleep with him. Once she does so, he breaks his promise. When Lord Mark tells Milly that Kate does love

Densher, she turns away from life in an act of will, the one act she has chosen herself. She has used her illness to focus her life and thus attain a kind of identity.

There is evidence that Kate expects nothing tangible from her association with Milly. Kate returns to London and does not leave when she has the opportunity "for thinking of — Venice" (388), i.e., Milly. Further, she abandons Lancaster Gate and all its advantages to return to her father. As she offered to do at the beginning of the novel, she goes to make a home for him because she is all he has. She has once more only herself to offer; she brings him no trophies, no income. Her only compensation, the one idea she holds to, is her hope that Milly has been satisfied, "which ... is what I've worked for." She wants her to have had "the peace of having loved" (364). And when the letter from the New York lawyer does come, Kate is not concerned with amounts; it is in itself "the proof" (392) of Milly's love. Kate recognizes Milly's triumph in the generosity of her spirit: "She died for you then that you might understand her. From that hour you *did*," she tells Densher. "And I do now. She did it for *us* ... I used to call her ... a dove. Well she stretched out her wings, and it was to *that* they reached. They cover us" (402 – 3). In choosing the money over Densher, Kate accepts their protection.

Milly's bequest, like Alice James's to Katharine Loring, is confirmation that Milly understands the value of the gift Kate tried to give. Densher could have prolonged Milly's life but chose not to, preferring to satisfy his English gentleman's sense of honor — closely allied as it is to the need to control — by refusing to lie to one woman after he had promised another he would do anything necessary, thus demonstrating that he loves his idea of himself more than he loves either of them. This treachery moves Kate to accept her freedom from him and choose Milly's gift as her own, for it is clear to her that she and Densher will "never be again as [they] were" (403). Finally Milly's love has freed Kate both from the necessity of marrying for money and of marrying Densher, whose ultimatum that she must choose either the money or him once again demonstrates his determined adherence to the official ideological position.

Kate's and Milly's affection for each other manifests itself by their trying to help each other satisfy social expectations; in her first scene with Densher, Kate explains to him that there are many things women can do for each other that a man wouldn't understand. Kate and Milly seem unable to express their affection without a male intermediary. Through Densher's assistance, Milly at last manages to give her fortune to Kate. As far as the money is concerned, Milly always meant to help Kate; financial aid, after all, is the only kind Kate has ever needed. When Milly finds out that Kate is pledged to Densher, she leaves him the fortune that will make him, in Aunt Maud's eyes, an acceptable husband for Kate. Milly squares everyone with this bequest. She colludes in keeping up the illusion everyone has tried so hard to maintain for her. To leave the money directly to Kate would tell Susan, Sir Luke, Aunt Maud, and Kate herself that their efforts for her happiness have been in vain.

Although marriage is foremost in the minds of Kate and Milly as well as in the minds of those wanting to marry them or marry them off, it is not the only relationship that concerns them. When Densher, seen in the context of parody, is demoted from his privileged position as ideological spokesman, the voices of Kate and Milly can be heard in dialogue with each other, and in a dialogue that subverts the values of the power structure. That James sympathizes with their subversion is suggested by the fates of heroines in other novels from his late period, where women are punished when they make the traditional choice of marriage. Verena is taken off by Ransom (that parody of a Southern gentleman), the tears in her eyes "not the last she was destined to shed" (370). In *Portrait of a Lady*, Isabel goes back to a despicable husband, unable to avert her tragedy because, like most nineteenth-century women, she cannot escape from a disastrous marriage (Fowler, 69). Recognizing both the social emphasis on marriage and its inadequacies, these later novels clearly portray the ambiguities in the condition of nineteenth-century women.

In offering this rewriting of *The Wings of the Dove*, am I merely emulating the Scrutineers, those petit bourgeois critics, "at once hair raisingly radical and really rather absurd," and only comforting myself by feeling "that by reading Henry James [I belong] to the vanguard of civilization itself?" (Eagleton, 34). Or can I assure myself that this enterprise, if not helping the bag lady, is at least not actively conspiring to keep her on her corner?

Bakhtin believes that the individual is not a discrete social entity nor a novel a discrete cultural phenomenon; both, constituted in polyphony, are supported by a web of intertextual relationships. While it does not overthrow the official monologue, Kate's and Milly's dialogue, even when muted in the second volume, coexists in dynamic opposition to it. The rich ambiguity of James's text is of some consequence here. Reading with an ear alive to the possibilities of heteroglossia we might, as Vygotsky suggests, learn — and teach others — who we are not, who we might yet become. As long as we decline the invitation to join the center we can avoid becoming parodic characters ourselves;

we can bear witness to the marginal everywhere, whether they are characters in Jamesian novels or bag ladies on the streets of Hollywood.

Works Cited

Bakhtin, M. M. *The Dialogic Imagination*. Ed. Michael Holquist. Trans. Caryl Emerson and Michael Holquist. Austin: University of Texas Press, 1981.

Belsey, Catherine. *Critical Practice*. London and New York: Methuen, 1980.

Booth, Wayne C. "Freedom of Interpretation: Bakhtin and the Challenge of Feminist Criticism," *Bakhtin: Essays and Dialogues on His Work*. Ed. Gary Saul Morson. Chicago and London: University of Chicago Press, 1981; rpt. 1986.

Crowley, J. Donald and Richard A. Hocks, eds. "Editors' Commentary," *The Wings of the Dove*. New York: Norton, 1978.

Eagleton, Terry. *Literary Theory: An Introduction*. Oxford: Basil Blackwell, 1983; rpt. 1985.

Edel, Leon. *The Life of Henry James: Volume 2*. Harmondsworth, Middlesex: Penguin Books, 1963; rpt. 1977.

Emerson, Caryl. "The Outer Word and Inner Speech: Bakhtin, Vygotsky, and the Internalization of Language," *Bakhtin: Essays and Dialogues on His Work*. Ed. Gary Saul Morson. Chicago and London: University of Chicago Press, 1986.

Faderman, Lillian. *Surpassing the Love of Men*. New York: William Morrow, 1981.

Fowler, Virginia. *Henry James's American Girl*. Madison: University of Wisconsin Press, 1984.

James, Alice. *The Death and Letters of Alice James*. Ed. Ruth Bernard Yeazell. Berkeley: University of California Press, 1981.

James, Henry. *The Bostonians*. New York: The New American Library, 1979.

_____. *The Wings of the Dove*. Ed. Donald Crowley and Richard Hocks. New York: Norton, 1978.

Krook, Dorothea. "Milly's and Densher's Ordeal of Consciousness" in *The Wings of the Dove*. Ed. Crowley and Hocks. New York: Norton, 1978.

Matthiessen, F. O. "James's Masterpiece" in *The Wings of the Dove*. Ed. Crowley and Hocks. New York: Norton, 1978.

Morson, Gary Saul. "Preface: Perhaps Bakhtin," *Bakhtin: Essays and Dialogues on His Work.* Ed. Gary Saul Morson. Chicago and London: University of Chicago Press, 1981; rpt. 1986.

Rowe, John Carlos. *The Theoretical Dimensions of Henry James.* Madison: University of Wisconsin Press, 1984.

Sears, Sallie. "Kate Croy and Merton Densher" in *The Wings of the Dove.* Ed. Crowley and Hocks. New York: Norton, 1978.

Shklovsky, Victor. "Sterne's *Tristram Shandy:* Stylistic Commentary," *Russian Formalist Criticism: Four Essays.* Trans. Lee T. Lemon and Marion J. Reis. Lincoln and London: University of Nebraska Press, 1965.

Spivak, Gayatri Chakravorty. "Explanation and Culture: Marginalia," *Humanities in Society* 2 (1974): 201 – 221.

————. "Feminism and Critical Theory," *For Alma Mater: Theory and Practice in Feminist Scholarship.* Eds. Paula A. Treichler, Cheris Kramarae, Beth Stafford. Urbana and Chicago: University of Illinois Press, 1985.

————. "French Feminism in an International Frame," *Yale French Studies* 62 (1981): 155 – 184.

————. "Revolutions That As Yet Have No Model: Derrida's *Limited Inc,*" *Diacritics* 10 (December 1980): 29 – 49.

Vygotsky, Lev. *The Psychology of Art.* Trans. Scripta Technica, Inc. Cambridge, Mass.: The M.I.T. Press, 1971.

Ward, J. A. "Social Disintegration in *The Wings of the Dove*" in *The Wings of the Dove.* Ed. Crowley and Hocks. New York: Norton, 1978.

Wegelin, Christof. "The Lesson of Spiritual Beauty" in *The Wings of the Dove.* Ed. Crowley and Hocks. New York: Norton, 1978.

3

Prolegomenon for an Ecofeminist Dialogics

Patrick D. Murphy

I

Pluralistic humanism has run its course. What may have encouraged individual growth and intellectual diversity for some components of the culture is now producing a *laissez-faire* attitude that truncates the debate over cultural values through nonjudgmental or "undecidability" postures.[1] As Gerald Graff has trenchantly suggested, "real disagreement has become rare, for the multiplicity of tongues leads not to confrontation but to incommensurability and talking at cross-purposes" (190). Pluralism has never included everybody, but has always established the parameters of acceptable difference: "our cultural discourse is a totality which does not contain everything — did not, for example, contain women, who were decisively not *only* the relative creatures the culture had imagined them to be" (Tarantelli, 180; see Marini, 150).

The various cataclysms of the twentieth century that dethroned the idealist humanism that posited the linear progression of western civilization did not dethrone the anthropocentrism of religious and secular humanism, nor did they disrupt the androcentrism that arises from the patriarchal base of Western culture. Similarly, the theoretical projects that arose to challenge humanism have produced an energetic skepticism and a shifting of foci of theoretical and critical attention, but they have not promoted a worldview that enables any kind of affirmation of new values or a praxis that enables the application of such values in the physical world. In marked contrast to critical maladies of enervated humanism, solipsistic skepticism, and paralytic undecidability, a triad of (re)perceptions has appeared, which, if integrated, can lead toward an affirmative praxis: the Bakhtinian dialogical method, ecology, and feministics.[2] Dialogics enables the differential unification of ecology and feministics that can produce a new perception of the relationship of humanity and world, and a praxis that works toward the decentering dealienation of andro/anthropocentric humanism and the reintegrative, affirmative dissolution of the intellectual isolation of "radical" skepticism. Dialogics encompasses Marxist dialectics through emphasizing the unity of opposites and their interanimating dynamic tension (see Lenin, 192 – 238 and 359 – 63; Mao, 117 – 25).[3] At the same time it reveals that the most fundamental relationships are not resolvable through dialectical synthesis: humanity/nature, ignorance/ knowledge, male/female, emotion/intellect, conscious/unconscious. And, Bakhtin's conception of centripetal/centrifugal tension provides a means of countering totalization so that any "totality" is continuously recognized as already a relativized, temporal centripetal entity in need of centrifugal destabilizing.

II

Ecology and feministics provide the groundings necessary to turn the dialogical method into a livable critical theory, rather than a merely usable one, applicable only to literature, language, and thought. As Gayatri Chakravorty Spivak candidly observes, "one must fill the vision of literary form with its connections to what is being read: history, political economy — the world. And questioning the separation between the world of action and the world of the disciplines. There is a great deal in the way" (95). And one of the "deals" in the way consists of critical theories that only work in the classroom but cannot be applied to the rest of one's interpretive behavior, by means of which we act in the world.

Ecology means fundamentally the study of the environment in its interanimating relationships, its change and conservation, with humanity recognized as a part of the planetary ecosystem. The study of ecology, then, is not a study of the "external" environment that we enter, or a management system for the raw materials at our command; it is a study of interrelationship, place, and function, with its bedrock being the recognition of the distinction between things-in-themselves and things-for-us. The latter entities result from intervention, manipulation, and transformation. And, as a corollary, if we can render other entities things-for-us, the reverse also exists: other entities can render us things-for-them. Ecology is a means for learning how to live appropriately in a particular place and time, so as to preserve, contribute to, and recycle the ecosystem (see Rolston, 14 – 27). As Adrienne Rich expresses it, "I need to understand how a place on the map is also a place in history, within which as a woman, a Jew, a lesbian, a feminist, I am created and trying to create" (8; see also Snyder, *Old Ways,* 63 – 64).

In a very basic way, the recognition of the difference between things-in-themselves and things-for-us, and the corollary of us-as-things-for-others, leads directly into feministics, particularly an inter-rogation of gender. Only through recognizing the existence of the "other" as a self-existent entity can we begin to comprehend a heter-archical gender dyad in which difference exists without binary oppo-sition and hierarchical valorization. Feministics, committed to exposing, critiquing, and ending the oppression of women, overthrow-ing patriarchy and phallocentrism, demands male recognition of the "other" as not only different but of equal ontological status. All four of the fundamental relationships identified above, humanity/nature, ig-norance/knowledge, male/female, and emotion/intellect, are impli-cated in and conceptually affected by patriarchal structure in all of its intertwined physical and intellectual manifestations. As the poet Sharon Doubiago dramatically states it, "because of sexism, because of the psychotic avoidance of the issue at all costs, ecologists have failed to grasp the fact that at the core of our suicidal mission is the psycho-logical issue of gender, the oldest war, the war of the sexes" (4).

But that first recognition of the "other" as self-existent entity is just that, a first step. It enables the further recognition of interrelation-ship and interanimation, but on a dyadic heterarchical basis rather than on a hierarchical use-value or exchange-value basis. Barbara Johnson notes that only a romantic androcentrism can phallaciously raise autonomy over all other relationships: "Clearly, for Thoreau, pregnancy was not an essential fact of life. Yet for him as well as for every human being that has yet existed, someone else's pregnancy is the very *first* fact of life. How might the plot of human subjectivity be reconceived (so to speak) if pregnancy rather than autonomy is what raises the question of deliberateness?" (190; see Keller, 106 – 7). Such a question arises only as a result of feminist interrogation. But it not only interrogates autonomy but also affirms relationship, privileging by im-plication nurturing over engendering. This privileging provides a nec-essary corrective to the androcentric-based difference between the definitions of "fathering" and "mothering" in our culture, which in themselves have significant ecological implications, the former of un-limited expansion and the latter of sustaining.

But heterarchy does not simply return us to pluralism. Hazel Henderson, in explaining heterarchy, speaks of such a viewpoint as meaning subset plurality within a system without dominant/subordinate ranking and argues that "hierarchy is an illusion generated by a fixed observer" (212). Thus we can recognize that biogender differences exist, can occur in both genders, and should not be comparatively evaluated to determine which are more "useful" or "superior." Rosemary Reuther makes the case that "without sex-role stereotyping, sex-personality stereotyping would disappear, allowing for genuine individuation of personality. Instead of being forced into a mold of masculine or feminine 'types,' each individual could shape a complex whole from the full range of human psychic potential for intellect and feeling, activity and receptivity" (210). At the same time, such a heterarchical viewpoint would necessarily challenge any effort to maintain and cultivate sociogender differences because these would limit subset plurality and serve oppressive and exploitative purposes. This would lead to specific political practices that would subvert existing social structures and participate in the process of evolving new structures. Such evolution in turn serves a basic ecological function: "A healthy, balanced ecosystem, including human and nonhuman inhabitants, must maintain diversity" (King, 119). And that diversity will occur within ecosystem homeostatis, which is "an achievement and a tendency. Systems recycle, and there is energy balance; yet the systems are not static, but dynamic" (Rolston, 14). The capitalist myth of unlimited expansion is actually a static ideal, no different from the dream for a perpetual motion machine.

Using the health of the ecosystem as the fundamental criterion for judgment enables us to introduce a new conception of value to oppose those that dominate capitalist and state capitalist economies. In opposition to either use value or exchange value as the criterion of worth, we need to develop a criterion of ecological value, which emphasizes interrelationship, maintenance, and sustainment. I would argue that just such heterarchical differentiation explicitly, and a sense of ecological value implicitly, guides much of Carol Gilligan's *In A Different Voice*. As she suggests, "through this expansion in perspective, we can begin to envision how a marriage between adult development as it is currently portrayed and women's development as it begins to be seen could lead to a changed understanding of human development and a more generative view of human life" (174). The triad of dialogics, feministics, and ecology, in that order, clearly appears in this remark concluding her book.

In terms of judgmental criteria, feminists have criticized Marxists for subordinating the struggle against women's oppression to the class

struggle and for emphasizing the conditions and relations of production over those of reproduction. Such criticisms are directed against
the limitations of a determinist interpretation that privileges the history of class struggle over the larger history of human inequality based
on gender oppression and reproductive exploitation. Oppression and
exploitation, gender and class, are intimately and inseparably linked,
but with a significant difference. Specific conditions and relations of
production and the classes that arise from them are historically transient. But gender, like pigmentation, will exist with any relations of
production, and will continue to produce a dynamic tension born of
difference that can potentially result in oppression. The relations of
reproduction, unlike those of production, are necessarily more dialogical than dialectical. And the struggles to overthrow both patriarchy
and capitalism need to be placed in an even larger context: the relationship of humanity within nature. The recent development of an
ecological feminism (ecofeminism) has begun this process of intertwining the dyads of female/male and nature/humanity.

The weaknesses regarding gender oppression and sociogender
differences in "Deep Ecology" demonstrate the inability of environ-
mentalism on its own to produce a sufficient livable theory and all-
sided praxis (see Devall and Sessions on Deep Ecology; for critiques
see Doubiago, Salleh, Warren, Zimmerman, and Murphy, "Sex-
Typing"). Feminist thought has to be employed to bring to consciousness and thus enable the breaking of patriarchal habits of perception.
But environmentalists have not initially recognized the identity of in-
terests. Ynestra King noted only a few years ago that

> For the most part, ecologists, with their concern for nonhuman na-
> ture, have yet to understand that they have a particular stake in end-
> ing the domination of women because a central reason for woman's
> oppression is her association with the despised nature they are so
> concerned about. The hatred of women and the hatred of nature are
> intimately connected and mutually reinforcing. (118)

King argues that domination of man over woman is the prototype for
other forms of domination, but it is unlikely that they can be chrono-
logically separated since they are founded on the same conception of
reality. More important, however, are the four principles that King establishes as the base for ecofeminism: (1) the oppression of women and
the building of "Western industrial civilization" are interrelated
through the belief that women are closer to nature; (2) life on earth is
heterarchical, "an interconnected web"; (3) a balanced ecosystem of

human and nonhuman "must maintain diversity"; (4) species survival necessitates a "renewed understanding of our relationship to nature, of our own bodily nature and nonhuman nature around us" (119–20).

Ariel Kay Salleh critiques Deep Ecology in terms of its failure to make the paradigm shift necessary to achieve its professed goals. Specifically, she argues that it takes an anti-class posture, but ignores oppression, and that it remains trapped in a "tacit mind-body dualism" that downplays the significance of ideology as a material force in the world. "The feminist consciousness," declares Salleh, "is equally concerned to eradicate ideological pollution, which centuries of patriarchal conditioning have subjected us all to, women and men" (342). She concludes that the proponents of Deep Ecology remain locked in the old dualistic paradigms because they have not as yet denounced and sought to overthrow "the suppression of the *feminine*." And this "is not just a suppression of real, live, empirical women, but equally the suppression of the feminine aspects of men's own constitution which is the issue here" (344).

Karen J. Warren begins her discussion of ecofeminism with this very problem of dualism, and for her the strength of ecofeminism is that it "encourages us to think ourselves out of 'patriarchal conceptual traps,' by *reconceptualizing* ourselves and our relation to the nonhuman natural world in nonpatriarchal ways" (7). Much of Warren's essay is given over to a critique of liberal feminism, Marxist feminism, radical feminism, and socialist feminism, and their shortcomings, which necessitate a "transformative feminism" that will "make a responsible ecological perspective central to feminist theory and practice" (18).

But how are all of these interrogational and transformative strands to be woven into a philosophical net with a self-conscious method of critique and affirmation? Ecofeminism needs a philosophical method not only to link its fundamental aspects but also to enable it to remain an active, developing critique guiding praxis rather than a monological political dogma or an abstract interpretive instrument. That method is dialogics.

III

The Bakhtinian dialogical method is becoming widely recognized. But some character traits are less known and more neglected than others. It seems no accident that *Freudianism: A Marxist Critique*, published under Vološinov's name, is the last Bakhtinian text to be reissued and appear in paperback, although it was one of the earliest works published. Except for the well-quoted "Discourse in Life and Discourse in Art," it is the text least related to literature and literary theory per se, but one of crucial importance for Bakhtin's concept of the utterance, particularly in terms of the "inner word" and in terms of a larger conception of the dialogical method as reaching beyond aesthetic texts.[4]

In opposition to what was perceived as Freudian psychoanalysis, *Freudianism* presents dialogical conceptions of the self, the psyche, and the "content of consciousness," which initiate the recognition of the constitution of the individual as a *chronotopic relationship*, i.e., a social/self construct developing within given social, economic, political, historical, and environmental parameters of space and time (Bakhtin, *Dialogic*, 85). The "other" in its various manifestations, therefore, including *parole*, culture, place, class, race, and gender, participates in the formation of self. The individual occurs as chronotope within the "story" of human interaction with the physical world, but that narrative is only a historical fiction organized by means of a limited perspective through which beginnings, middles, ends, and motivations are substituted for the nonhuman centered, contiguously structured universal story that allots us only episodes — the self in and as part of the other. This self/other as interpenetrating part/part and part/whole relationships rather than dichotomy is fundamental for understanding the mutually constitutive character of the dialogics-ecology-feministics triad. Both ecology and feministics are deeply concerned with the conception of the "other" as part of effecting crucial paradigm shifts in human understanding.

Just as the other participates in the formation of the self, so too does the self as individual-in-the-world participate in the formation of the other in its various manifestations. And, just as the self enters into language and the use of *parole*, so too does the "other" enter into language and have the potential, as does any entity, to become a "speaking subject," although centripetal structures and cultural forces hinder such a realization. The implications of this other as speaking subject need to be conceptualized as including more than humans, and as potentially being constituted by a speaker/author who is not the speaking subject but a renderer of the other as speaking subject (Bakhtin, *Problems*, 47 – 57). The pivotal questions here will be the degree to which language is recognized as one type of sign system, the degree to which volition is assumed as a prerequisite for becoming a speaking subject, and the degree to which the other speaking subjects who do not use the *parole* of human beings can "speak" in a sign system that can be understood by humans.

In *Freudianism,* Bakhtin attacks Freudian psychology as being

based on "a *sui generis* fear of history, an ambition to locate a world beyond the social and the historical, a search for this world precisely in the depths of the organic" (14). In contrast, he claims that "outside society and, consequently, outside objective socioeconomic conditions, there is no such thing as a human being. Only as a part of a social whole, only in and through a social class, does the human person become historically real and culturally productive" (15). All this is true in contradistinction to the ahistorical biologistic bent under attack, but it is true only insofar as we are talking of a person as a sociocultural historical entity. Yet a human being is also a biologically developed entity. In his effort to reinsert the human being into history and culture, Bakhtin artificially removes that being from the environment. It has been the view of both feminist and post-Marxist psychoanalytic study that the psychological dimensions of the individual need to be analyzed as an integral part of the whole being, and not as a narrowly defined originary center, but the tendency remains to isolate qualitatively that being from the world.

Bakhtin emphasizes from the opening of *Freudianism* the significance in psychology of the conflicts between inner and outer speech and various levels of inner speech, that communication between the conscious and the unconscious consisting of specific utterances that have a speaker and a respondent, a "self" and an other "self," which are not identical but are parts of the same mind (23 – 24). Jacques Lacan views the unconscious as being "structured like a language," and some French feminists, such as Hélène Cixous, also view it as having language at least as it is constituted by means of the "Imaginary." But Bakhtin points out that this use of language always appears in the form of utterances made by the conscious speaking subject, even when mediating messages from the unconscious.

As Bakhtin insists, "every utterance is the product of the interaction between speakers and the product of the broader context of the whole complex social situation in which the utterance emerges" (*Freudianism*, 79; see *Speech Genres*, 71). Even the articulation of the unconscious is a social interrelationship by virtue of its minimal dynamic of being an utterance (79). This point is reinforced by Bakhtin's claim that "any speaker himself is a respondent to a greater or lesser degree" (*Speech Genres*, 69). Thus, the "other" is always implicated in psychical activities, indicating that the "self" itself is not singular, unified, or total, but is multiple, through the non-identity of the conscious and unconscious and self-conceptions and drives (see Smith, ch. 5). It is precisely this recognition of non-identity and the need for inner dialogue, specifically between "masculine" and "feminine" aspects of the psyche, that Salleh sees missing from the propositions of Deep Ecology and seriously impairs its subversion of patriarchy's hegemony. As Cixous's attempts to write the Imaginary indicate, as in "The Laugh of the Medusa," all efforts to articulate the mind involve social interaction. Even as she seeks to "break" the language, she does so in a sociohistorical context and through orienting her ideas toward an audience that is expected to participate actively in the constitution of meaning ([Bakhtin]/Vološinov, *Marxism,* 102; see *Speech Genres,* 111).

To the degree that we are able to articulate the mental activities of our unconscious as well as conscious verbally, these articulations are oriented toward the rest of the world and our position in that world. And they are articulated by means of words that always already introduce that other world to us as a result of the historicity of *parole.* But this also applies to articulation by means of other semiotic structures, which are also either culturally or naturally constituted so that the audience for them has the potential for responsive understanding (see [Bakhtin]/Vološinov, *Marxism,* 10 – 12). I would argue that, like the unconscious, the nonhuman also articulates itself by means of various "dialects," and neither requires volition to do so.

In addition, Bakhtin argues for calling "the inner and outward speech that permeates our behavior in all its aspects 'behavioral ideology.'" He goes on to say that "this behavioral ideology is in certain respects more sensitive, more excitable and livelier than an ideology that has undergone formulation and become 'official.' In the depths of behavioral ideology accumulate those contradictions which, once having reached a certain threshold, ultimately burst asunder the system of the official ideology" (*Freudianism,* 88). Here one sees implicit the fundamental tension between centripetal and centrifugal forces, with the centrifugal privileged for its desystematizing power. The upshot of all this is that even at the level of the articulation of the unconscious, the individual is already socially interacting, laying the basis for an impact upon the world that has been affecting that individual.[5] What is suggested here is the role of the individual through self-reflection and self-conscious articulation of thought in transforming ideology (*Freudianism,* 90). This occurs as a result of the individual undergoing, reflecting on, and articulating the differences between experiences in social reality and the natural world that do not square with the official ideology, and then developing subject-positions that enable resistance (Smith, ch. 1).

If, indeed, psychoanalysis and self-analysis involve a dialogue of the conscious and unconscious, which together constitute the life of the mind, then conscious/unconscious form an unsynthesizable dialogical relationship. Freud's recognition that the unconscious could not be abolished led him to attempt to keep it in check through the Superego. Others predating Freud attempted a similar maneuver in the realm of the intellect/emotion dyad, believing that rationality and reason, products of enlightenment, would enable one to overcome the emotions. Emotions, of course, were the province of the feminine. Surprisingly enough, despite the obviously oppressive character of this hierarchical assignation of reason and emotion to the differing genders, we see its repetition in the attempted Lacanian identification of the unconscious with the female (see Jardine, "Gynesis," for a critique of this position). And yet again, we have both within each of us, emotion and intellect, conscious and unconscious, and at various times one serves us better than the other in our worldly encounters. Dialogics lets us recognize the mutually constitutive character of these dyads, with each aspect at specific times being constituted as a center of mental activity and requiring the other to act as centrifugal force preventing the solidification of that center into dogma. If emotion and instinct arise from historical natural influences on the evolution of the species, then their exertions on our behavior, their entering into consciousness, are a form of the natural world "speaking" to us through signs that our conscious renders verbally. To deny "emotion" as feminine and/or "instinct" as primitive nature is to reserve the role of speaking subject only for the ego and to deny a voice to the "other," which is in reality a part of ourselves.

The dialogical relationships of the intellect/emotion and humanity/nature dyads can only be ascertained through attempting to facilitate the coming into verbal being of both sides of the dyad. And here one of the limitations of Bakhtin's formulations reveals itself in his limiting a conception of the other to participants in human society. Ecology has to be brought to bear to break dialogics out of the anthropocentrism in which Bakhtin performs it (see, for example, "Discourse in Life," 95). Such a limitation renders it impossible for any aspect of the nonhuman to be rendered as a speaking subject, whether in artistic texts, other texts, or human behavior. Although he does argue that the object of the utterance is a living participant, a third constitutive factor of the utterance, which can be the external/nonverbal world to which the speech act is oriented, it remains an object ("Discourse," 101 – 2). And yet, does not instinct itself, which arises from outside or prior to "society," become a speaking subject through the unconscious and through emotions, which themselves create electrochemical changes in the human body?

Numerous authors and artists have attempted to render nature as a speaking subject, not like the romantics to render nature an object for the self-constitution of the poet as speaking subject, but as a character within texts with its own existence. I think here of the efforts of such writers as Dorothy Wordsworth, Robinson Jeffers, Mary Oliver, John Haines, Ursula Le Guin, Gary Snyder, and Linda Hogan. There is not the space to argue here for their degrees of successful rendering of the nonhuman as speaking subject, but I think these attempts become most successful when they include human characters as well, enabling the differential comparison of self and other. An ecofeminist dialogics requires this effort to render the other, primarily constituted by androcentrism as women and nature (and actually as the two intertwined: nature-as-woman and woman-as-nature), as speaking subjects within patriarchy in order to subvert that patriarchy not only by decentering it but also by proposing other centers. Speaking at the Center for the Study of Democratic Institutions, Gary Snyder called for establishing "a kiva of elders" to represent the nonhuman within democratic institutions:

> Historically this has been done through art. The paintings of bison and bears in the caves of southern France were of that order. The animals were speaking through the people and making their point. And when, in the dances of the Pueblo Indians and other people, certain individuals became seized, as it were, by the spirit of the deer, and danced as a deer would dance, or danced the dance of the corn maidens, or impersonated the squash blossom, they were no longer speaking for humanity, they were taking it on themselves to interpret, through their humanity, what these other life-forms were. That is about all we know so far concerning the possibilities of incorporating spokesmanship for the rest of life in our democratic society. (*Turtle Island*, 109; see also Silko, Rodman)

That may have been about all we knew fifteen years ago, but feministics has taught us much since then about incorporating at least part of the rest of life into our discourse, constituting women as speaking subjects. The point is not to speak for nature, but to work to render the significance presented us by nature into verbal depiction by means of speaking subjects, whether this is through characterization in the arts or through discursive prose. To quote Snyder again:

> What we must find a way to do, then, is incorporate the other people — what Sioux Indians called the creeping people, and the standing people, and the flying people, and the swimming people — into the councils of government. This isn't as difficult as you might think. If

we don't do it, they will revolt against us. They will submit non-
negotiable demands about our stay on the earth. We are beginning to
get non-negotiable demands right now from the air, the water, the
soil. (*Turtle Island*, 108)

I don't share his optimism about the facility of this move, but I
believe in its necessity and applaud Le Guin's depiction of it in *Always
Coming Home*. When a person cries out in pain, is it volitional? When
selenium poisons ground water, causes animal deformities, and re-
duces the ability of California farmers to continue to overcultivate
through irrigation land with little topsoil, are these signs that we can
read? And in reading such signs and integrating them into our texts,
are we letting that land speak through us or are we only speaking
for it?

Nonhuman others can be constituted as speaking subjects rather
than merely objects of our speaking, although even the latter is pref-
erable to silence. The analogy I would use is that of men adopting
feminist theories, practices, or interpretations. Far too often men continue attempting to speak *for* women, with the following result: "when
male theorists borrow the language of feminist criticism without a willingness to explore the masculinist bias of their own reading system, we
get a phallic 'feminist' criticism that competes with women instead of
breaking out of patriarchal bounds" (Showalter, 127). It is possible,
however, for men to render women as speaking subjects by means of
their application of feminists theories, criticism, and scholarship
(Heath, 8–9, 27–28). The feminists who have constituted themselves
as speaking subjects have enabled some men to render that voicing.
Such rendering will always occur within the limitations of the author's/
speaker's refractive mediation, and there will certainly always be two
voices there — the feminist speaking subject and the rendering male
author — just as there will be with the nonhuman speaking subject and
the rendering human author. In neither case does this excuse waging
the struggle for such rendering. Richard Ohmann makes the point
that

If [men] are "in" feminism at all, we were dragged into it kicking and
screaming, and now that we're there we should think of ourselves as
on extended probation, still learning. What we do there with our experiences, our competence, and our gender and class confidence, is a
matter to be negotiated through caution, flexibility, improvisation, listening, and often doubtless through a strategic fading into the wall-
paper. But I don't see drawing back from the knowledge that
feminism is our fight, too. (187)[6]

"Caution, flexibility, improvisation, listening" are certainly attributes of the best ecological and feministic work to date practiced by both women and men and imply a strongly dialogical orientation toward critical work. And yet, how does one maintain such a stance and avoid tendencies toward dogmatism and totalization? Dialogical rigor.

IV

At the end of each of the preceding parts, I have emphasized application of the dialogical method to avoid interrogative sclerosis and ideological calcification. Bakhtin himself presents a dyad that both explains the need to oppose dogmatism and totalization, that clarifies the heterarchical yet partisan character of dialogics, and provides a conceptual framework for being able to critique and affirm without absolutes. That dyad is centripetal/centrifugal, a mutually constituted relational unity of opposites: "Alongside the centripetal forces, the centrifugal forces of language carry on their uninterrupted work; alongside verbal-ideological centralization and unification, the uninterrupted processes of decentralization and disunification go forward" (*Dialogic*, 272). In language and ideology this dyad continuously manifests itself as center and margin, and has been a crucial basis for the development of deconstruction. Yet, deconstruction has found itself unable to affirm much beyond pleasure and play — hardly sufficient for the process of reconstruction that occurs following the overthrow of any outmoded system of thought, government, culture, or community. A paradigm shift requires not merely the scuttling of the previous paradigm but the institution of a new one, which in its turn will also need scuttling.

The struggle is not to abolish any type of centering, but to recognize the relative nature of centers and their dynamic relationship with margins. Given the cultural and ideological hegemony of capitalism in the United States, ecofeminists must necessarily comprise part of the margin, serving as a centrifugal force attempting to break up, to fragment the totalizing discourse that perpetuates business as usual. At the same time, those working within the margins must recognize that at any given moment they are forming a center from/on which to work. But there are centers and there are centers. One type serves as foundation, cast in stone and rendered immovable, on which to stand; the other serves as pivot, a base on which to step and from which to move on to another center-as-pivot. The distinction here is that between

-isms and -istics, dogmas or beliefs, and perspectives or hypotheses.

In an article defending Deep Ecology, George Sessions suggests the problems with failing to distinguish between -isms and -istics. He recognizes and opposes the way some forces within the ecological movement in America have become misanthropes as a result of an ecocentrism that requires an absolute "Earth First" position. At the same time, Sessions argues that "the Age of Ecology involves a major 'paradigm shift' to an ecocentric mode of understanding the world ... The ecocentric perspective involves a biological, as well as a cultural, understanding of the human species resulting in a new awareness of the place of humans in the ecological web and of the ecological limitations of humans in the Earth community" (66). This definition of an "ecocentric mode of understanding," it seems to me, is far more dialogical than the beliefs of many adherents of ecocentrism, including some that Sessions cites. Yet he himself is caught up in a non-dialogical nostalgic conception of ecocentrism that would render its present day formulations essentially identical with ancient and primal ones: "When we realize that over 99% of all humans who have ever lived on Earth have been hunters/gatherers, then it is clear that ecocentrism has been the dominant human perspective throughout history" (66). Here Sessions confuses conditions and existence with beliefs about that existence and overlooks the philosophical and experiential distances between our ancestors and ourselves.

To substitute ecocentrism for anthropocentrism does not constitute the significant paradigm shift that Sessions, as well as the rest of us, wish to see occur because it allows for the continued belief in and promotion of static absolutes. We have seen this same problem arising in Marxism with the establishment of the dialectic not as a method but as a blueprint in which the "synthesis" is idealistically preordained. Nostalgia is another dimension of the absolutist tendencies of -isms, which reinforces static idealizations. If ecocentrism and androgyny existed once long ago in a virtually unblemished state, then we need only to get back to that state and find the answer that has already existed rather than to create a relative answer that will invariably be flawed and inadequate to the complexities of the question that required it. The recognition of such inadequacy provides the skeptical self-interrogation necessary to maintain any answer as a pivot rather than a foundation. In like manner, different elements within the feminist movement have set specific goals and principles for themselves that need to be continuously revisioned if participants are not to end up asking "is that all there is" without any method for projecting the next step.

Not long before his death Bakhtin wrote that "there is neither a first nor a last word and there are no limits to the dialogic context" (*Speech Genres,* 170). The dialogic method is a way to incorporate that decentering recognition of a permanent *in media res* of human life and a constantly widening context for human interaction and interanimation within the biosphere and beyond. Coupled with the two basic pivots outlined here, ecology and feministics, dialogics provides a method by which we may yet effect one of the paradigm shifts necessary to break down the dualistic thinking of patriarchy that perpetuates the exploitation and oppression of nature in general and women in particular. At the same time, it warns us that once we do succeed in overthrowing patriarchy and its socioeconomic systems, a new host of problems and contradictions will arise, as yet unenvisioned, that will require new debate, new answers, and new pivots. Ecofeminist dialogics provides a place and method by which to step and dance, but not to stand.

Notes

1. This criticism of the concept of "pluralism" includes a self-critique of my use of that term in "Sex-Typing."

2. "Feministics" defines the orientation of feminist-anchored practices, including political activism, women's studies, feminist critique and gynocriticism, and feminist theory; but recognizes that there is neither a monolithic "feminism" nor "feminist theory," and that much valuable feminist critical work is non- or anti-theoretical; it also implies the non-dogmatic multivocality, suspicion of *-ismness,* and self-critique that abounds in feminist work.

3. I take up the relationship and difference of dialogics and dialectics in greater detail in "Dialectics or Dialogics."

4. Although a few proponents of Bakhtin have initiated such reaching, dialogics remains primarily a method of literary criticism or rhetorical studies, for which it serves very well. But my point is that not only need it not be as limited as most adoptions of it suggest, even in the case of such broader essays as Don Bialostosky's and Charles Schuster's, or as limited as Bakhtin himself allowed it to be, but that it must not remain so limited if it is to realize its effective potential in the world.

5. In relation to this point, see Bakhtin's discussion of primary and secondary speech genres in *Speech Genres,* 60 – 63, and the remarks on the materiality and ideological value of semiotic materials in *Marxism,* 10 – 12.

6. Cary Nelson observes that feminism does not need men for its theoretical development (157). While I agree with this in relation to theory and to any

particular critical innovation or realization, I have to disagree with the idea of
a lack of a "need" for men in relation to the potential for ideological and political victories on the part of feminist struggles, given the balance of forces in
the world today.

Works Cited

Adams, Hazard, and Leroy Searle, eds. *Critical Theory Since 1965*. Tallahassee:
    Florida State University Press, 1986.

Bakhtin, Mikhail. *The Dialogic Imagination: Four Essays by M. M. Bakhtin*.
    Trans. Michael Holquist and Caryl Emerson. Ed. Holquist. Austin:
    University of Texas Press, 1981.

_____. *Problems of Dostoevsky's Poetics*. Trans. and ed. Caryl Emerson. Theory
    and History of Literature 8. Minneapolis: University of Minnesota
    Press, 1984.

_____. *Speech Genres & Other Late Essays*. Trans. Vern W. McGee. Ed. Caryl
    Emerson and Michael Holquist. Austin: University of Texas Press,
    1986.

[Bakhtin]/V. N. Vološinov. "Discourse in Life and Discourse in Art." In [Bakh-
    tin]/Vološinov, *Freudianism*, 93 – 116.

_____. *Freudianism: A Marxist Critique*. Trans. I. R. Titunik. Ed. Titunik and
    Neal H. Bruss. New York: Academic Press, 1976.

_____. *Marxism and the Philosophy of Language*. Trans. Ladislav Matejka and I.
    R. Titunik. Cambridge: Harvard University Press, 1986.

Bialostosky, Don. "Dialogics as an Art of Discourse in Literary Criticism."
    PMLA 101.5 (1986): 788 – 97.

Bruss, Neal H. "V. N. Vološinov and the Structure of Language in Freudian-
    ism." In [Bakhtin]/Vološinov, *Freudianism*, 117 – 48.

Cixous, Hélène. "The Laugh of the Medusa." *Signs* 1 (1976). Reprinted in
    Adams and Searle, 309 – 20.

Devall, Bill, and George Sessions. *Deep Ecology: Living as if Nature Mattered*.
    Salt Lake City: Peregrine, Smith, 1985.

Doubiago, Sharon. "From Mama Coyote Talks to the Boys," *Upriver/Downriver*
    #11 (1988): 1 – 5.

Gilligan, Carol. *In A Different Voice: Psychological Theory and Women's Develop-
    ment*. Cambridge: Harvard University Press, 1982.

Graff, Gerald. *Literature Against Itself: Literary Ideas in Modern Society*. Chicago:
    University of Chicago Press, 1979.

Heath, Stephen. "Male Feminism." In Jardine and Smith, 1 – 32.

Henderson, Hazel. "The Warp and the Weft: The Coming Synthesis of Eco-Philosophy and Eco-Feminism." In *Reclaim the Earth: Women Speak Out for Life on Earth.* Ed. Leonie Caldecott and Stephanie Leland. London: The Women's Press, 1983.

Jardine, Alice A. "Gynesis." *Diacritics* 12 (1982). Reprinted in Adams and Searle, 560 – 70.

————. "Men in Feminism: Odor di Uomo or Compagnons de Route?" In Jardine and Smith, 54 – 61.

————, and Paul Smith, eds. *Men in Feminism.* New York: Methuen, 1987.

Johnson, Barbara. *A World of Difference.* Baltimore: Johns Hopkins University Press, 1987.

Keller, Evelyn Fox. *Reflections on Gender and Science.* New Haven: Yale University Press, 1985.

King, Ynestra. "Toward an Ecological Feminism and a Feminist Ecology." In *Machina Ex Dea: Feminist Perspectives on Technology.* Ed. Joan Rothschild. New York: Pergamon Press, 1983. 118 – 29.

Lacan, Jacques. "The Mirror Stage." In *Ecrits,* 1977. Reprinted in Adams and Searle, 734 – 38.

Le Guin, Ursula K. *Always Coming Home.* New York: Bantam, 1986.

Lenin, V. I. *Philosophical Notebooks.* Vol. 38 of *Collected Works.* Trans. Clemens Dutt. Ed. Stewart Smith. 4th ed. 45 vols. Moscow: Foreign Languages Publishing House, 1961.

Mao Zedong (Mao Tsetung). "On Contradiction." In *Selected Readings from the Works of Mao Tsetung.* Peking: Foreign Language Press, 1971, 85 – 133.

Marini, Marcelle. "Feminism and Literary Criticism: Reflections on the Disciplinary Approach." In *Women in Culture and Politics: A Century of Change.* Ed. Judith Friedlander, et al. Bloomington: Indiana University Press, 1986. 144 – 63.

Murphy, Patrick D. "Dialectics or Dialogics: Method and Message in the Classroom." *The GRIP Report* 8. Proceedings of the Sixth Annual Meeting of the GRIP Project, May 20 – 22, 1988, Carnegie Mellon University, Pittsburgh.

————. "Sex-Typing the Planet: Gaia Imagery and the Problem of Subverting Patriarchy," *Environmental Ethics* 10 (1988): 155 – 68.

Nelson, Cary. "Men, Feminism: The Materiality of Discourse." In Jardine and Smith, 153 – 72.

Ohmann, Richard. "In, With." In Jardine and Smith, 182–88.

Reuther, Rosemary Radford. *New Woman/New Earth: Sexist Ideologies and Human Liberation.* New York: The Seabury Press, 1975.

Rich, Adrienne. "Notes Toward a Politics of Location." In *Women, Feminist Identity and Society in the 1980s: Selected Papers.* Ed. Myriam Díaz-Diocaretz and Iris M. Zavala. Philadelphia: John Benjamins, 1985. 7–22.

Rodman, John. "The Dolphin Papers." *On Nature: Nature, Landscape, and Natural History.* Ed. Daniel Halpern. San Francisco: North Point Press, 1987. 252–80.

Rolston, Holmes, III. *Philosophy Gone Wild: Essays in Environmental Ethics.* Buffalo: Prometheus Books, 1986.

Salleh, Ariel Kay. "Deeper than Deep Ecology: The Eco-Feminist Connection." *Environmental Ethics* 6 (1984): 339–45.

Schuster, Charles I. "Mikhail Bakhtin as Rhetorical Theorist." *College English* 47 (1985): 594–607.

Sessions, George. "Ecocentrism and the Greens: Deep Ecology and the Environmental Task." *Trumpeter* 5.2 (1988): 65–69.

Showalter, Elaine. "Critical Cross-Dressing: Male Feminists and the Woman of the Year." In Jardine and Smith, 116–32.

Silko, Leslie Marmon. "Landscape, History, and the Pueblo Imagination." *On Nature: Nature, Landscape, and Natural History.* Ed. Daniel Halpern. San Francisco: North Point Press, 1987. 83–94.

Smith, Paul. *Discerning the Subject.* Minneapolis: University of Minnesota Press, 1988.

Snyder, Gary. *The Old Ways.* San Francisco: City Lights Books, 1977.

———. *Turtle Island.* New York: New Directions, 1974.

Spivak, Gayatri Chakravorty. *In Other Worlds: Essays in Cultural Politics.* New York: Methuen, 1987.

Tarantelli, Carole B. "And the Last Walls Dissolved: On Imagining a Story of the Survival of Difference." In *Women in Culture and Politics: A Century of Change.* Ed. Judith Friedlander, et al. Bloomington: Indiana University Press, 1986. 177–93.

Warren, Karen J. "Feminism and Ecology: Making Connections." *Environmental Ethics* 9 (1987): 3–20.

Zimmerman, Michael E. "Feminism, Deep Ecology, and Environmental Ethics." *Environmental Ethics* 9 (1987): 21–44.

4

Irigarayan Dialogism: Play and Powerplay

Gail M. Schwab

Dialogic Thinking and Thinking Dialogics

The contributions of Mikhail Bakhtin and his circle to linguistics, philosophy, and literary criticism have been enormous, and they promise only to continue to grow and develop as scholars in all branches of these disciplines become more familiar with the ideas and concepts involved. The very existence of an anthology entitled *Feminism, Bakhtin and the Dialogic* underlines Bakhtin's increasing importance for women's studies and for feminism itself. One of the ways in which *we*, that is to say that small but fairly vocal group of scholars considering ourselves to be feminists, can make use of Bakhtinian linguistic philosophy is in the re-reading and re-interpreting of the writings of the French feminist, Luce Irigaray.

Frequently criticized as apolitical and essentialistic, Irigaray, one of the most radical feminist thinkers writing today, has often been compartmentalized, and thus conveniently marginalized, by American feminist scholarship. There are many reasons for this, some of them too polemical (can that really mean too "dialogic?") to go into here, but one of the main reasons is Irigaray's own style of thought and expression. Dialogic herself, she is easily misinterpreted because she speaks in many voices. A traditional monologic reading of Irigaray will privilege one voice over all the others, or silence one or more voices, but I will argue that Irigaray should not, indeed cannot, be read monologically. The Bakhtinian dialogic linguistic model articulates her textuality at the same time as it allows us to grasp the inappropriateness of any monologic interpretation of her work.

In a now oft-quoted passage from chapter three of *Marxism and the Philosophy of Language* we read:

Utterance, as we know, is constructed between two socially organized persons ... The *word is oriented toward an addressee,* toward *who* that addressee might be: a fellow-member or not of the same social group, of higher or lower standing (the addressee's hierarchical status), someone connected with the speaker by close social ties (father, brother, husband and so on) or not. There can be no such thing as an abstract addressee, a man unto himself, so to speak. (All italics represent Vološinov/Bakhtin's emphasis.)[1]

Luce Irigaray's *Parler n'est jamais neutre* (*To Speak is Never Neutral/Non-Gendered*)[2] offers what might be called an existential illustration of this Bakhtinian concept of the social origin of language. Irigaray, addressing the *Séminaire d'histoire et sociologie des idées et des faits scientifiques* (Seminar of the History and Sociology of Scientific Facts and Ideas), of the University of Provence, Marseille, is aware of and inhibited by the prestige of the "hard" sciences (a phallocentric term if ever there was one). In these sciences truth is considered solid and graspable, that is apolitical, non-gendered and impersonal, and facts are not spoken by anyone for anyone but "speak for (and by) themselves" in a crystalline neutral medium. Irigaray openly declares her distress:

Depuis longtemps, je n'ai pas éprouvé une telle difficulté à l'idée de parler en public. Le plus souvent, je peux anticiper à qui je vais parler, comment parler, comment argumenter, me faire comprendre, plaider, voire plaire ou déplaire. Cette fois je ne sais rien, parce que je ne sais pas qui j'ai devant moi. Revers de l'impérialisme scientifique: ne pas savoir à qui l'on s'adresse, comment parler.[3]

She is uncomfortably aware of the falsehood of such a position. In Bakhtinian terms,

word is a two-sided act. It is determined equally by *whose* word it is and *for whom* it is meant. As word, it is precisely *the product of the reciprocal relationship between speaker and listener, addresser and addressee.* Each and every word expresses the "one" in relation to the "other." I give myself verbal shape from another's point of view. ... [4]

Language cannot be cut loose from person, time, and place to float freely in some ideal, impersonal, non-time and non-place. Bakhtin's critique of structuralist linguistics is well-known and need not be restated here. What is important in this context is Irigaray's insistence on articulating the contingent, social nature of her own language.

Irigaray's acute and painful sensitivity to the dialogic nature of language is rare — particularly in academic colloquia where the one who speaks is only minimally concerned with the one who listens, or is even indifferent to whether anyone listens at all. She will not, or cannot, speak from a position of neutral impersonality.

> Pourquoi un sujet ne dirait-il pas: *je sens ainsi, je vois telle chose, je veux ou je peux ceci, j'affirme cela?* Ce doit être une question de temps? Un frein dans les découvertes. Mais ce frein ne se sait plus comme tel et se prétend vérité. Or le "je" est parfois plus vrai que le "on" ou le "il." Plus vrai parce qu'il dit ses sources.[5]

I, Luce Irigaray, can speak *to* someone, but *"truth"* will not simply speak itself. As she faces her audience in Marseille, the empty space she feels and the silence she hears, where other bodies and other voices should have been, have the unexpected effect of wiping out knowledge. *"Cette fois je ne sais rien, parce que je ne sais pas qui j'ai devant moi."* "I don't know *anything* [my emphasis] because I don't know whom I have before me." Knowledge itself is here a function of dialogue.

No other feminist writer is so profoundly dialogic as Irigaray. Her theoretical stance has always been that of a respondent or a questioner. She engages another in dialogue, reacts to the other, interacts. *"La Tache aveugle d'un vieux rêve de symétrie"* ("The Blind Spot in an Old Dream of Symmetry"), the principal essay of the 1974 *Speculum,* is a reading of Freud, and in it Irigaray points out metaphysical assumptions, contradictions and quirks in the materiality of the language of the Freudian text. She quotes Freud, makes puns, jokes and comments, asks questions, quotes Freud again. . . . She never totalizes her ideas into a conclusion which could then be read as "Irigaray's final word on Freud." Her questions and comments stand. They maintain themselves alongside the bits and pieces from the Freudian text.

Irigaray will later claim this interrogative/citational method as her method. She writes in the dialogue "Questions" which is at the center of *Ce Sexe qui n'en est pas un* (*This Sex Which is Not One*), *"Je n'apporterai donc pas des définitions à l'intérieur d'un discours questionné."*[6] No definitions. No answers. Only questions. Jane Gallop entitled one of her essays on Irigaray in *The Daughter's Seduction* "Impertinent Questions."[7] She further wrote in "The Father's Seduction," another essay from the same collection:

> The process of questioning is a specific dialectic shattering of stable assumptions and producing contextual associations. . . . Irigaray's uncertain, indeterminate attempt to respond to questions without giving

definitive answers thus attempts to really engage the questions, to dialogue with something *hetero* (other) rather than being trapped in the
homo (same).[8]

Irigaray herself underlines the specifically relational character of
her thought when she claims that what she really wants and intends to
do is *"faire la noce avec les philosophes."* Jane Gallop has boldly translated
Irigaray's *"faire la noce"* as "have an orgy with the philosophers,"[9] and
the French expression does indeed imply those excesses of food, drink,
and sex that orgies involve. Irigaray and her philosophers are going to
comingle and interpenetrate. She is going to deal with them with the
same irreverent eroticism she used on Freud in *Speculum*. There will
be a promiscuous contiguity of her language(s) and theirs, a metonymic intertwining. They're going to have an orgy — and the end
product will be an enrichment of each by the other. Neither partner
will die in a mystic One. Nor will they together sire a little offspring —
a Hegelian synthesis. Difference is not to be bred out, but sought out
and maintained. For this reason I should prefer to minimize the significance of Jane Gallop's term "dialectic" and rather underline the second term she uses, the Bakhtinian term, "dialogue."

Phallocentric Discourse and the Dialogic Challenge

As Toril Moi has pointed out in *Sexual/Textual Politics*, Irigaray
wrote *Speculum*, a French *doctorat d'état* in philosophy, in order to challenge philosophical discourse, which she calls the "master discourse"
or the "discourse of discourses."[10] She carries her challenge even further in the 1984 *Ethique de la différence sexuelle* (*The Ethics of Sexual
Difference*), and in the 1985 *Parler n'est jamais neutre*, for while she is
living it up with the philosophers, she also invites the scientists to join
in the fun. The double orgy had actually already begun in *Speculum*
where, after all, Irigaray takes on philosophy in Plato, Plotinus, Descartes, and science in Freud. This distinction between science and philosophy is in fact an artificial one, since Irigaray's concept of a
"philosophe" would seem to be akin to the eighteenth-century Didero-
tian model. Philosophers and scientists are not two separate groups;
the scientist is a philosopher and the philosopher a scientist. If philosophy is the master discourse, its right-hand man is scientific discourse.
Together they set the standard for Truth, that one Truth which has no
gender, no race, no class (no pun intended).
Ethique de la différence sexuelle is the published series of lectures

given at the Erasmus University where Irigaray held a visiting chair in philosophy in 1982. Each of her seminars is grouped around the reading of one or more classic texts: Plato's *Banquet,* Spinoza's *Ethics,* Descartes's *Les Passions de l'âme.* There are also texts from Aristotle, Hegel, Merleau-Ponty, Levinas. *Ethique de la différence sexuelle* is an unsettling work on first reading — unsettling because it would appear that the party is already over. Irigaray seems too methodical, almost anti-Irigarayan. Her seminars show little of the stylistic dash and adventuresome spirit of "The Blind Spot" or of *This Sex Which is Not One.* They are more didactic and professorial, more serious in tone and more traditional, even though the old Irigarayan themes have not really changed. She continues to criticize a conception of human sexuality which overvalues the penis. She has not given up attacking logic and phallocentric discourse, but she does all of this in a more traditionally logical and methodical way than she had done it before.

Moi has severely criticized Irigaray for this seeming inconsistency in style and method, which she sees as already apparent in certain essays of *This Sex Which is Not One,* notably in *"Le marché des femmes"* ("Women on the Market") and *"La mécanique des fluides"* ("The Mechanics of Fluids").[11] Moi has called Irigaray a "deconstructionist": She is a reader of the text of western culture, a critical reader who, as Moi writes, "knows how to expose the flaws and inconsistencies of phallocentric discourse."[12] "The Blind Spot" is something of a deconstructionist masterpiece.

Moi closely analyzes what she calls Irigaray's mimetic technique for deconstructing phallocentric discourse.

> Irigaray's mimicry in *Speculum* becomes a conscious acting out of the hysteric (mimetic) position allocated to all women under patriarchy. Through her acceptance of what is in any case an ineluctable mimicry, Irigaray doubles it back on itself, thus raising the parasitism to the second power. Hers is a theatrical staging of the mime: miming the miming imposed on woman. Irigaray's subtle specular move (her mimicry *mirrors* that of all women) intends to *undo* the effects of phallocentric discourse by *overdoing* them.... The question, however, is whether and under what circumstances this strategy actually works.[13]

Here is Irigaray's position vis-à-vis the specular economy of western culture: Mimicry is indeed one of Irigaray's most effective strategic moves, but it is not the only one in her repertoire, and she does not use it exclusively to deconstruct.[14] Irigaray does not mimic Freud *only* to deconstruct him. She opens his text up for further inquiry. Her specular move is intended not only to mirror but to provoke ... speculation.

What was finished off, closed, monologic, is now opened up for dialogue. The mirror image ultimately remains in the economy of the *homo* if it is not used to engage with the *hetero,* to use Jane Gallop's terms. To insist exclusively on Irigaray's mimicry per se is to ignore her dialogism.

> It is difficult to see how Marxist discourse is undermined by her mimicry. Rather it would seem that Irigaray is using Marx's analysis in an entirely conventional way.[14]

The conventionality of Irigaray's use of Marxist theory in "Women on the Market" is somewhat debatable, but is not the issue here. Marxist discourse, inevitably one of the social languages of educated Europeans, is certainly part of Irigaray's internal dialogue. To use Marxist discourse for one's own purposes is to make a typical dialogic move. If Irigaray's purpose here is not the deconstruction of Marx, but the illustration of certain economic bases of women's position in culture, why should she necessarily be principally concerned with the undermining of Marxist discourse?

"Women on the Market" and "The Mechanics of Fluids," along with most of the essays of *Ethique de la différence sexuelle* or of *Parler n'est jamais neutre,* are indeed very different from *Speculum,* but in them Irigaray is setting up a different type of dialogue. The difference in tone results not from a naïve recuperation of the language of patriarchy, but from a change in tactics or strategy. Jane Gallop has remarked, perspicaciously, that behind the Freud of *Speculum* Irigaray perceived the "ghost" of Lacan.[15] The extraordinary mimetic technique and the challenging, often mocking, tone of *Speculum* result directly from this interchange with Lacan and his disciples.

Gallop has also shown that this "polemic defensiveness"[16] is typical of Irigaray's pieces on Lacan and on psychoanalysis in general.[17] In the later essays Lacan and the Lacanian group are not the targeted interlocutors, at least not so prominently or exclusively. The exchange tends to be less contentious. In *Ethique de la différence sexuelle,* for example, Irigaray engages at once with more distant partners in her philosophers, and with more intimate ones in her students, and as she wrote in the passage quoted in the beginning of this essay:

> Je peux anticiper à qui je vais parler, comment parler, comment argumenter, me faire comprendre, plaider, voire plaire ou déplaire.[18]

Irigarayan textual production is always a function of dialogue.
Dialogue is at the heart of the entire project of *Ethique:* In the

title essay of the book she conceptualizes herself and her historical, social, and philosophical position in Rotterdam. She inserts herself into a series of relations.

> Venir à Rotterdam pour enseigner la philosophie ne représente pas n'importe quoi. Aventure de pensée, aventure de découverte, ou re-découverte, d'un pays qui a abrité plusieurs philosophes. Les a tolérés et encouragés dans leur travail.[19]

And she proudly adds, *"Je ne manquerai pas á cette histoire."*[20] The deliberate reference to Spinoza in the title of the book indicates that she has placed herself in a certain history. She is carrying on a tradition and is aware of it. The texts written by those other *philosophes* in Holland are an integral part of Irigaray's project. In the same way that Freud was *in* "The Blind Spot," Descartes, Spinoza, Plato are *in Ethique de la différence sexuelle*. Their words become Irigaray's. Her words are theirs.

To try to divide up *Ethique,* carefully rendering unto Irigaray the things that are Irigaray's, and unto Plato the things that are Plato's, would be to try to inscribe the text into that marketplace economy, so brilliantly analyzed by Irigaray, where all things are carefully branded with a patronym. In Irigarayan textuality, words and ideas are not, any more than are women in Irigarayan sexuality, objects of exchange in a "homo/hommo-sexual" economy.[21] Questions and anxieties of "influence" and "originality" become fruitless here, the remnants of the pederastic relation.[22] Language circulates freely, breaking down barriers or seeping across them; it flows according to the mechanics of fluids Irigaray would oppose to the anal, "homo/hommo-sexual" mechanics of solids. It cannot be divided up, branded, possessed. Each word is the confluence of many streams of thought.[23]

Despite the rather grandiose title and conventional tone which would seemingly relate *Ethique de la différence sexuelle* to a systematizing philosophical praxis, it is not a totalizing work any more than was "The Blind Spot." Less full of fireworks, it nevertheless shoots off in all directions from *agape* to *eros,* to maternity, to time and space, to a critique of scientific discourse. Irigaray continues to refuse to produce a monologic, unified, phallocentric text. She consistently rejects a monologic, unified, phallocentric truth.

She tells her colleagues in Marseille that she feels the

> angoisse d'un pouvoir absolu qui plane dans l'air, d'un jugement d'autorité partout imperceptiblement là, d'un tribunal à la limite sans juge, ni avocat, ni accusé! Mais le système juridique est en place. Il y a une vérité à laquelle il faut se soumettre sans appel, contre laquelle

on peut faire des infractions sans le vouloir ni le savoir. Cette instance
suprême s'exerce à votre corps défendant.[24]

The remainder of her talk, and indeed the whole of *Parler n'est jamais
neutre,* is a series of strategies designed to shake this one truth, to dis-
orient judge and jury, and bring down the entire "judicial system." She
asks questions, new questions, unexpected, unsettling questions of science, and it is not only the answers to these questions (typically not to
be found in Irigaray's text) which would be revolutionary. The questions themselves, hitherto unasked, or marginalized, or trivialized,
move "hard" scientific discourse itself into a position of dialogic
responsibility.

To mention only a couple of examples:

> Si je vous dis que deux ovules peuvent engendrer un nouveau vivant,
> cette découverte vous semble-t-elle possible, probable, vraie? Pure-
> ment génétique ... Ce type de découverte va-t-il être encouragé, y
> compris par des crédits? Va-t-il être diffusé par les médias?
>
> La contraception masculine est-elle possible hormonalement? Oui?
> Non? Pourquoi? Si elle l'est, cette information est-elle diffusée, sa
> pratique encouragée[25]

Such questions demand not only new research and new experiments.
They drive the speculum deep into science. They require that science
study its own image, and this self-reflexivity reveals cracks in the mirror which supposedly reflects reality and also outlines the knotty surface of the supposedly smooth neutrality of scientific language.

The neutral questions science seeks to answer are actually gendered questions. Their gender is revealed in the absence of those other
questions, the ones Irigaray forces out into the open, the ones which
had not been asked seriously, or had been dismissed outright as
unscientific.

Science reveals itself not as a dialogue with or even an interrogation of "facts," but as the imposition of an ideology on data, data which
is in itself by no means neutral. The collection of data is reflective of
certain choices — choices which are inevitably political and gendered.
Scientific discourse is the paradigm of monologism, defined by Ken
Hirschkop as "a strategy of response toward another discourse, albeit
a strategy which aims to ignore or 'marginalize' the opposite
discourse."[26]

In an attempt to silence the voices of gender, race, class, and difference, scientific discourse will pretend they are non-existent, or at

the very least inappropriate to scientific inquiry. The "monologue" of science is a dialogue which denies itself in order to deny the other. It assumes the position of "naturalness," of neutrality, which subsumes the Other into the Same. *"Parler n'est jamais neutre,"* counters Irigaray, and her critique, typically pluralistic and de-centered, articulates the hidden political dialogue within scientific discourse at the same time as it opens it up for a new external dialogue, where the Other and difference would not be erased but re-inscribed in language.

Dialogics and Power

Irigaray has been accused of being essentialistic, notably by Moi who sums up and analyzes the criticisms leveled at her by other supposedly more political feminists.[27] The basis of the case against Irigaray would seem to rest with her "identification" of a certain multivoiced, dialogic textual praxis with the morphology of female sexuality. This is the by-now notorious "women's writing." Her descriptions of women's writing, imagistic, elliptical and poetic as they are, should not be read literally as definitions, particularly by so sophisticated a reader as Moi.

The morphology of the female body, which has erogenous zones all over, anywhere from head to foot, and where eroticism is not centered, focalized in a single organ, becomes a metaphor through which to grasp a textuality which is diverse, plural, circular, centrifugal — in fact, multivoiced and dialogic. "Women's writing" is no more a "representation" of the female body than phallocentric discourse is a "representation" of the penis. Women's writing is a textual strategy in precisely the same way as phallocentric discourse is a textual strategy: the one is open dialogism, the other that closed-off dialogism we have called monologism. Women's writing then becomes a feminist strategy for challenging philosophic and scientific discourse; it becomes the weapon for a new and revolutionary philosophy and science.

Moi recognizes Irigaray's contribution to feminism in her deconstructions of philosophical phallocentrism, but then faults her as naive when it comes to power politics.

> The material conditions of women's oppression are spectacularly absent from her work. But without specific material analysis, a feminist account of power cannot transcend the simplistic and defeatist vision of male power pitted against female helplessness that underpins Irigaray's theoretical investigations.[28]

As Moi herself shows, many French feminists do tend to be more concerned with post-modernist theories of textuality than with "material analysis,"[29] but this is most definitely not the case with Irigaray, and to read her as apolitical is to minimize the deep personal commitment she has made, the challenge that she has taken directly into the patriarchal intellectual establishment, and for which she has been ostracized (witness her expulsion from the Ecole Freudienne at Vincennes). French intellectuals are a notoriously clique-ish set, and Irigaray has had to become an outsider, definitely a black sheep if not something of a scapegoat. It is difficult to see how Irigaray could be considered an ivory-tower intellectual in any case. What really *is* important is that Irigaray's *engagement* can be read quite clearly in her texts.

Sexual/Textual Politics was first published in 1985, which means that Moi, who had access to Irigaray's more theoretical and poetic philosophic writings from which "material analysis" is supposedly absent, did not know, could not have known at that time, *Ethique de la différence sexuelle* or *Parler n'est jamais neutre*. Criticism which was perhaps partially valid in 1985 (from a certain point of view) can no longer withstand close scrutiny. One might say that after *Speculum*, after her orgy with the philosophers, Irigaray was able to turn her attention to more practical feminist concerns. As I have shown, in the later texts Irigaray's critique of phallocentrism does not stop with the "master discourse" but is extended to scientific discourse as well. I have called scientific discourse the right-hand man of philosophic discourse, but if knowledge is power, the sciences, source of technology, are also the right-hand men of the capitalist power structure or of any other existing political or economic power structure. Irigaray's challenge to science carries post-modernist theory across the threshold which to so many of us seems an impenetrable barrier. She calls the hard sciences to account — something few intellectuals in the humanities or the social sciences would dare to attempt.

Finally, Irigaray's most recent work, as yet largely unpublished, has been overwhelmingly "material." For the past few years she has been conducting large-scale experimental research on sexual difference in language use across an international linguistic base, in an effort to determine how women use language differently from men. Her findings lead her to conclude that "the material conditions of women's oppression" *are* recuperable in language usage, and further, that it is language which must change.[30] It is here that Bakhtin can help us once again to understand Irigaray's radicalism. Katerina Clark and Michael Holquist write:

Language invokes the political concept of freedom because language is struggle against the necessity of certain forms. Language is a unitizing noun developed for the action of what is a scattered and powerful array of social forces. Whether or not social interaction is conceived as class struggle, social forces are never conceived otherwise than as being in conflict ... Bakhtin argues that language is where those struggles are engaged most comprehensively and at the same time most intimately and personally. It is in language, not in the nation-state, that social force finds its most realized expression. "Each word ... [writes Bakhtin] is a little arena for the clash and criss-crossing of differently oriented social accents."[31]

As has been pointed out by Wayne Booth,[32] Bakhtin was not aware of a feminine "differently oriented social accent" in this clash and criss-crossing. Irigaray's work adds that differentiated voice to the conflict, and the linguistic changes she calls for will inevitably transform relationships, alter the dynamics of the status quo, and unbalance the existing power structures. Ultimately, then, the dichotomy between textual analysis and material analysis disappears, as does the rather specious line I have drawn between Irigaray's earlier and later texts. The battle against women's oppression begins at the level of language, of textuality, and will be fought out there.

In conclusion, I would argue that to accuse Irigaray of insufficient political consciousness is to ignore the dynamic political potential of dialogism. Dialogic textuality, by articulating otherness, inevitably articulates the powers attempting to marginalize or eliminate otherness. As the power struggle is dragged out into the open in dialogics, all monologic positions are undermined, and revealed as ultimately untenable, self-contradictory.

In *Feminist Dialogics,* Dale Bauer writes:

The feminist struggle is not one between a conscious "awakened" or natural voice *and* the voice of patriarchy "out there." Rather precisely because we all internalize the authoritative voice of patriarchy, we must struggle to refashion inherited social discourses into words which rearticulate intentions other than normative or disciplinary ones.[33]

This problematical binary opposition "in here/out there" is one of the traditional psychological conundrums Bakhtin's linguistic model helps us to get beyond. Caryl Emerson, in a telling contrast between Lacan and Bakhtin, writes that the dialogue between inner and outer speech is central to both approaches. In each case, the gap between inner and outer can be a cause of pain: in Lacan it is the pain of desire, in Bakhtin, the pain of inarticulateness ... [34]

Inarticulateness being the lack of words, of our own words to express our particular experience(s). The feminist, woman in general, lives this pain, lives on the edge of this gap, and one of Irigaray's greatest accomplishments is to have shed light down into the fissure, using the paradigm of woman's sexuality—this sex which is not one—which in phallocentric terms is non-existent, nothing, empty space where something should be. Irigaray's project of inscribing this "nothing," this empty space, and of thereby turning it into "something" can be understood in Bakhtinian terms as a "re-socialization" (Caryl Emerson's word) of an inner conflict. Caryl Emerson writes that Bakhtin

does not deny the reality of internal conflicts, but he does socialize them, thus exposing their mechanisms to the light of day. If enough individuals experience the same gap, it is re-socialized: there develops a political underground, and the potential for revolution.[35]

Neither Dale Bauer nor Caryl Emerson was writing about Irigaray, but it would be difficult to articulate her project, her political position, or her methods more precisely. Recognizing her unavoidable position within patriarchy, and within its language, Irigaray struggles to produce a textuality which "rearticulates intentions (the feminist ones) other than normative or disciplinary ones," and to develop the potential for revolution. Why *"faire la noce avec les philosophes"* (or *les scientifiques*)? Because their language is in us, is us. Let us use it, if we can, in such a way as to let our voices be heard. Feminist dialogics both articulates women's position within the patriarchal power structure and opens up the possibility for modification of that structure. We might ask ourselves whether there exists a more radical political position.

I agree with Toril Moi that essentialism, no matter how utopian, is dangerous for feminism. We cannot risk being trapped in our own Imaginary, since the Symbolic Order, since Political Reality, are too threatening to be ignored, even temporarily. But it is time to set aside the essentialistic reading of Irigaray. Reading her through a dialogic model allows us to grasp both her philosophic method as she criticizes patriarchal textuality, and her politics as she advocates a non-patriarchal textuality. The essentialistic reading of women's writing is a monologistic, reductionist, imaginary vision of what is actually a call to dialogics. Monologistic textuality has traditionally silenced the female voice: Irigarayan dialogics may let it be heard.

Notes

1. V. N. Vološinov/Mikhail Bakhtin, *Marxism and the Philosophy of Language* (Cambridge, Massachusetts, 1986), p. 85.

2. The clumsiness of the translation attempts to reproduce the complexity of meanings of the French *"neutre,"* which can be translated as the relatively innocuous English "neutral," but also means "non-gendered," or might even perhaps be rendered as "neutered," that is "de-gendered."
This translation and all others are my own, unless otherwise indicated.

3. Luce Irigaray, "Le Sujet de la science est-il sexué?" *Parler n'est jamais neutre* (Paris, 1985), p. 309. "It's been a long time since I've experienced such difficulty with the idea of speaking in public. Most often, I can anticipate to whom I'm going to speak, how to speak, how to construct an argument, make myself understood, plead a case, even please or displease. This time I don't know anything because I don't know whom I have before me. The disadvantage of scientific imperialism: not to know whom one addresses, how to speak."

4. Vološinov/Bakhtin, p. 86.

5. Irigaray, "Introduction," *Parler,* p. 9. "Why would a subject not say: *I feel this way, I see such and such, I want or I can this, I affirm that?* Maybe it's a question of time? A brake on discovery? But this brake does not recognize itself as such and claims to be truth. Well 'I' is sometimes truer than 'one' or 'he.' It's truer because it tells its origin."

6. Luce Irigaray, "Questions," *Ce Sexe qui n'en est pas un* (Paris, 1977), p. 120. "I will therefore bring no definitions into a questioned discourse." My readings of *Speculum* and of *Ce sexe qui n'en est pas un* owe a great deal to Jane Gallop, one of the very best readers of Irigaray. I gratefully acknowledge this debt.

7. Jane Gallop, "Impertinent Questions," *The Daughter's Seduction* (Ithaca, 1982), pp. 80–91.

8. Ibid., "The Father's Seduction," pp. 64–65.

9. Ibid., p. 78.

10. Toril Moi, "Patriarchal Reflections," *Sexual/Textual Politics* (New York, 1985), p. 129.

11. The translations of the two preceding titles are from Catherine Porter's translation of *Ce Sexe qui n'en est pas un, This Sex Which is Not One* (Ithaca,

1985). "Women on the Market" is a particularly fine rendering of Irigaray's title, and for this reason I wish to retain it.

12. Moi, p. 138.

13. Ibid., p. 140.

14. To use Marx for strictly feminist purposes strikes me as entirely unconventional to begin with. Does not the "conventional" Marxist position on feminism reject "gender struggle" and subordinate women's issues to class struggle? This was certainly Simone de Beauvoir's position for many years — the abolition of class was to abolish gender discrimination.

15. Gallop, "Impertinent Questions," p. 80.

16. Ibid.

17. As a case in point I would cite the article *"Misère de la psychanalyse,"* originally published in *Critique* in 1977, and included in *Parler n'est jamais neutre* (pp. 253 – 279). Irigaray wrote the article to avenge (I can think of no more appropriate term to account for the tone of this article) the suicide of a friend of hers, a woman psychoanalyst. Nowhere is Irigaray more sarcastic; nowhere is her mimicry more biting or bitter. The dialogue with psychoanalysis is one in which Irigaray has always had a deep personal stake.

18. See footnote 2 for translation.

19. Luce Irigaray, *"Ethique de la différence sexuelle,"* *Ethique de la différence sexuelle* (Paris, 1984), p. 113. "Coming to Rotterdam to teach philosophy does not represent just anything. Adventure of thought, adventure of discovery, or rediscovery of a country which sheltered several philosophers. Tolerated them and encouraged them in their work."

20. "I will not fail this history."

21. *"Homme"* is the French noun for "man," and "homo/hommo" is one of Irigaray's favorite puns, especially in *This Sex Which is Not One.* The word-play underlines the "sameness" and "maleness" of a certain sexual economy and has nothing to do with homophobia.

22. Gallop, "The Father's Seduction," pp. 63 – 65. Jane Gallop uses the term "pederasty" to characterize a certain relationship of disciple to authority figure.

23. Ibid., "The Ladies' Man," pp. 39 – 42. I here apply Jane Gallop's analysis of the "mechanics" of the fluidity of female sexuality to a certain conception of language, a conception which I find particularly Bakhtinian.

24. Irigaray, "Le Sujet de la science . . . ," p. 308. "Anguish of an absolute power which hovers in the air, of an authoritative judgement, imperceptible but everywhere present, ultimately of a tribunal with neither judge nor lawyer

nor accused. But the judicial system is in place. There is a truth to which one must submit without appeal, which one can violate without wanting to or knowing. This supreme jurisdiction is in power without your being aware of it."

25. Ibid., p. 309. "If I tell you that two eggs can engender a new living being, does this discovery seem to you possible, probable, true? Purely genetic? Is this type of discovery going to be encouraged, and by authorities as well? Is it going to be publicized by the media?" "Is masculine contraception hormonally possible? Yes? No? Why? If it is, is this information publicized, is the practice encouraged?"

26. Ken Hirschkop, "A Response to the Forum on Mikhail Bakhtin," *Bakhtin: Essays and Dialogues on His Work,* Gary Saul Morson, ed. (Chicago, 1986), p. 75.

27. Moi, *cf.* sub-texts of her article entitled "Womanspeak: A Tale Told by an Idiot," and "Idealism and Ahistoricism," pp. 143 – 149.

28. Ibid., p. 147.

29. This distinction between "material analysis" and "textual analysis" is a problematical one. What is more material than language? Does the question even make sense? I hope to show that it does not, but for now I retain Moi's distinction for the purpose of making my case.

30. I thank Luce Irigaray for passing unpublished texts on to me and for discussing them with me. I apologize to the reader for not being able to present these materials in detail. Irigaray does not wish them to be cited before their publication. I here refer only in the most general way to her conclusions, and can go no further. The new book should be out in French early in 1990.

31. Katerina Clark and Michael Holquist, *Mikhail Bakhtin* (Cambridge, Massachusetts, 1984), p. 220. Quote from Vološinov/Bakhtin, p. 41.

32. Wayne C. Booth, "Freedom of Interpretation: Bakhtin and the Challenge of Feminist Criticism," in Morson, pp. 145 – 176.

33. Dale Bauer, "Gender in Bakhtin's Carnival," *Feminist Dialogics: A Theory of Failed Community* (Albany, 1988), p. 2.

34. Caryl Emerson, "The Outer Word and Inner Speech: Bakhtin, Vygotsky, and the Internalization of Language," in Morson, p. 32.

35. Ibid., p. 32.

Works Cited

Bauer, Dale. *Feminist Dialogics: A Theory of Failed Community.* Albany: State University of New York Press, 1988.

Clark, Katerina and Michael Holquist. *Mikhail Bakhtin*. Cambridge, Massachusetts: Harvard University Press, 1984.

Irigaray, Luce. *Ce Sexe qui n'en est pas un*. Paris: Minuit, 1977.

―――. *Ethique de la différence sexuelle*. Paris: Minuit, 1984.

―――. *Parler n'est jamais neutre*. Paris: Minuit, 1985.

―――. *This Sex Which is Not One*, Trans. Catherine Porter. Ithaca, New York: Cornell University Press, 1985.

Moi, Toril. *Sexual/Textual Politics*. New York: Methuen, 1985.

Morson, Gary Saul, ed. *Bakhtin: Essays and Dialogues on His Work*. Chicago: University of Chicago Press, 1986.

Vološinov, V. N./Mikhail Bakhtin. *Marxism and the Philosophy of Language*. Trans. Ladislav Matejka and I. R. Titunik. Cambridge, Massachusetts: Harvard University Press, 1986.

5

Critical Imperialism and Renaissance Drama: The Case of *The Roaring Girl*

Deborah Jacobs

To be effective, feminist criticism cannot become simply bourgeois criticism in drag.
　　　　　　Lillian Robinson, Sex, Class, and Culture

If we treat the opposition between male and female as problematic rather than known, as something contextually defined, repeatedly constructed, then we must constantly ask not only what is at stake in proclamations or debates that invoke gender to explain or justify their positions but also how implicit understandings of gender are being invoked and reinscribed.
　　　　　　Joan W. Scott, Gender and the Politics of History

Mikhail Bakhtin's grotesque and carnivalesque figures understandably appeal to a variety of critics interested in the "subversive" potential of "marginal" or "marginalized" subjectivities. But much Bakhtinian work, including some feminist Bakhtinian work, tends to romanticize marginality — a not too surprising tendency given Bakhtin's own indulgence in an increasingly romantic and nostalgic treatment of "the folk" at the end of *Rabelais and His World*. Yet, while Bakhtin generally emphasizes the differences between the culture in which Rabelais wrote and his own highly repressive, much less festive and humorous one, it is precisely contemporary criticism's ongoing failure to acknowledge cultural difference that marks much feminist and historicist work on pre-bourgeois literature, work apparently grounded in Bakhtinian or similar models of resistance.[1] For while experience has taught feminism to "read" otherness more responsibly across contemporary cultures, that is, while radical differences are

73

now readily acknowledged among women across race, class, age, ethnicity, and sexual preferences, many feminisms still cling to an essential female or feminist body over historical time. My essay begins by raising objections to the transhistorical and transcultural thematization of models of subversion and resistance — Bakhtin's carnival, his grotesque body, and other not necessarily Bakhtinian figures of excess — and concludes by exploring the implications of this particular sort of a-historicity for feminist politics.

Baldly stated, the problem is one of cultural and critical imperialism. As Peter Stallybrass and Allon White argue in *The Politics and Poetics of Transgression*, the bourgeoisie

> is perpetually rediscovering the carnivalesque as a radical source of transcendence. Indeed that act of rediscovery itself, in which the middle classes excitedly discover their own pleasures and desires under the sign of the Other, in the realm of the Other, is constitutive of the very formation of middle-class identity. (201)

In their view, twentieth-century critics (feminists, New Historicists, Bakhtinians, and others) "find" everywhere — *in* writings by and about women or other marginal and marginalized figures and *on* Renaissance and other non-bourgeois bodies — their own themes of resistance and subversion. Remarkably, those bodies turn out to be gendered and hierarchized in ways that resemble the bourgeois (perhaps feminist, perhaps not, but always progressive and "liberal") individualized subject. I will argue that these readings "novelize" non-novelistic and pre-novelistic literature; they gobble up semiotically the materials even of another culture and time, asking them questions specific to a novelistic (middle-class, individualized) subjectivity as if they are the only questions in town. Indeed, "novelized" questions — those concerned with, among other things, a "sovereign" individual consciousness or subjectivity — may be the appropriate questions to ask nineteenth- and twentieth-century texts: texts produced under the conditions in which such questions emerged; texts wherein definitions of resistance and subversion or representations of individual or collective hopes, dreams, and aspirations might have more relation to a certain contemporary subject's consciousness. And similarly, a Bakhtin to which gender has been added for the 1990s would seem to have more applicability to these texts.[2] It does seem clear, however, that the novel — the genre and method of middle-class individualized consciousness — has produced, privileged, dehistoricized, and depoliticized a certain way of reading, one we are only beginning to repoliticize. "Novelized" reading renders its own motives and politics invisible and remakes in the reader's own image Renaissance and other pre-novel-era figures: Shakespeare, for instance, or in the case of my argument, a roaring girl. As Tennenhouse has it, these figures somehow "testify to the timelessness of the modern individual, [one's] own ambitions, fears and desires" (*Power*, 7).

Let me illustrate how a "novelized" reading might proceed vis-à-vis Thomas Dekker and Thomas Middleton's *The Roaring Girl* (1611).[3] I will then try to clarify the nature of my objections to this reading. I want to offer Dekker and Middleton's stage production about a roaring girl's role in an otherwise highly stock city comedy as a text ripe for facile reception, for "novelizing" by our culture and its various meaning-makers including both feminists and Bakhtinians. Because the central figure, Moll Cutpurse, is instrumental in disrupting two male-originated plots — the senex figure's attempt to thwart his son's marriage to a woman slightly beneath him in rank, and a lecherous gallant's seductions of a citizen wife — the play's tone, its "message," and its central character have been claimed as subversive.[4] Moreover, intertwined with the roaring girl's active role in both plots is her successful attempt to set both ranks of men straight concerning the reading of her body. That is, Moll asserts that she is neither "monster" (as old Sir Alex believes) nor "whore" (as Laxton assumes) simply because she cross-dresses. And in the "novelized" reading I am trying to illustrate, these assertions will stand for a challenge to "patriarchal authority" (but as "authority" and "patriarchy" are defined by twentieth-century standards and contexts. I put these words in quotes to emphasize the way we take for granted their transhistorical currency).

In "Crossdressing, The Theatre, and Gender Struggle in Early Modern England," for instance, Jean E. Howard argues that certain cross-dressers (and she points, for one, to Moll Cutpurse in Dekker and Middleton's play) "protested the hierarchal sex-gender system and the material injustices that it spawned" (436). Her essay argues, further, that cross-dressing generally had a "subversive or transgressive potential" and that it "threatened a normative social order" (418). From a similar perspective, Mary Beth Rose, in "Women in Men's Clothing: Apparel and Social Stability in The Roaring Girl," finds the titular character "an embodiment of *female independence* boldly challenging established social and sexual values" (368, my emphasis). Rose goes on to assert that, taken along with the related social commentary, the artistic representation of the man-woman "suggest[s] a deep cultural ambivalence in the British Renaissance about *female independence and equality between the sexes*" (368, emphasis added). Notice how both arguments rely on a phraseology usually associated with liberal humanist ideals; I am suggesting that we need to examine more carefully the transposition of historically specific values onto representations of the pre-bourgeois subject.

Let me point very briefly to the lines from *The Roaring Girl* that have been marshalled to demonstrate that this Renaissance play and its main character resist and subvert "patriarchy" and "the state" in the same way a contemporary subject might. Many of Moll Cutpurse's bawdy and clever speeches are, after all, hilariously appropriable for feminist purposes in the late twentieth century. Consider the following lines which, at some point or another, Rose and Howard offer in support of their feminist arguments:

> I have the head now of myself, and am man enough for a woman. Marriage is but a chopping and changing where a maiden loses one head and has a worse i' the place. (2.2.45 – 8)

> I scorn to prostitute myself to a man,
> I that can prostitute a man to me. (3.1.116 – 17)

> I have no humor to marry; I love to lie o' both sides o' the' bed myself; and again, o' th'other side, a wife, you know, ought to be obedient, but I fear me I am too headstrong to obey; therefore I'll ne'er go about it. (2.1.38 – 42)

The delight we experience as twentieth century feminists reading these lines has more to do with our own experiences in culture than with the Renaissance staging of the body of a roaring girl in 1611. Certainly, as Stallybrass and White argue, "Thinking the body is thinking social topography and vice versa" (192); body images "speak social relations" (10). But in finding a feminist or subversive body on the Renaissance stage, we risk finding not necessarily the body being staged (under specific historic and political circumstances), but the one we want to find — that is, our own body, our own "social topography." We ask, "What would our own bodies mean in this situation?" when we could be asking, "Why was this cross-dressing body staged in this way at this time?" Semiotically we should not ask, "What does the sign mean?" but "How is the sign used?" To ask *why* a body is staged in a certain way at a certain time; to ask how a sign is used rather than what it might mean, is to ask what might be thought of as pre- or non-novelistic questions, questions more appropriate to pre-novelistic texts. By pre-novelistic texts, I mean texts produced before modern bourgeois consciousness grew up along with its genre — the novel — that helped to produce it and which erased and continues to erase (especially in some subgenres) the specific political uses which are made of semiotic materials. It does so by mass-reproducing the transhistorical thematizing of the world that can ask of texts only one sort of question, (a question that I would phrase as something like, "Where am 'I' in this text?").[5]

What follows is an alternative reading of the play's codes, one that I hope will provide a radical contrast to a "thematization" of either Bakhtin's theories or Dekker and Middleton's *The Roaring Girl*. I argue that Bakhtin's grotesque and mass bodies *can* help us imagine an alternative social formation to our own, but not if we inscribe them with current and insufficiently historicized gender codes.

The figure Bakhtin provides in *Rabelais and His World* is an entire, two-halved social formation. It includes the classical, closed or aristocratic body and its counterpart, the excessive and open, grotesque or mass body. It is not possible to talk about the grotesque or mass body without taking into account the other half of the figure, the aristocratic body which has authority over it. Nor can we speak of the closed or classical body without invoking a grotesque or mass one which threatens to debase it. An evocation of either half of Bakhtin's figure always calls its "other," the other half of the social formation, into being.

Consider, for the purpose of clarification, the social formation in Shakespeare's *The Tempest* where it might seem that the Sycorax/Caliban social unit should be read as the grotesque or debasing half of Bakhtin's figure. Yet, as earlier and rightful rulers of the island, are they not in a homologous (if inferior) relationship to the Prospero/Miranda (Ferdinand) grouping?[6] That is, just as Prospero, Miranda, and Ferdinand are representative of the English aristocratic or noble body, Sycorax and Caliban represent the "native" nobility, the island's indigenous aristocracy.[7] Since all occupy the same space in the social formation — the same half of the Bakhtinian figure — other bodies than Caliban's must be sought to fill in the grotesque or debasing half of Bakhtin's figure. We look to Trinculo and Stephano for the true grotesques who would substitute some debased formation for the existing social order.

To return to *The Roaring Girl*, Moll Cutpurse's body — merely because it is female and enormous — is *not* the grotesque or subversive body in this play. But if we are looking for "sex-gender hierarchies" with which we are familiar, in which we can locate ourselves, we can't see (to cite Dekker and Middleton's "Prologue") that this "[Moll] flies/ With wings more lofty." Her staged body, like Caliban's, is a variation of the noble or closed body, something homologous to it. To locate the grotesque body in Moll Cutpurse, then, is a mistake because her body is "called up" to maintain the social order. She is, after all, a staged and controlled figure instrumental in perpetuating the status quo; that is, she triumphs in various ways over anyone perceived as disruptive of the social order. The more properly grotesque bodies that would threaten this order are the lascivious gallants and loose citizens' wives of the subplot, the two misshapen undesirables Trapdoor and Tearcat, and the underworld criminals who communicate clandestinely through "canting," an anti-language not ratified by the social order. Significantly, the roaring girl defeats Laxton (a gallant who promotes the improper exchange of women in the subplot); she outwits and drives out Trapdoor exposing him to be a conniving, disloyal subject; and she recuperates (and renders innocuous) the "cant" of the underground figures. At every point in the play where there is a potential debasing of the social order, the figure of Moll Cutpurse, as an instrument of the state (in a state-sanctioned production), deflates these challenges.[8] This play may, in fact, be staging some sort of resistance, but it is not written on Moll's body, and it certainly does not triumph.

The above reading of Moll's body allows "problem" sections of the play which must be ignored in a thematized (often contemporarily gendered) reading to make sense differently. For instance, Moll's own reading of her own body must be glossed over (or left out) in order to interpret her as a subversive figure. Thus both Rose's and Howard's essays can deal with Moll's declaration of cultural difference only by resorting to textual and ideological gymnastics. Rose simply clips a quotation in half, offering only the lines that can be appropriated for her purpose. She uses only the beginning of Moll's speech delivered upon her defeat of Laxton at Grays Inn Field in order to argue that Moll is taking men and their complicity in women's whorishness to task. Rose cites the following lines:

> If I could meet my enemies one by one thus,
> I might make pretty shift with 'em in time,
> And make 'em know she that has wit and spirit,
> May scorn to live beholding to her body for meat;
> Or for apparel, like your common dame,
> That makes shame get her clothes to cover shame. (3.1.143–48)

However, the following dropped lines serve to problematize Rose's reading which foregrounds Moll's "subversiveness." The larger context of the scene and this speech reverse the roles Rose would find. That is, Laxton and the women he would turn to whores "threaten" the social order; Moll clearly champions it, as the omitted lines attest:

Base is that mind that kneels unto her body,
As if a husband stood in awe on's wife:
My spirit shall be mistress of this house
As long as I have time in't. (3.1.149–52)

And when Rose brings the dropped lines back, several pages later, it is in order to account for Moll's strange insistence on her chastity by equating virginity and autonomy (385), a problematic equation in the Renaissance to say the least. (A Renaissance woman's autonomy, her very leaving of the house unaccompanied, was almost without exception read as indicating sexual promiscuity. See the quotation from Howard below.)

Howard's essay also makes these particular lines conspicuous in their absence. Howard, more than Rose, however, foregrounds the importance of the play's insistence on Moll's chastity (437). In other words, Howard quite rightly makes much of a feature of the text that declares its cultural difference from, not its sameness to, bourgeois culture. But at the same time, instead of allowing this "oddity" to raise questions about cultural difference, Howard explores ways to transform it into a feature of our own culture's consciousness:

> This insistence [on Moll's chastity] can be read as a way of containing the subversiveness of her representation, of showing her accepting the central fact of the good woman's lot — i.e., that she not use her sexuality except in lawful marriage. Another way to read the insistence on chastity is to see it as an interruption of that discourse about women which equates the mannish independence with sexual promiscuity. (437)

Any reading of Moll's "insistence on chastity," it seems, should be preferred to one that shows its support of the social structure, since the latter denies us a view of Moll as a subversive, excessive, or feminist figure. Nevertheless, Moll's description of her own body valorizes not a grotesque, excessive or debased body, but a classic, enclosed and chaste one, one that in Stallybrass and White's terms (following Mary Douglas) "excludes filth" (191).

The refusal to read Moll's control over her own body as anything other than a sign of gender struggle (as a twentieth-century Eurocentric feminist might define it) is characteristic of a kind of historical criticism that is willing to historicize context but not an individual subject's consciousness. Such a reading characterizes as well a feminist discourse that is willing to rigorously historicize the material conditions of women's existence but still retains a transhistorical resistant "woman" and is, furthermore, determined to find "her" in other cultures, despite the high cost (especially to feminism) of ignoring the signs and codes that might deny her existence. To reiterate a (not very original) point, the problem shared by these brands of feminism and historicism is that the historically earlier individuals they represent appear remarkably like "us." It is as if "we" are "there."[9] While we can admit that institutions, social conditions and objects — that is, contexts — undergo change, we insist on exempting human consciousness from this possibility; we insist on locating it outside history. It is "always already there — gendered, desiring, ready to be tossed about by historical circumstances and riddled with conflicts" (Armstrong, 348).

I have elaborated this position at length, not because it explicitly addresses Bakhtinian analysis but because the cross-cultural and transhistorical tendencies I am identifying as still prevalent in recent critical thought are in conjunction with the concerns I have about a wholesale, undiscriminating "genderfying" of Bakhtin. I want to qualify the kind of dialogics — the hearing of different cultural voices — for which this collection calls. Any dialogic reading, and especially a feminist dialogics, must be painstakingly historicized; it must operate under the assumption that consciousness as well as context changes over time and culture.

To return, then, to the lines that Rose severs and Howard rationalizes, Moll tells us — as alien and painful as it may be to present-day feminists — exactly how her body is to be used in this play.

> Base is that mind that kneels unto her body,
> As if a husband stood in awe on's wife:
> My spirit shall be mistress of this house
> As long as I have time in't. (3.1.149–52)

Notice how Moll's body is presented not as disruptive or resistant, but as absolutely contained and controlled by her "spirit," just as the husband does not stand "in awe on's wife" and the state does not stand in awe of its subjects. I'm arguing that this roaring girl's body as staged in this play figures Bakhtin's entire two-part social formation described earlier. That is, the relation between her "spirit" and her "house" (her body) is to be read as homologous to that between state and subject or husband and wife. Just as Moll's body, in her view, should be ruled by its mistress "spirit," a wife should be ruled by her husband and a subject by its monarch. In other words, Dekker and Middleton's roaring girl does not challenge or threaten to subvert the social order; on the contrary, Moll's body — the same body Rose and Howard read as excessive and (therefore) subversive — is used to reinforce and champion the very order their readings would have her threaten.

Without placing undue interpretive emphasis on the play's ending, I want to suggest nevertheless that the final scene becomes remarkably intelligible in this alternate reading. The marriage scene — a scene that in Renaissance drama serves to reaffirm the existing social order and which can't be easily reconciled to a reading of Moll as subversive — makes sense when we, like Sir Alex, learn to see how Moll's figure is "used" in this particular situation (and not what it might "mean" to us today). Again, Moll herself summarizes her role as one of "service" to the existing order, and the play ends with the following mutual recognition of that role:

> Moll. *Father and son*, i ha' done you simple *service* here.
>
> Seb. For which thou shalt not part, Moll, unrequited.
>
> S. Alex. Thou'rt a mad girl, and yet I cannot now Condemn thee. (5.2.206 – 9, emphasis added)

But I am not really interested in replacing Rose's and Howard's readings of this play with a truer truth or a more valid reading. I do believe, however, that the "specific political conditions"[10] have arrived under which the "novelized" readings I have critiqued above no longer prove adequate or useful to feminism. And let me return to a point I glossed over earlier: that the costs to feminism of turning a deaf ear to the voices of cultural difference, the costs to feminism of taking for granted a gendered culture outside history will be terribly high. To look for origins along feminist lines is to imagine that we are something other than historical products; it is to posit our present social formations, including systems of gender, as essential, primal, transhistorical. If, on the other hand, we resist such a reified notion of culture; if we resist the impulse to ask "where am I in this text?", perhaps some cultural differences heretofore rendered invisible by the very limits of the questions we have asked will emerge. Finally, if we keep insisting "we are there," if we cannot admit to a past in which gender might be less central or radically different, how will we ever be able to imagine a future that is just as different? Much is at stake.

Notes

1. Inadequately examined applications of Bakhtin's categories are not limited to the work of literary critics. Theorists such as Joseph Natoli, in his introduction to *Tracing Literary Theory*, and Mary Russo in her essay, "Carnival and Theory," (both cited below) participate in what I see as ahistorical and problematic uses of Bakhtin's grotesque body. My critique of Natoli's piece is too broad to be elaborated here; primarily I take issue with his assertion that the grotesque body (and he refers to the "body" of contemporary theory as such) can somehow eventually "replace" the classical, "official body" (Natoli xviii). But the former finds existence only in relation to the latter; they invoke and are invoked by one another, contain and are contained by one another. My critique of Russo's otherwise very useful piece is much more specific and limited to the way she transhistoricizes and transvalues gender via Bakhtin's figure of the hag and the way it is to be interpreted as subversive across time and culture. For more adequately historical treatments of Bakhtin's figures, see the essays in this volume as well as the recent *Bakhtin and Cultural Theory* (eds., Ken Hirschkop and David Shepherd, Manchester UP, 1989).

2. If a Bakhtinian analysis can be of use to Renaissance scholars it will be so precisely because Bakhtin does not acknowledge gender (as we know it) to be a useful category of analysis in early modern Europe. To add a contemporary understanding of gender to Bakhtin's ideas of carnival is to take away a powerful analytic tool, one powerfully useful in analysis of earlier or other cultures wherein gender is configured differently and/or is less central semiotically. I hope the argument of my essay will clarify this point and the following: that it is not necessarily anti-feminist to deny a transhistorical fixed relevance of feminism's primary category: gender. For elaboration of this point see Joan Scott's book cited below, especially the essay, "Gender as a Useful Category of Historical Analysis."

3. All citations to *The Roaring Girl* are to Frazer and Rabkin's anthology, *Drama of the English Renaissance II*.

4. Little attention has been given *The Roaring Girl*; Rose's piece and Howard's piece are the best to date. There is also a new edition of the play introduced and edited by Paul Mullholland. In addition, a few general works mention the play or Moll's character along the lines of cross-dressing.

5. That the novel, generally and inclusively, is guilty of this transhistorical phallacy, is a large claim indeed, but one that seems worth making. For an excellent reading of the novel's place in the construction of the bourgeois subject see Armstrong's *Desire and Domestic Fiction: A Political History of the Novel* (New York: Oxford, 1987). See also Bakhtin's "Epic and Novel." He certainly has such a point in mind when he writes that the novel is "the only genre that was born and nourished in a new era of world history and therefore it is deeply akin to that era ... " (4). Bakhtin asserts throughout "Epic and Novel" that

there is really only one contemporary genre — the novel; among other things, I believe he attends here to the novel as a *method* of bourgeois consciousness as well as a representation of it: a method of reading and interpreting that I am calling (probably not with any originality) "novelization."

6. My reading of this aspect of *The Tempest* is influenced by Len Tennenhouse's lectures delivered at the University of Minnesota.

7. For another example of this earlier cultural logic see Thomas Harriot's *A Briefe and True Report of the New Found Land of Virginia* (New York: Dover Publications, 1972) and the engravings published with the report.

8. Howard marshals the very same details to make an entirely different point, one more in keeping with a (liberal) materialist feminist position.

9. See Nancy Armstrong's essay (cited below) for another and fuller elaboration of this problem with a slightly different emphasis.

10. The phrase is Daniel Cottom's from *Text and Culture* (cited below). I share with Cottom the position that an interpretation's validity, its "rightness" or "wrongness," can only be discussed in terms of its political implications, that "no way of reading is wrong except as it may become so under specific political conditions" (13).

Works Cited

Armstrong, Nancy. "Introduction: Literature as Women's History." *Genre* 19.4 (1986): 347–69.

Bakhtin, Mikhail. "Epic and the Novel." *The Dialogic Imagination*. Ed., Michael Holquist and trans. Caryl Emerson. Austin: University of Texas Press, Slavic Series, 1981.

_____. *Rabelais and His World*. Trans., Helene Iswolsky. Bloomington: Indiana University Press, 1984.

Cottom, Daniel. *Text and Culture: The Politics of Interpretation*. Minneapolis: University of Minnesota Press, 1989.

Dekker, Thomas and Thomas Middleton. *The Roaring Girl. Drama of the English Renaissance II: The Stuart Period*. Eds., Russel A. Frazer and Norman Rabkin. New York: MacMillan, 1976. 333–368.

Howard, Jean E. "Crossdressing, The Theatre, and Gender Struggle in Early Modern England." *Shakespeare Quarterly* 39.4 (1988): 418–440.

Natoli, Joseph, ed. *Tracing Literary Theory*. Chicago: University of Illinois Press, 1987.

Robinson, Lillian S. *Sex, Class, and Culture*. New York: Methuen, 1978.

Rose, Mary Beth. "Women in Men's Clothing: Apparel and Social Stability in *The Roaring Girl.*" *English Literary Renaissance* 14 (1984): 367–391.

Russo, Mary. "Female Grotesques: Carnival and Theory." *Feminist Studies/Critical Studies.* Ed., Teresa de Lauretis. Bloomington: Indiana University Press, 1986.

Scott, Joan Wallach. *Gender and the Politics of History.* New York: Columbia University Press, 1988.

Stallybrass, Peter and Allon White. *The Politics and Poetics of Transgression.* Ithaca: Cornell University Press, 1986.

Tennenhouse, Leonard. Lectures. The Body in Literature before 1700: The Aristocratic Body and its Others. Delivered in the English Department at the University of Minnesota, 1989.

――――. *Power on Display: The Politics of Shakespeare's Genres.* New York: Methuen, 1986.

6

Style and Power

Josephine Donovan

The current popularity of Mikhail Bakhtin's works among Western critics lies mainly in the fact that several of his key concepts — in particular that of the dialogue — seem to reinforce the pluralist ideal of liberal humanism. In my view, this is not why Bakhtin should be of interest to feminist critics; rather, it is because he, like other Marxist critics, recognized that literature exists in a political context and therefore literary devices reflect and refract the power differentials of the author's society. Style in this view is not innocent or neutral — i.e., purely aesthetic — but rather is, as Richard Ohmann termed it, "an epistemic choice," a political expression.[1]

There are, to be sure, problems inherent in a feminist use of Bakhtin. One is that he is largely ignorant of women's literature; this gap is particularly glaring in his remarks on the rise of the novel — a genre to which women made major contributions.[2] Second, as Wayne Booth points out, despite his emphasis on dialogue (in his study of Rabelais, for example), "nowhere ... does one find any hint of an effort to imagine any woman's point of view or to incorporate women into a dialogue. And nowhere in Bakhtin does one discover any suggestion that he sees the importance of this kind of monologue, not even when he discusses Rabelais' attitude toward women."[3] Third, Bakhtin's work is often ambiguous and contradictory, perhaps because of his need to satisfy censors.[4] He is therefore particularly amenable to appropriation for a variety of conflicting purposes.

Nevertheless, because there are so few works that conceive style in political terms, and because of the specificity of his insights, certain of Bakhtin's ideas should prove useful to feminist critics who are constructing women's literary history. His concept of the novel as the locus of a counterhegemonic resistance to the centralized authority of official disciplines is a particularly attractive one for feminists, because it is clear that various stylistic devices women writers used in the early novel or proto-novel express just such a resistance to subordination.

Bakhtin contrasts the novel with classical genres, which he equates with official discourse; they depend upon "a hierarchical distance" (18). The epic, for example, is "walled off" from the present and has no "place" for the "openendedness, indecision, indeterminacy" characteristic of the novel's worldview (16). The novel, in fact, connects to "a zone of maximally close contact between the represented object and contemporary reality in all its inconclusiveness" (31), where classical genres and "official" languages maintain a distance from the "zone of familiar contact" (20). The authoritarian "word of the fathers" therefore cannot be used in the novel, because the novel problematizes all received truths (342), denying the "absolutism of a single and unitary language" (366), expressing a "liberation ... from the hegemony of a single and solitary language ... an absolute form of thought" (367).

Bakhtin sees the novel, therefore, as a somewhat anarchic, insubordinate genre that reflects a kind of popular resistance to centralizing official establishments and unifying disciplines.[5] "The novel is associated with the eternally living element of unofficial language and unofficial thought (holiday forms, familiar speech, profanation)" (20). In addition to its use of living vernaculars, the novel challenges official discourse through irony and through its positioning in the "zone of contact" between literature and life. The latter means that the novel exists on a kind of boundary line between the literary and nonliterary, routinely incorporating "extraliterary genres," such as letters, diaries, etc. (33).

The novel's use of irony is almost definitional with the genre. Unlike classical genres such as the epic where the hero is presented nonironically — ("There is not the slightest gap between his authentic essence and its external manifestation"; "his view of himself coincides completely with others'" [347]) — characters, events and knowledge in the novel are problematized through the use of critical irony. In the novel, Bakhtin notes, "the object is broken apart, laid bare (its hierarchical ornamentation is removed): the naked object is ridiculous; its 'empty' clothing ... is also ridiculous. What takes place is a comical operation of dismemberment" (23 – 24).

If we accept Bakhtin's characterization of the novel as a form that reflects a counterhegemonic resistance to the "word of the fathers," it does not take much of a leap to understand why women might have been attracted to the genre. First, women had been excluded from training in official discourses — Latin and classical rhetoric — for centuries, and thus barred from "official" literary production, which until very recently required a knowledge of classical literature. Second, women were historically positioned in the "unofficial" world of the vernaculars. As Walter J. Ong notes, after about 700 A.D., "Learned Latin, which moved only in artificially controlled channels through the male world of the schools, was no longer anyone's mother tongue, in a quite literal sense. Although from the sixth or eighth century to the nineteenth, Latin was spoken by millions of persons, it was never used by mothers cooing to their children."[6] Third, women lived in the "familiar zone of contact" that became the prime matter of the novel. Fourth, what little historical experience women had in writing (eighty percent of Western women were illiterate until the early nineteenth century) was in unofficial forms such as letters, diaries, and informal, family biographies. Finally, because in the early eighteenth century the novel was a new, amorphous and popular genre, there were no "official" critical axioms by which it had to be judged. Writers were therefore relatively free to proceed as they wished, contingent only upon readers' approval.

Women's political location in the unofficial margins, in short, was the context that determined the epistemic choices early women novelists made in their writing. Their style, which was characterized by an ironic use of indirect discourse, the use of the "plain style" in prose, the "dashaway" epistolary mode, and paratactic syntax, reflected a political resistance to hierarchical subordination. All of these stylistic devices — together with their habitual use of nonliterary forms — express a preference for unofficial, nonsubordinate, everyday modes and a resistance to the imposition of authoritarian official dicta.

The blurring of the boundaries between the literary and nonliterary in women's early literary production can perhaps best be illustrated by Jane Barker's proto-novel, *A Patch-work Screen for the Ladies* (1723). Barker chooses as her structural model an item from women's "unofficial," domestic world — a patch-work screen — constructing her fiction as pieces of fabric, some of which are extraliterary forms such as recipes.[7] An object that is functional in the use-value production that characterized women's economic sphere thus becomes, in Barker's conception, a model for an artistic product — and the line between the two is not clear. A "maximally close" "zone of contact" is maintained between literary representation and reality.

Moreover, the patchwork construction is paratactic; that is, pieces of narrative are placed side by side without the subordination seen in hypotactic syntax. (Parataxis derives from the Greek *paratassein*, "to place side by side," while hypotaxis stems from *hypotassein*, "to arrange under," *hypo* meaning *under*.)[8] Barker does not rank the literary kinds that go to make up her composition; a "serious" or "official" literary genre, such as a Pindaric ode, is treated with the same degree of stylistic seriousness as a recipe or a medical prescription — all of them are cast in verse. Thus the ode is not given priority but is rather leveled to the same status as other elements in the work.

In his comments on stylistic traditions in Western literature, Erich Auerbach notes that hypotaxis, which is characteristic of classical Ciceronian rhetoric, "looks at and organizes things from above," where in parataxis the "causal, modal, and even temporal relations are obscured." Events simply proceed "single file" with no apparent overarching organization.[9] Clearly parataxis is closer to the real world, if experienced relatively naively, without a pre-existing organizational schema; it reflects the associative, random connections of consciousness in immediate response to its environment, where hypotaxis distances the thinker or writer from material reality. Parataxis could thus be characterized as an "unofficial" style, where hypotaxis expresses the rhetorical distancing characteristic, Bakhtin noted, of "official" modes.

There are many reasons women might have been inclined toward paratactic construction. One is that they were not trained in classical rhetoric with its modes of subordination. Second, in their domestic, use-value production, women did not experience a hierarchical division of labor; rather, they performed a variety of tasks sequentially, but none of these tasks held a priority (as opposed to exchange-value production where intellectual and manual labor are separated with the former held in higher esteem and with labor acutely specialized and repetitive). Third, there is some evidence — provided by contemporary theorists — that women's epistemology remains more integrated with the environment than men's (perhaps because of their base in use-value production), that women's "mode of thinking," to quote Carol Gilligan, "is contextual and narrative rather than formal and abstract."[10] Finally, women may have preferred nonsubordinating forms in part as a resistance to the imposition of alien "official" disciplines upon their own lives and upon their familiar environment.[11]

Another early proto-novel, perhaps on a par in importance with Barker's *Patch-work*, is Celia Fiennes's *Journeys*, probably written in 1702. Here again the informing structure is paratactic, the only unifying thread being the author's picaresque peregrination through the countryside. Fiennes makes few judgments — aesthetic or moral; little or no critical perspective or explanatory theory is provided. As in folk art, events, people, and landscape all exist on the same unsubordinated plane. Again, Fiennes's paratactic, non-judgmental structure may derive from her lack of education, her lack of perspectives through which to judge. Or it may reflect the worldview of an oppressed group that has little knowledge of the causes of events. As Philip Fisher suggests in his study of the American sentimentalist novel, for the oppressed there are few temporal or causal explanations for events; they just seem to happen suddenly.[12] The only perceivable order is that they happen one thing after another without subordinating, explanatory conjunctions.

Some critics have suggested that women modernists such as Gertrude Stein and Virginia Woolf employed a paratactic style.[13] More recently, in a computer analysis comparing stylistic structures in women's and men's prose, Mary Hyatt discovered that women writers favored polysyndeton, a paratactic figure that connects ideas through a series of "and" phrases. Hyatt comments,

> a predilection for polysyndeton lessens the opportunity for grammatical subordination, for if a string of items is joined equally by the same connective, there can be no hierarchical value assigned to the items. And the emphasis is the emphasis of unpredictability, for the reader does not know when the list will end. But it is also the emphasis of *sameness*. The effect is often one of childishness and naivete, simply because no judgment is being made about the relative importance of the items.[14]

A related stylistic feature of the writing of the early women novelists (and their precursors) was the use of the plain style in prose. Margaret Cavendish, the Duchess of Newcastle, for example, exclaimed in 1653, "Give me a *Stile* that *Nature* frames, not *Art*," while Mary Wollstonecraft in 1792 announced, "I shall disdain to cull my phrases or polish my style ... I shall not waste my time in rounding periods. ... I shall try to avoid ... flowery diction. ... "[15]

In his study of seventeenth-century stylistic transitions away from Ciceronian rhetoric with its rounded periods and hypotactic constructions, Morris Croll describes the "loose period," a feature of the plain style that was used heavily in the novel. Unlike the syllogistic, subordinating design of the Ciceronian period, which involves rhetorical distance from what Bakhtin labeled the "zone of contact" between experienced reality and representation, the loose period attempts

> to express ... the order in which an idea presents itself when it is first experienced. It begins, therefore, without premeditation, stating its idea in the first form that occurs; the second member is determined by the situation in which the mind finds itself after the first has been

spoken; and so on throughout the period. Each member being an
emergency of the situation.[16]

In *The Rise of the Novel*, Ian Watt similarly observes that in the
epistolary style of the novel "everything was subordinated to the aim
of expressing the ideas passing in the mind at the moment of writing."[17] In *Literary Women*, Ellen Moers called this the "dashaway" style
characterized by its "breathless, disorganized 'artless' informality."[18]
Not surprisingly this was considered a woman's style.

Nineteenth-century American writer Caroline Kirkland apologetically termed hers a "gossiping" style and used another model from
women's domestic production — knitting — to explain its construction.
In *A New Home* she noted she used "a rambling gossiping style," recognizing that "this going back to take up dropped stitches, is not the
orthodox way of telling one's story; and if I thought I could do any
better, I would certainly go back and begin at the very beginning; but
I feel conscious that the truly feminine sin of talking 'about it and
about it,' the unconquerable partiality for wandering wordiness would
cleave to me still."[19] Thus, Kirkland realizes that she is resisting an
"orthodox" official narrative mode in using an "unofficial" style based
on another kind of women's use-value praxis, knitting. Here again we
find a blurring of the boundaries between the literary and nonliterary
and a rejection, albeit apologetically, of official prescripts. Not surprisingly, her work, *A New Home — Who'll Follow?*, is a borderline "novel"
between fiction and nonfiction — a fictionalized autobiographical narrative of her pioneering experiences in the early nineteenth-century
Midwest.

This dashaway, gossipy, epistolary style clearly suggested a naive,
uncontrolled sensitivity, one that was immediately responsive to its environment and not submissive to rhetorical distancing designs, such as
seen in the hypotactic Ciceronian period of "official" prose. It also
allowed the speaker to express subversive thoughts, which could later
be justified as having been made under the excitement of the moment.

The stylistic devices women employed in the early novel (as well
as, in some cases, before and after) reflect their oppressed political
position. Located on the margins, in unofficial zones, women used
forms derived from their familiar everyday world, forms that expressed a paratactic nonsubordinating sensitivity, and which, finally,
registered a resistance to the hierarchical subordinations of official
modes, the "word of the fathers." In this way women contributed enormously to the creation of the dialogic counterhegemonic consciousness
that Bakhtin saw embodied in the novel.

Notes

1. Richard M. Ohmann, "Prolegomena to the Analysis of Prose Style," *Style in Prose Fiction*, English Literature Essays, 1958 (New York: Columbia University Press, 1959), p. 14. See Ken Hirschkop's criticism of the liberal appropriation of Bakhtin, "A Response to the Forum on Mikhail Bakhtin," in *Bakhtin: Essays and Dialogues on His Work*, ed. Gary Saul Morson (Chicago: University of Chicago Press, 1986), pp. 75–76.

2. See Dale Spender, *Mothers of the Novel* (New York: Pandora, 1986); Jane Spencer, *The Rise of the Woman Novelist* (New York: Basil Blackwell, 1986); Josephine Donovan, "The Silence Is Broken," in *Women and Language in Literature and Society*, ed. Sally McConnell-Ginet, Ruth Borker and Nelly Furman (New York: Praeger, 1980), pp. 205–18; and Donovan, "Women and the Rise of the Novel," *Signs* 16, no. 3 (Spring 1991).

3. Wayne C. Booth, "Freedom of Interpretation: Bakhtin and the Challenge of Feminist Criticism," in *Bakhtin*, ed. Morson, pp. 165–66. Booth himself, however, evinces a condescending attitude toward feminist criticism (see p. 156, n. 15). See also my reservations about a feminist rush to Bakhtin in a letter to the editor, *Tulsa Studies in Women's Literature* 6, no. 2 (Fall 1987): pp. 371–73.

4. Gary Saul Morson, "Who Speaks for Bakhtin?" in *Bakhtin*, ed. Morson, p. 15.

5. Bakhtin's critique of formalist literary criticism similarly rejects it as a mathematizing discipline that ignores and elides the anomalous, the random, the marginal, the "unofficial," in short the real political and social context of literature and language. See V. N. Vološinov, *Marxism and the Philosophy of Language*, 2d ed., trans. Ladislav Metejka and I. R. Titanik (New York: Seminar Press, 1973), pp. 60, 71, and M. M. Bakhtin, *The Dialogic Imagination: Four Essays*, ed. Michael Holquist, trans. Caryl Emerson and Michael Holquist (Austin: University of Texas Press, 1981), pp. 292, 352. In the latter work Bakhtin insists there is no unitary language or literary structure; rather, "village sewing circles, . . . workers' lunchtime chats, etc., will all have their own types" (97).

6. Walter J. Ong, S. J., *The Presence of the Word* (New Haven: Yale University Press, 1967), pp. 250–51. These points are elaborated in Donovan, "Silence."

7. This analysis is developed at greater length in Donovan, "Women and the Rise of the Novel."

8. *Webster's New Collegiate Dictionary* (Springfield, Mass.: G. and C. Merriam, 1974), pp. 832, 564; see also Vološinov, *Marxism and the Philosophy of Language*, p. 144.

9. Erich Auerbach, *Mimesis: The Representation of Reality in Western Literature*, trans. Willard Trask (1946; reprint ed., Garden City, N.Y.: Doubleday Anchor, 1957), pp. 62, 91, 185.

10. Carol Gilligan, *In a Different Voice: Psychological Theory and Women's Development* (Cambridge: Harvard University Press, 1982), p. 19. For a survey of these theories see Josephine Donovan, *Feminist Theory: The Intellectual Traditions of American Feminism* (New York: Ungar, 1985), pp. 173 – 76. For other theories about women's use of the patch-work, paratactic construction, see Elaine Showalter, "Piecing and Writing," in *The Poetics of Gender*, ed. Nancy K. Miller (New York: Columbia University Press, 1986), pp. 222 – 47; and Rachel Blau DuPlessis, "For the Etruscans," in *The New Feminist Criticism: Essays on Women, Literature, and Theory*, ed. Elaine Showalter (New York: Pantheon, 1985), p. 278.

11. I document women theorists' resistance to Cartesian mathematizing disciplines in "Animal Rights and Feminist Theory," *Signs* 15, no. 2 (Winter 1990).

12. Philip Fisher, *Hard Facts: Setting and Form in the American Novel* (New York: Oxford University Press, 1985), p. 116 – 17.

13. On Woolf, see Sydney Janet Kaplan, *Feminine Consciousness in the Modern British Novel* (Urbana: University of Illinois Press, 1975), p. 81, n. 11. On Stein, see Shari Benstock, "From the Editor's Perspective," *Tulsa Studies in Women's Literature* 3, nos. 1 – 2 (Spring-Fall 1984): 15. For my further thoughts on women's style see Josephine Donovan, "Sarah Orne Jewett's Critical Theory: Notes toward a Feminine Literary Mode," in *Critical Essays on Sarah Orne Jewett*, ed. Gwen L. Nagel (Boston: G. K. Hall, 1984), and "Feminist Style Criticism," in *Images of Women in Fiction: Feminist Perspectives*, ed. Susan Koppelman Cornillon (Bowling Green, Ohio: Bowling Green Popular Press, 1972).

14. Mary Hyatt, *The Way Women Write* (New York: Teachers College Press, 1977), p. 67.

15. Margaret [Cavendish] Countess of Newcastle, *Poems and Fancies* (1653; reprint ed., Yorkshire, England: Scholar Press, 1972), p. 106; Mary Wollstonecraft, *A Vindication of the Rights of Woman* (1792; reprint ed., Baltimore: Penguin, 1975), p. 82. See also Donovan, "Silence," pp. 213 – 16.

16. Morris Croll, *Style, Rhetoric and Rhythm: Essays*, ed. J. Max Patrick, et al. (Princeton: Princeton University Press, 1966), p. 68.

17. Ian Watt, *The Rise of the Novel* (Berkeley: University of California Press, 1957), p. 194.

18. Ellen Moers, *Literary Women* (Garden City, N.Y.: Doubleday Anchor, 1977), p. 97.

19. Mrs. Mary Clavers [Caroline Kirkland] *A New Home — Who'll Follow?* (1839; reprint ed., New York: Garrett Press, 1969), p. 140.

Works Cited

Auerbach, Erich. *Mimesis: The Representation of Reality in Western Literature,* trans. Willard Trask. 1946. Reprint ed. Garden City, NY: Doubleday Anchor, 1957.

Bakhtin, M. M. *The Dialogic Imagination: Four Essays,* ed. Michael Holquist; trans. Caryl Emerson and Michael Holquist. Austin: University of Texas Press, 1981.

Benstock, Shari. "From the Editor's Perspective." *Tulsa Studies in Women's Literature* 3, nos. 1–2 (Spring-Fall 1984).

[Cavendish,] Margaret, Countess of Newcastle. *Poems and Fancies.* 1653. Reprint ed. Yorkshire, England: Scholar Press, 1972.

Croll, Morris. *Style, Rhetoric and Rhythm: Essays,* ed. J. Max Patrick, et al. Princeton: Princeton University Press, 1966.

Donovan, Josephine. "Feminist Style Criticism." In *Images of Women in Fiction,* ed. Susan Koppelman Cornillon. Bowling Green, Ohio: Bowling Green Popular Press, 1972.

_____. *Feminist Theory: The Intellectual Traditions of American Feminism.* New York: Ungar, 1985.

_____. "Sarah Orne Jewett's Critical Theory: Notes Toward a Feminine Literary Mode." In *Critical Essays on Sarah Orne Jewett,* ed. Gwen L. Nagel. Boston: G. K. Hall, 1984.

_____. "The Silence Is Broken." In *Women and Language in Literature and Society,* eds. Sally McConnell-Ginet, Ruth Borker, and Nelly Furman. New York: Praeger, 1980.

_____. "Women and the Rise of the Novel" *SIGNS,* 16, no. 3 (Spring 1991).

DuPlessis, Rachel Blau. "For the Etruscans." In *The New Feminist Criticism: Essays on Women, Literature, and Theory,* ed. Elaine Showalter. New York: Pantheon, 1985.

Fisher, Philip. *Hard Facts: Setting and Form in the American Novel.* New York: Oxford University Press, 1985.

Gilligan, Carol. *In a Different Voice: Psychological Theory and Women's Development.* Cambridge: Harvard University Press, 1982.

Hyatt, Mary. *The Way Women Write.* New York: Teachers College Press, 1977.

Kaplan, Sydney Janet. *Feminine Consciousness in the Modern British Novel.* Urbana: University of Illinois Press, 1975.

[Kirkland, Caroline]. Mrs. Mary Clavers. *A New Home — Who'll Follow?* 1839. Reprint ed. New York: Garrett Press, 1969.

Moers, Ellen. *Literary Women*. Garden City, N.Y.: Doubleday Anchor, 1977.

Morson, Gary Saul, ed. *Bakhtin: Essays and Dialogues on His Work*. Chicago: University of Chicago Press, 1986.

Ohmann, Richard M. "Prolegomena to the Analysis of Prose Style." In *Style in Prose Fiction*. English Institute Essays, 1958. New York: Columbia University Press, 1959.

Ong, Walter J., S. J. *The Presence of the Word*. New York: Yale University Press, 1967.

Showalter, Elaine. "Piecing and Writing." In *The Poetics of Gender*, ed. Nancy K. Miller. New York: Columbia University Press, 1986.

Spencer, Jane. *The Rise of the Woman Novelist*. New York: Basil Blackwell, 1986.

Spender, Dale. *Mothers of the Novel*. New York: Pandora, 1986.

7

Radical Writing*

Peter Hitchcock

In his analysis of the work of George Eliot, Raymond Williams discusses the concept of "a knowable community," the tension between the voice of the educated observer and the lived relations described.[1] The success of the narrative does not depend on the sublimation of the one by the other, but on the ways in which the dynamism of both is preserved and empowered. Williams uses this concept to show how the knowledge of community existence increasingly becomes problematic in English fiction from the nineteenth century on. The fissures between the voice of the author and the communities to some extent authored proved to Williams that community knowledge is fragmentary and dispersed among a whole range of communicative levels. The knowable community of working-class novels are particularly problematic because, in general, they do not form an archive of what the knowable community was: they do not constitute a relic so much as a blueprint. With this in mind, I turn to the fiction of a writer whose perspectives on the intersubjectivity of knowable communities are focused through generations of working-class *women*, a focus that provides us with some equally problematic correlatives to identity and memory; namely, gender and history.[2]

The work of Pat Barker, an English novelist whose fiction about English working-class women provides a veritable commentary on what communication can mean to their identity relations,[3] is an open testimony to the complex matrix of gender and class subjectivities where utterances are always formed and sometimes undermined by the conscious and unconscious projections of audience and response.

---

*In memoriam Maude Hitchcock 1897 – 1990. Another "Century's Daughter."

Barker does not assume that questions of women's and working-class resistance coalesce around a more or less unified set of grievances. The fact that the Bakhtinian voicing of her work cannot be read as one voice does not reassert the divisive incommensurability of women's and working-class issues but rather suggests that this heterogeneity is itself the hallmark of a significant counterhegemonic discourse. The possibilities of such an alliance not only enable an understanding of the workings of radical fiction, but also clarify the role of intersubjective voicing in women's history which, I believe, is where the knowable community now has its most important resonance.[4]

Working-class writers are often put in the uncomfortable position of either following the lead of non-proletarian and sometimes anti-proletarian culture or, in committing themselves to developing a specifically working-class voice, thereby relegating themselves to the margins of cultural debate. The net result of these effects is to produce either isolated writers who appear to have transcended the limitations of their individual existence or writers who are shuffled in with literary movements to which they do not aspire. Women's writing, for example, has its own specific discontinuous history; yet this process itself has highlighted major problems of historiographic and aesthetic concern. The alterity of difference which has been so important to feminist theories of subjectivity is playing an increasing role in problematizing the different positions from which women's voices may emerge, including those of race and class. Pat Barker, for one, understands the difficulties of attempting to voice the non-identity in difference of gender and class which may confine her work to the periphery of both countertraditions. How, then, does she grapple with this dilemma?

Pat Barker has been called a practitioner of the nearly extinct art of the working-class novel. This is not quite accurate for several reasons, chief of which is that such comments tend to ameliorate the role of feminist consciousness in her stories. Barker's fiction complicates theories of dialogic feminism, for here is work that bears in its very letter the idea that women's writing is social discourse, heterogenous not despite its class orientation, but through its class position. The *Union Street* of the title of her first novel is the locus of a particular sign community, the working-class of northeast England in the 1970s, whose particular sign use is geographically and socio-economically determined: more important than this, the major interlocutors of the narrative are the women of the community, a fact which counteracts both the working-class hero syndrome of much proletarian fiction and also the preponderance of writing about bourgeois women which has dominated much of the history of this sphere of British cultural production. *Union Street* is full of the voices of working-class women: they populate and over-populate the street and the language of the novel and, although the book is divided into seven chapters, each about a woman who lives in or around Union Street, it is the communality of the language and the experiences conveyed which gives the narrative its politico-aesthetic strength.[5] The language itself is no guarantee, however, of gender/class authenticity. Rather than reproduce the text through an emphasis on intentionality, dialogism asserts an infidelity in language, a propensity to displace, but a displacement enmeshed in determinate and dynamic social relations. Radical writing is a refraction more than a reflection of existence in sign.

Barker shifts the question of political solidarity from the limits of individual expression to the voices of collective subjectivity defining the tenuous strands of community relations. It must be said at the outset that this is proposed from within the novel of realism, which itself has provided a host of constraints to the voices of women and the working-class in history.[6] Yet Barker remains resolute in exploring the criss-crossing patterns of gender and class oppression by 1) articulating the interconnections of voice and place in community identity and 2) constructing a history "hidden from history" in the recollections of community memory.

The first evidence of this trajectory occurs in Kelly Brown's story in *Union Street* (1982). Kelly is wandering alone, searching and yet not consciously. It is something that she has done quite often since being brutally attacked and raped. She meets an old woman, Alice Bell, whose story is the last of the book; she is a woman who is also searching, for peace of mind, and an end befitting the dignity of her life. Their solidarity is a strong statement on the sisterhood of class:

> "At least in the Home you'd get your meals." [Kelly] paused. Then burst out, "And they'd see you were warm. They'd see you had a fire."
>
> "Is not the life more than meat and the body than raiment?"
>
> She [Alice] wasn't quoting. She had lived long enough to make the words her own. Again silence. . . .
>
> "There's no other way. They're trying to take everything away from me. Everything." She smiled. "Well, this way they can't. That's all." . . .
>
> "I won't tell anybody," she said. She looked down at their hands: the old woman's cracked and shiny from a lifetime of scrubbing floors, her own grubby, with scabs on two of the knuckles. They sat together for a long time.[7]

Kelly and Alice sit together not simply because of their prior lone-liness, but because of their mutual recognition, formed around the concept of a threatening "they" — a "they" with many names in this story and specific resonance for the English working-class women de-scribed. "They" for Kelly are the Establishment, the school, the head-master, the middle-class, the adults who don't understand her and, in particular, the man who has raped her; for Alice, too, "they" are the Establishment and the middle-class, the "mean" men who had been her husbands, the parsimonious social services who only exist for her when she is too worn out to fend for herself, the rational beings who have calculated her expendability; "they" are those who invented the "Workhouse" with its "Home" as the sensitive successor, the home for the elderly poor while her actual home is "taken" from her. The "us and them" sociology of the poor may seem simplified but it is no less real, and it has a history.[8] Even in her dire situation, Alice makes one last effort to die the way she wants; while Kelly, young as she is, already sees that "they" must be opposed or the only freedom from necessity will be death. Not only can we register solidarity in their speech, but this knowledge is also written in their hands, in the unspoken of their existence. This too is figured in the dialogism of the oppressed.[9]

The meaning of this intergenerational solidarity for Barker is complex, although within the framework of the narrative it may simply tie the first story to the last in the book, Alice's. Meetings like Kelly and Alice's are specifically about the words with which to speak commu-nity. As Bakhtin has pointed out, there are no class-defined words, but there is a constant struggle to make those words one's own, as Alice suggests. Oppressed subjects often find their voices constrained or drowned out, and their daily vicissitudes bear witness to their resist-ance to such processes. For Barker, resistance is made all the more necessary by economic crisis which informs the background to her first novel (specifically the 1973 miners' strike which would topple Edward Heath's Conservative government the following year). If the first level of "utterance context" is Kelly and Alice's exchange in the scene above, Barker is quite insistent that this context is itself overdetermined by the broader climate of "us and them" class-relations which surfaced so strongly during Heath's regime. Yet none of the characters are simply a mouthpiece for these relations: they mediate class effects in every-day life. When Alice Bell "talks politics" with Mrs. Harrison, she does so not as a unionist, but as a woman well aware that a miners' strike can mean cold nights for the poor and the old in particular. Still, she defends the miners in the recognition that their sacrifice is at least the equivalent of hers; this, however, may not always be so evident to the reader, especially following Alice's dire attempt to get more coal for her fire. Neither Alice nor Barker poses easy solutions to the dilemmas that may bind even solidarity, which makes *Union Street* much better historical evidence than some utopian idealization of the workers' defeat of the Heath government.

Perhaps the most important aspect of Alice's testimony is her historical sense of what it means to be a working-class woman. This memory is etched in her consciousness as well as on her hands. She draws a parallel between the immiseration of the English working class in the early seventies with her experience of the hardships of the thirties, and now finds herself more poorly fed and housed than ever. Alice's projection of the subjective is more than just a handy agglomeration of details; her memories are her active present — an ongoing process that Raymond Williams has explored under the rubric of structures of feeling or "affective elements of consciousness."[10] But how does a working-class woman "make the words her own?"

Feminist dialogics provides an important development. For instance, Patricia Yaeger has shown how women's writing can "plagiarize" patriarchal discourse without being reducible to it.[11] The notion of ventriloquy is a relatively unexplored component of dialogic strategies (although, to be sure, it is generally analyzed under the rubric of parody in Bakhtin's work on Dostoevsky). In particular, Yaeger's discussion about how appropriation of phallocentric language can help "free" women's heteroglossia represents a crucial departure from French feminism's preoccupation with the theoretical *impasse* of *parler femme*.[12] Hers is a feminist reworking of the centrifugal forces that Bakhtin identifies in language and in part may explain the processes through which the subaltern subject may make the language her own.

Elements of Bakhtin's work on dialogism could also inform radical feminist criticism through a *class* consideration of appropriation and the appropriated. Dialogism is nothing if not the concretization of text and context: without a specific socio-historical context, for instance, Bakhtin's conception of the utterance simply has no meaning, except perhaps in the abstract systemization of language forms (with all the monologic tendencies that may belie). In short, dialogism is the working proof of the multi-accentuality of the sign, but sign overdetermined by social specificity. Of course, this indeterminacy has theoretical analogues of varying degrees. Emphasize indeterminacy in the sign and you are forced to collapse the social in a typically Baudrillardian denial of the referent; emphasize determinacy and you may end up with a form of vulgar economism where every human subject is calculated. Dialogism is not some happy medium between such extremes, but neither does it view them as mutually exclusive.

Dialogism, then, must be engaged in the same way that it critiques sign, as a determinate analytical tool of indeterminate sign formations. For it to transcend this (to become, in other words, the indeterminate mirror of which it speaks) would be to transcend its own dialogicity to become, as Robert Young has astutely pointed out, yet one more instance of theoretical monologism.[13] Although Bakhtin described sign as Janus-faced, this has much more to do with its ideological function than undecidability (it is certainly the case, however, that undecidability itself may be read in terms of ideology and ideological effects). Since struggle intersects in sign, it follows that the speaking woman subject, or in Luce Irigaray's terms, *parler femme*, is not a problem of invention, creation, or absolute ownership of sign.[14] Man, like the bourgeoisie, attempts to monopolize sign by conditioning the circumstances or contexts in which sign use and interaction take place. Masculinist ideology at the level of sign is in this sense doomed to its own subversion, for it cannot completely orchestrate the conditions on which it may be founded. The situation, of course, is complicated by the intersection of more than one struggle in sign at one and the same time: a working-class accentuation may yet embody a racist terminology; a masculinist orientation may well also contain a proletarian impulse; or a bourgeois utterance may also have a feminist inclination. No one utterance will coincide with a sign community; one problematic for a feminist dialogism, therefore, may be how to measure different and sometimes contradictory community accentuation across what appears as the same utterance.

From the opening pages of *Union Street,* the omniscient narrator is a practitioner of one of Bakhtin's favorite arts, double-voiced discourse, an ability which allows the narrator to move in and out of the language of the sign community.[15] This, however, is not the reflection of the bourgeois liberal sympathies of an author willing to get inside the consciousness of her or his characters. The point about Bakhtin's notion of double-voiced discourse is that it requires "lived social relations," not impressions, to build its semantic field. Thus, bodies "jack-knifing" against the cold, or "sandpapering" arms with dirty hands, constitute one level of descriptive power; "jammy-bugger," "on the hump," and "pinched" blankets represent another. When Barker's prose purples, these voices run at the same time:

> Mrs. Brown looked suddenly older, rat-like, as her eyes darted between Arthur and the girl. Kelly, watching, said, "I don't know what you're on about tea for, our Linda. If you're late again you're for the

chop. And I don't know who you'd get to give you another job. 'T'isn't everybody fancies a filthy sod like you pawing at their food." "Language!" said Mrs. Brown, automatically. (8)

By alternating prose styles and continually shifting narrative point of view, Barker builds a mother/daughter tension in a way remarkable for its economy. Here we have not only the language of the characters, their reported speech, but also description that they would use of this exchange. In addition, we have the narrator's interlocutions on the matter (for instance, Mrs. Brown becoming rat-like) and a subtext that gives the passage its theme. Only Kelly in this scene, a girl who will be sexually brutalized later in the story, does not hear the sexual jealousy of this dialogue and, significantly, is chastised for her "language." In the following exchange, Mrs. Brown adopts a middle-class voice in order to impress her new "fancy man" (who is as working-class as she is). Kelly will have nothing to do with such airs and graces because they bear little relation to her mother's and Kelly's realities as working-class women.

"Well," said Mrs. Brown, her voice edging upwards, "I'd better see what there is for breakfast."
"I can tell you now," said Kelly. "There's nowt."
Mrs. Brown licked her lips. Then, in a refined voice, she said, "Oh, there's sure to be something. Unless our Linda's eaten the lot."
"Our Linda's eat nothing. She's still in bed."
"Still in bed? What's wrong with her?"
"Day off. She says."
"Day off, my arse!" The shock had restored Mrs. Brown to her normal accent. "Linda!" Her voice rose to a shriek. (6)

Mrs. Brown's practical equation of male with middle class is a relatively consistent strategy throughout the book and emphasizes how multiple voicing, in this case of an individual character, organizes what Bakhtin calls a social purview or world view. Barker's comments on the problems of telling this story are an interesting correlative in this regard. Initially she found that, without meaning to, she "kept undermining [her] characters by slipping into middle-class style language and distanced observation."[16] Even in the version that we have, there are moments of this sort, but in most of the key narrative events in the story Barker's prose does not retreat or condescend in this way. For instance, while Kelly is raped she remains silent, a silence forced by fear of death, but the prose itself resists this ultimate act of monologism: " ... even when he had succeeded in forcing her hand to close around the smelly purple toadstool, it wasn't enough. He forced her down and spread himself over her, his breath smelling strongly of peppermint and decay" (29). Resistance is also registered in this example where Lisa's labor begins:

> The pains were stronger too. Very strong. There was something mechanical about their strength, their remorseless regularity. She felt them as extreme heat, as though she were being forced to stand too close to a furnace, to watch the door open, slowly, knowing that the heat would be strong enough to sear her eyeballs and burn her skin. Then as the contraction ebbed, as the door closed, came cold and ashen darkness . . .
>
> People appeared and stood by the bed . . . At first she spoke to them, but as the day wore on speech became too much of an effort. (128)

We also learn of the ageing prostitute Blonde Dinah not just through her dialogue with others, but in the internal speech of one of her "customers," the just-as-worn-out George Harrison.

> Well, she wouldn't would she? Her old stalking grounds. But he listened to her talk. The cracked and seamed face lit up, her voice came out warm and spluttery between badly fitting teeth, and her hands, shaping the darkness, re-created a community, as she talked about the past, about the people she had known. He found himself wondering about her, about what she was like, like . . . well, like. She must get sick of it surely, not to mention sore. Gladys . . . but then Gladys was different . . . well, anyway, Gladys didn't go too much on that sort of thing. But perhaps Dinah didn't either? Perhaps it was a job, like cleaning lavatories out was just a job? (226–227)

The social relations that conjoin to produce oppression marked by male violence, prostitution, and childbearing are not the monopoly of the lives of working-class women; nor is the language used to communicate these relations. Barker's point is to suggest, however, that the specific struggles of such women have received scant cultural expression, and even less cultural critique, and that this requires a little more than a tactical reorientation of writer and reader: it needs an alternative culture of writing and reception. Such an approach may not only question the formal limitations of the novel, but also the critical tools employed in the "value-free" appreciation of working-class women's writing. Barker is surely right to bemoan the lack of tradition on which to build and draw strength for her work, but in a sense this is where the power of her radical writing may lie, for such work announced itself by its non-traditional or even anti-traditional intonations. These resist assimilation by a bourgeois male hegemony because her combinations of voices are precisely those which certain structures of domination prefer not to (or cannot) hear: ideologically, a hegemony may well invoke its own contradictions but its intention, at least, is to silence them.

One of the achievements of *Union Street* is that the women's lives portrayed are not catapulted into the realm of the spectacular, of variations that provide them or their readers' miraculous relief (one might say catharsis, or sublimation) from the dire social relations of their existence. The effect of this is not one of hopelessness, but a lesson in the discourse of resistance. Working-class voices build and multiply not despite social relations, but through them. It is small wonder, therefore, that there is so much activity alongside the voices in the stories of *Union Street* because for the working class, and particularly its women, there is always work to be done. The narratives of Lisa, Muriel, and Iris all bear the brunt of both a sexist division of labor and the class extraction of surplus value from their labor. Labor for women may also mean childbirth, as it does for Lisa. It is Joanne's narrative, however, that most firmly asserts this social purview in the very texture of its language.

Like Kelly, Joanne is being forced to grow up quickly. As a working-class teenager she is lucky to find far from glamorous work in the cake factory. Joanne has an upwardly mobile boyfriend, Ken, who is getting himself educated at the local Poly and gets her pregnant in the meantime. The man who really loves her is a midget, Joss, who is the butt of local humor but is the only person who seems to understand her (interestingly, his first name is actually Joyce, the surname of a local man who gassed himself after his wife left him). When Joanne stays over at Joss' place we hear: "She could just imagine all the jokes. Step ladders. Everybody the same size in bed. All that. Even her own mother had had a bloody good laugh, but she wouldn't be laughing when she heard about last night" (70). Now the short, sharp nature of Joanne's thought processes might seem to some just another example of the "restrictive codes" of the lower orders were it not for Barker's dialogic rendering of the "utterance contexts" of Joanne's existence. Here is Joanne at the factory:

> The noise was horrific as usual. There was no possibility of conversation. Even the supervisor's orders had to be yelled at the top of her voice and repeated many times before anybody heard. At intervals, there were snatches of music. It was being played continuously but only

> the odd phrase triumphed over the roar of the machines. Some of the women moved their mouths silently, singing or talking to themselves: it was hard to tell. Others merely looked blank. After a while not only speech but thought became impossible.

> The first sponge cake reached Jo. She began the sequence of actions that she would perform hundreds of times that day. It took little effort once you were used to it and, provided the cakes continued to arrive in a steady stream, it could be done almost automatically.

Most bourgeois fiction shrinks from the representation of work, much less the thoughts of those who do it. This sequence begins in ordinary fashion with what Bakhtin calls "objectified discourse." This disinterested approach ("distanced observation"), however, won't do the job and so the discourse becomes, intentionally or not, double-voiced. At the very point when work appears to silence the worker, the worker's voice begins to seep through: "It took little effort once you were used to it." The sometimes staccato delivery is in part a product of work, but it is not completely deadening, "Almost, but not quite." Barker's novel underlines that such consciousness cannot be rendered independently of the socio-economic determinations of class-inflected language. Joanne's position as a woman within the working class is asserted time and time again in her story so that man, particularly the Ken variety, may seem a mutation of the work process, another source that threatens silence and must also be resisted.

After telling Ken about the baby, she walks toward home with him, but he stops her under a railway bridge and forces her into sex. A train passes overhead as Joanne realizes that Ken is trying to "screw" the baby out of her. His "terrible, monotonous power" is compared to the "deadly and monotonous" power of the train, "almost matching the thrusts of Ken's bum." She fights back: "With deadly corrosive hatred she began to move against him, imposing upon him the rhythm of the train, which was at first exciting, and then terrible and then, abruptly, ridiculous, so that he lost his erection and slid ignobly out of her" (100 – 101). The discourse on power here is never quite the author's own, for there is a "sideward glance" to the voice of another, Joanne's, and her apprehension of the equation of mechanism and man. We know from Joanne's factory experience that she is no stranger to monotonous power. Man and machine are only articulated together when they are seen to curtail women's desire; this theme is consistent in Barker's writing, from her analysis of the labor of prostitution in *Blow Your House Down* to the topos of the ball and chain that knocks down Liza's house in *The Century's Daughter*.

That much maligned term, "the language of class," is here not interpreted as the transparent voice or enunciation of individual characters within the narrative, although from what has been said so far, I am obviously interested in these utterances. Class language, however, is not just Joanne, or Alice, or Kelly speaking but the *way* they speak and the conditions through which their interactions take place. But while Barker attempts to show the interrelations of her characters as community experience, she also resists the temptation to represent them as a "slice of life" snapshot by developing a diachronic insistence as community memory. In *Union Street* this memory is suggested most strongly in Alice's narrative, although the most developed example appears in Barker's third novel, *The Century's Daughter,* through the recollections of Liza, whose birth on the stroke of midnight 1900 gives the book its title.

I would like to consider Liza's memory as a working through of the problem of collective identity. Barker's story is a curious assembly of anecdote and confession — like *Union Street* an intergenerational narrative, but this time emerging in the alternating voices of Liza Jarrett, an old woman on the verge of death, and Stephen, a social worker, whose job is (initially) to persuade Liza to move so that her house can be torn down for a new development project. Liza's memory brings us through the century of her "lived relations," from Edwardian England to its "post-industrial" ghost; from the twilight of Victoria to the harsh realities of Thatcher — all the while casting Liza's gendered class position in a different light.

For many critics of this novel, the idea of a "gendered class position" is obviated by its working-class milieu. Isabel Scholes, for instance, complains that Liza is an "unstoppable bore" who is "old, not wise" and "larger issues" like the "disintegration of working-class culture" are touched upon only to be "trivialized."[17] Paul Driver, in an otherwise enthusiastic review, remarks that the novel is a "consciously 'working-class' fiction whose claim to reality status might be found off-puttingly vehement."[18] Such comments raise an issue about the "acceptable" bounds of working-class women's narrative — even within the laudable commitment of Virago Press (Barker's publisher). The historical claims of Liza, however fragmented or "trivial," call into question some of the more glaring assumptions about identity in women's working-class communities. I want to consider this aspect in relation to Barker's story in two ways: first, in the language or memory (where language is the construction of meaning, not just the words that are spoken); and second, the organization of time and space in the narrative as an analysis of what Bakhtin has called "chronotope." In partic-

ular, I want to explore the possibilities suggested by Reva Brown in her
comments on *The Century's Daughter* that "one is left, however, with the
impression that, beneath the storyline, there is an amount of 'special
pleading' for working-class life as valuable and interesting because of
the necessity to struggle for existence and not despite it. Perhaps she
[Barker] is right."[19] Perhaps, with the enjoinder that this is not history
as "plea," but memory as resistance.

Like *Union Street,* from the first page *The Century's Daughter* is
marked by vari-directional double-voiced discourse featuring, in this
case, Liza's active voice and Stephen's interior commentary:[20]

> "No point being eighty, is there?" said Liza, "If you can't be a bit
> outrageous?" And certainly she looked it, Stephen thought, with her
> scarlet headscarf tilted crazily over one eye, giving her the look of a
> senile pirate. "I'm sorry I didn't let you in when you come before.
> Thought you were some bloody do-gooding cow from the social."
> That — give or take an udder — was exactly what he was, but he
> didn't want to risk rejection now by saying so. Instead he handed her
> the letter he'd brought with him.

Although Liza does most of the talking here it is clear that the
reader learns as much about her from the unuttered response of her
listener, who Liza will talk to precisely because she does not believe him
to be a social worker (which, of course, he is). In contrast, Stephen
stays quiet, not in deference to Liza's age but because, as a bearer of
bad news, he believes Liza to be senile (which she is not). Their mutual
misrecognition (unlike the understanding of Kelly and Alice) keeps
their narratives separate. In effect, they will "speak" on a different
discursive level—even as the characters themselves learn more of each
other.

The storehouse of Liza's memory is the register of existence sym-
bolized or metamorphosed in the metal box beneath her bed. Lyn Pykett has recently commented on the significance of Liza's box of
memorabilia: "The box is a matrilineal inheritance, passed on from
Liza's grandmother to her mother and finally to Liza. It is almost literally an objective correlative for that matrilineal heritage which Liza
recognizes as she relives her life through the memories released from
the box."[21] Pykett's point is well-taken, for the associative effects inspired by the box temper "links in a chain of women stretching back
through the centuries, into the wombs of women whose names they
didn't know" (211). History measured in the births and deaths of
working-class women, in the labor of their labor, in the material bonds

of birth and upbringing? This is a very different form of history from the measured empiricism of surplus value and union men. It is not that these histories are inseparable, but that the evaluative criteria of the latter has tended to obscure or obviate the experience of the former. Liza's story is indeed a fiction, but its fictionality marks memory in the narratives of history.

In her collection of essays, *Sea Changes*, Cora Kaplan suggests that questions of social hierarchy and female subjectivity represent a "Pandora's box" for all feminist theory; feminism has not paid adequate theoretical attention to "other forms of social determination."[22] Liza's memory box is not a metonymic substitution for this problematic, or indeed a solution to it, yet there are ways in which the storytelling that the box inspires throws some light on the relationship between women's narrativization of history and "social determination." From the beginning of the novel the associations that Liza draws from the box dance like the women figures emblazoned upon it. The most important "piece" of history for Liza is the newspaper report announcing her birth at midnight, 1900. Stephen only partially understands the resonance of this documentary evidence and comments that Liza's mother must have been proud. Liza's response reveals some of the concrete realities of a working-class woman's life in Britain at the turn of the century: "We-ell, she was and she wasn't. She liked the newspaper bit all right — it was me she wasn't keen on. I was the seventh and she'd lost four. Three of them in one week. Took more than a bit of paper to make *her* jump for joy. Especially over a girl" (8). Of course, with squalid living conditions and even worse maternity care, child mortality rates were very high among the urban poor; but many children meant, or was taken to mean, many future breadwinners, especially if they were boys who could be channeled, sexist division of labor and all, into the mines or heavy industries.

Several critics have noted how Liza and Stephen are drawn together by their individual crises and loneliness (variously measured by the trials of Liza's age — much like Alice's in *Union Street* — and by Stephen's ambivalent feelings towards his parents, his homosexuality, and the related loss he has felt since his boyfriend left for the U.S.). Throughout their early meetings, however, Liza becomes significantly more aware of Stephen (not simply as a representation of authority, but as a potential audience and companion) than he is of her, even as a sensitive social worker. Thus, when she asks about "them" — those people who will evaluate whether or not she is "fit" to live alone — Stephen is initially surprised, but this foregrounds Stephen's awareness of his role in the deteriorating "welfare state," and the deteriorating state of

Liza's welfare. This, as it were, is the unspoken of their interaction and provides a bond that would otherwise be unlikely or artificial.

When Stephen or Mrs. Jubb (a helper) are not there, Liza fights her loneliness in the "few steps" that constitute her world by reaching for the box. She remembers the "full smell of the hot linen" as her mother, Louise, ironed; the goose grease when she was ill; and the time when Louise took her along when she went to clean at the Wynyard's mansion. The latter is a particularly harrowing experience, marked as it is by her father's protests (a matter of masculine pride, for he too worked for the Wynyards at the iron foundry). Even the crunching of her boots on the gravel driveway scares young Liza into silence but, like Joanne in *Union Street*, not necessarily acquiescence. When she wanders the house alone she thinks, "This is where they live, the Wynyards; this is where they eat and sleep and talk and laugh, and she remembered her father's hands, scarred with iron dust" (31). Later, after Mrs. Wynyard comes home unexpectedly, Louise's reaction is telling: "You're not supposed to be seen ... You're supposed to skivvy after 'em and get it all done and out of the way while they're flat on their backs, or out enjoying themselves. She doesn't fool me ... Some so-called *ladies*'d be sat in their own muck like loonies if they didn't have us to run round after them" (34).[23] But Louise had not said this to Mrs. Wynyard's face, and this is what confuses the young Liza, for Louise had in fact smiled as Mrs. Wynyard passed. Liza wanted to ask her why but could not and they walked home in silence, "every step was punctuated by the *flap-flap* of Louise's torn sole, sounding to Liza like the b-b-b-b-b of a blocked tongue" (34).

This memory, then, forms part of an education, for Liza comes to understand the strategic silence before authority, or the smiles that mean their opposite. Both, in their own way, may be mustered as dialogic resistance to hierarchy — whether at the workplace (for instance, the munitions factory where Liza toils) or the workplace called home. When Liza sees the "supervisor" talking to Elizabeth Wynyard at the factory, she knows the former is not "a lady" by "the tell-tale sagging of the knees. She had Miss Forster exactly placed." Similarly, Ellen, Liza's friend (and former Wynyard's maid) has Elizabeth "placed." She accuses her of "playing" by working at the factory and that for Liza and herself there was, by contrast, no choice involved. Later Liza asks Ellen why she could not meet Elizabeth halfway, and she replies, "Because she wouldn't know where halfway was." Liza's memory is full of these micro-social moments where she learns of the hierarchic "realities" of her existence, and eventually challenges them.

Not that her resistance is solely reserved for the bourgeoisie and its various manifestations; as a working-class woman her conflicts are not only inter-class but *intra*-class, specifically, with her husband Frank Wright. One of the reasons Frank occupies an important place in the narrative is that he uses his memory of the war (in which he was wounded in the throat) to speak tongues in the present of Liza's memory. Indeed, he holds seances to bring the voices of the dead back to the working-class community who had lost not just those voices, but the bodies which accompanied them. "He began to speak ... Or rather, he opened his mouth and voices poured out. One voice after another, and all different. Not as different, perhaps, as they had been in life, because there is a limit to what one damaged set of vocal chords can do, but different enough to be recognizable, and woman after woman leaned forward and strained to hear the voice of her son" (61). Although Liza is initially moved by this performance she doubts Frank's magical qualities; after all, he knew these men well enough to imitate them. But the way Frank represents community relations through his seances is ultimately seen as fraudulent by Liza because, whatever the therapeutic value for other members of the community, Frank does not project any social awareness into his personal relations. This, more than anything else, makes him a false historian.

Liza remembers the time when she was visiting the grave of her son Tom who was killed in the war and meets up with Lena Lowe (who had also lost a son in the war). It is a moment of solidarity and compassion but not sentimentality. She recalls the event in a dream:

> "She come to me in that mucky old mackintosh she used to wear. And she had something in her hands, something very bright, and I couldn't understand what it was, because I know they were jewels, and yet they seemed to be alive. Sapphires, rubies, diamonds; but brighter. And they were all moving about, and making this little squeaking noise, as if they were singing. And then I woke up, and I heard a voice say, 'The souls of the faithful are in the hands of God.' And I lay there and I thought, *Well, how daft. That wasn't God, it was Lena.*" (214)

Whereas Frank recalls images as a communion with God — as a form of ontological or metaphysical presence — Liza's memory and dreams seem firmly ground in the materiality of the everyday. The image of Lena in the dream underlines the importance of woman's bonding in community memory. Here, history is not constructed in the chronology of objectifiable events, but it is recorded in the disparate fragments of Liza "speaking" in her own way the collective experiences of her peo-

ple; the souls that "squeak" in the hands of Lena, the figures that
dance in the picture on the box. Memory is, therefore, both a resistance against the Franks of the this world and an expressive form of
"existence"; the communality of experience is a measure of intersubjective coherence. Remembrance is the key to Liza's identity as a working-class woman, an identity that may indeed challenge both categories
of subjectivity (working-class and woman).

Of course, this is not to say that history is merely storytelling, but
telling fiction can certainly make compelling history, as the following
personified palimpsest clearly shows: "You can never see your own
child clearly, she thought. Not the way other people see her, because
inside that face are all the other faces, hiding and revealing younger
faces still, until eventually the line disappears into the one face that is
like no other: the convulsed, bloody, purple face of a baby immediately
after birth" (206). In the course of this story, we read the multiple
inscriptions of history on the face, specific marks that may be missed
or forgotten against an historical narrative writing otherwise. Barker
dialogizes our sense of history so that we read, therefore, not just
about the First World War, but about Liza's experiences in the munitions factory; not just about childbirth, but about the specific socio-
economic conditions that render its physical hardships more so; not
just about the politics of eviction, but about the personal implications
of shattered communities. I would like to consider another way that
Barker asserts the importance of multivocal history by providing an
explanation of what may seem a curious interweaving of Liza's narrative with the story of Stephen, whose life touches on Liza's only at the
moment when hers is almost gone.

Chronotope in Bakhtin's writing refers to certain models of temporal and spatial relationships in the novel.[24] For Bakhtin, chronotope
not only allows him to make generic distinctions within the varying
discourses of the novel, but also suggests that the concept of "time-
space" offers a key interpretive model of the fundamental historicity of
the novel as form. Rather than summarize the varieties of chronotope
that Bakhtin develops (from the Greek romance to the novel of encounter) I will suggest that *The Century's Daughter* offers another model
of chronotopic relations. As noted above, Liza's obsession with the box
in this narrative is not for its contents so much as their associative
effects: the box itself is the chronotope locus of the story. For Liza it
represents a tangible relationship to the past which gives her a certain
dignity in the present — a present where, as she admits, she is prepar-
ing for death. The sequence of events she recalls may appear chrono-
logical, but do not represent the time/space of the traditional

biographer. Thus, the principle moments of this memory, "the long country of the past" (21), are, by turns: Liza at the age of ten — by which time her reputation as the "century's daughter" has been firmly established; four years later when Liza appears caught between girlhood and womanhood and wants to define herself as different from her mother; Liza at age seventeen when her brother Edward is killed in the war and she first meets Frank; the following year when Liza gives birth to Thomas Edward; Tom at age four and the haircutting incident; Liza a few months later, pregnant again, this time when the family is forced to move house and Frank is unemployed (here the narrative follows Liza through to the birth of her second child, Eileen, and the increasing violence and desperation of Frank who finally leaves in search of work and returns to die); 1940, with Tom in the service and Louise (Liza's mum) living with her; Tom's death and Liza's visit to the Jarrett graves (father, brother, and son); Eileen's pregnancy and the birth of Kath; Liza's visit to Eileen (now married and with a second child, Jenny, and two more, Keith and Sheila from Leonard's previous marriage); Kath getting into grammar school and later Liza's deranged attempt to kill her; Eileen and Kath's visit to the prison to see Keith; Liza at the pub with old friends; Kath leaving to live in London leaving Liza, at last, alone in the house (but for Nelson, the parrot), which leads to Liza's present and the slightly bizarre yet bitter circumstances of her death. Obviously, this is a way of telling the story as biography: piece together these scenes and you have the semblance of a life. But, I would argue, that is neither Barker's expertise in fiction, nor indeed does it represent the aesthetic strength of this narrative. The events of Liza's life as she recalls them hinge on particular moments of community and class knowledges among women.

The situation of her family while she is growing up, for instance, cannot be separated from an internal polemic concerning the social hardships of England's working-class before the First World War. Thus, while we learn of Liza's difficult relations with her parents (especially her mother, Louise) on a personal level, the time and space of the narrative encompasses any number of possible social determinants within these difficulties. For Louise life seems an endless cycle of childbirth and rearing, washing and ironing, and cleaning the "owner's" floors to make ends meet (the same owner who owns her husband's labor at the local ironworks). Liza's poverty is measured by her clothing ("lucky to have boots") and diet (tea means "doorsteps fried in dripping"). Liza's visits to the owner's house, "the Wynyard's mansion," signifies for her another life and, significantly, Stephen now lives at the Wynyard's (which has been split up into flats — in the age of the "post-industrial" the "owners" now live elsewhere). Indeed, when Stephen takes Liza back to the Wynyard's, it serves as a springboard for Liza's memory of Ellen Parker, who had worked at the Wynard's and later became a key organizer in the Labour Party. Liza tries not to sentimentalize either the Wynyard's house or those days because, as she says, whatever the community or solidarity, "women wore out by the time they were thirty." Thus, place is only important for its associative effects. It is not that Stephen has somehow come to fill the position of the "them" of Liza's youth (even given the nature of his specific task to get Liza to move) but more that Liza feels that there has been something lost and gained in comparative worker affluence and the niceties of the welfare state. She voices *this* experience as "we," "you," and "she":

> "Because that's where it went wrong you know. It was all *money*. You'd've thought we had nowt else to offer. But we *did*. We had a way of life, a way of treating people. You didn't just go to church one day a week and jabber on about loving your neighbour — You got stuck in seven days a week and bloody did it, because you knew if you didn't you wouldn't survive and neither would she. We had all that. We had pride. We were poor, but we were *proud*." (218)

For Liza this is not just nostalgia but a source of optimisim, as if there may be, through her experience, irreducible communal bonds. This is clearly a different use of memory from that which Jameson bemoans under the rubric of "the nostalgia mode," a cultural logic that quotes the past as a measure of aesthetic style. The "pastness" which Liza invokes grapples with a "real" history that impinges on or determines the present: it is the real foundation of her time/space relations.[25]

Stephen is present not because history marks him (as gay, as upwardly mobile working-class) as an outsider (as Liza is an outsider by age and worldview), but rather because he, in the brave new world of Thatcher's England, brings new experiences of life and death in community relations to bear on Liza's narrative. As Stephen listens to Liza, he wonders: "It startled him to realize that Liza had more faith in the future at eighty-four than he had at twenty-nine. He looked round at the people he worked with here and on the Clagg Lane estate, and it seemed to him that he was witnessing the creation of a people without hope" (219). If anybody, Stephen is the main source of sentimental comment in the novel, although the more he learns of Liza the more intrigued he becomes about the question of memory as an historical force, and in this at least he may be more than a witness to hopelessness.

I would like to give one more example of the chronotopic assemblage of memory in the novel. Although I am suggesting that *The Century's Daughter* is radically historical, its historicity does not appear as some "expressive causality" within the text: the moment of memory itself is a condition of the historical vision of the novel — including the simplifications and possible contradictions of Liza's "voice." In Chapter Six when Stephen again visits Liza, he tells her that his father is very ill and that his mother says that Dad has made up his mind to die. Given Liza's condition this exchange underlines how Liza's and Stephen's lives are intertwining — much as they do in their respective dreams about the figures on the box. Indeed, the more this process is accentuated, the more the box figures as a touchstone of Liza's memory and a condition of the present beyond it. When Stephen tells Liza that he is glad that she is alive, she responds, "Yes, son, I know you are," and she thinks of her dead son Tom and the labor of her own death (which she calls "work"). She drifts into the past once more, this time to the moment of Tom's birth — which again is marked by pain. This moment confirms her motherhood as separate from her mother (indicated in the argument over names) and the fundamental vulnerability of man, seen through the fragility of Tom's baby body with his barely covered brain and his testicles "like tiny crushable eggs." This sequence follows the family through to 1921 when Tom is four. As such, each "scene" makes some comment about the cultural construction of "man," whether it be Frank's interpellation as a subject in war speaking for the dead or Frank playing "soldiers" with Tom:

> "I thought it was time he had his hair cut."
> "*Cut*? You've bloody shaved it, man." She ran to Tom and picked him up in her arms.
> Frank was uneasy, but determined to fight back. "You can't keep him tied to your apron strings forever. He's a man."
> "A *man*? Frank, he's four years old."
> "High time he stopped looking like a lass. You don't want to make a Nancy of him, do you?" (97)

What Liza wants is a man who does not end up either dead or a brute, and if that means bringing up a "Nancy," then so much the better. This passage is immediately juxtaposed with a long section featuring Stephen and his dying father, Walter. Here the emphasis is on the failure of communication between father and son brought about by different conceptions of what "man" can mean. For Stephen, this usually works as a form of internal polemic, an "unspoken conversation," a dialogue that was "passionate, bitter, unrelenting in its intensity" (102). Stephen had not lived up to his father's expectations of "manliness"; yet now, as Walter lies dying, the cancer in his swollen stomach turns him, ironically, into something other than his image of man. "Stephen had never seen his father so nearly naked before, and the sight shocked him. The belly, what he half-derisively thought of as his father's 'pot,' clearly didn't belong with the rest of his body ... 'I wish it was labour' he [Walter] said, 'At least I'd know it had an end.'" Just to accentuate this transformation, Stephen sits up with Walter on his last night, but his father has him sleep in his bed with him instead. As Walter talks to him about his experience of unemployment one is reminded of Frank: "You talk about *passing* time, *killing* time, and you don't know what you're on about. You don't kill time, time kills you" (117). As he speaks to his son, Walter reveals that he has taken to watching young girls at the local school. And, as Stephen reflects on this, he thinks, "running through the entire conversation, had been one unspoken sentence: *You can't afford to judge me.*"

Neither Stephen nor Walter is a particularly well-drawn character, yet, as his father dies, Stephen comes to some understanding of the role that "masculinity" has played in his familial experience, the mutations of patriarchy with its ideology of breadwinner and attendant frustrations. Thus, to say that Stephen's story is a foil to Liza's is an understatement, for it is conceptually vital to the chronotope suggested. The reversal, not the complementarity, in his narrative throws Liza's recollections into relief. For instance, after his father's funeral Stephen spends one more night at his parent's home, but is tortured by the silence and death of his father seemingly penetrating his consciousness. He fights the silence and memory of his father by masturbating which, if it provides relief, does not leave Stephen with any sense of affirmation or renewal. When Frank dies, Liza is much more sanguine about the tasks before her: "She needed words powerful enough to ignite the silence that was densely packed into her, a voice that, fanned by the bellows of her lungs, would stream out of her mouth like a living torch" (167). Of course, voices are never enough, but the chronotope of community memory is a little more than denial or resignation.

Who are the inheritors of Liza's identity relations? Certainly not the youths who break into her house in search of money, empty the memory box onto the floor, punch Liza and leave her for dead. Nor does the logic of narration favor Stephen as a powerful resource against the "waning of affect" in our epoch, a dissolution here taken as the erosion of historical memory in community relations. Barker does not offer easy solutions; the tension evoked in the articulation of the knowable community remains a problem not just for women's working-class fiction, but for radical politics in general. The memory box of the century's daughter may be fictional, but it is also a resource of hope, a topos for the significance of women's history in the construction of the future. The nature of Liza's death does not kill the idea of this history but underlines that the intersubjective relations through which it is inscribed are under threat. Barker, like Benjamin, understands that "To articulate the past historically does not mean to recognize it 'the way it really was' (*Ranke*). It means to seize hold of a memory as it flashes up at a moment of danger."[26] This essay, then, ends perhaps as a preface to another one concerning the importance of women's historiography in telling the past as a way of making the future tell. Pat Barker's radical writing holds some lessons for this way of telling for, in the polyphony of women's voices which figure the social relations of her fiction, she suggests that we must retain our ears to hear beyond the single subject-centered reason that dominates the voice of authority. To render the past as dialogical is to make the future more so. If that ultimately takes us beyond the forms of single-authored culture, then so be it: it may make the knowable community a little more knowable, and a little less a contradiction in terms.

Notes

1. Raymond Williams, "The Knowable Community in George Eliot's Novels," *Novel* 2 (1969), pp. 255 – 68. The concept of the knowable community is also developed in a revised form in Williams's *The English Novel* (London: Paladin, 1974) and *The Country and The City* (London: Paladin, 1975). For a brief discussion of the importance of the knowable community to Williams's *oeuvre*, see Alan O'Connor, *Raymond Williams: Writing, Culture, Politics* (New York: Blackwell, 1989), pp. 68 – 79. We will see that I attempt to negotiate some of the limits to community knowledge using Bakhtin's conception of the dialogic. See in particular: M. M. Bakhtin, *The Dialogic Imagination*, ed. Michael Holquist. Trans. Caryl Emerson and Michael Holquist (Austin: University of Texas Press, 1981) and V. N. Vološinov, *Marxism and the Philosophy of Language*, trans. Ladislav Matejka and I. R. Titunik (New York: Seminar Press, 1973).

2. There is a growing body of theoretically sophisticated analysis of categories of gender and history, particularly as they pertain to the "women's

story" or "herstory." My point here is not to summarize such arguments but to register their importance to the very possibility of my project. The following works have been influential in this regard: "What's New in Women's History" by Linda Gordon and "Writing History: Language, Class, and Gender" by Carroll Smith-Rosenberg in *Feminist Studies/Critical Studies*, ed. Teresa de Lauretis (Bloomington: Indiana University Press, 1986), pp. 20 – 54; Joan Wallach Scott, *Gender and the Politics of History* (New York: Columbia University Press, 1988); the special issue of *Radical History Review* on "The Women's Story" 43 (Winter, 1989); *Sex and Class in Women's History*, ed. Judith L. Newton, Mary P. Ryan and Judith R. Walkowitz (London: Routledge, 1983); and Judith Newton, "History as Usual?: Feminism and the 'New Historicism,'" *Cultural Critique* 9 (Spring 1988), pp. 87 – 121. There is a sometimes obvious tension within and between these works concerning the production of women's history, whether from developments in linguistic and literary theory, or from autonomous theorization in feminist historiography itself. Broadly, the former has helped me to articulate questions of identity, and the latter, problems of memory in historical narrativization, although this is more evident in a longer version of the present essay.

3. Pat Barker has published four novels to date: *Union Street* (1982), *Blow Your House Down* (1984), *The Century's Daughter* (1986), and *The Man Who Wasn't There* (1989). All are published by Virago. Although I believe the themes of community identity and memory can be discussed in relation to all four of these works, I restrict myself to two of them, and as such, my analysis does not claim to represent the dialogic possibilities of Barker's writing across the full range of her work. The differences between each work are as instructive as their similarities.

4. The matrix that I will explore concerns the intersubjective grid suggested in Bakhtin's theory of dialogism, the historical knowledge produced by Barker's working-class women, and what both can mean for community identity. The discursive strategies of women's history articulate the most pronounced sense of the knowable community in our era.

5. For some readers of the book this is precisely what defines its weakness. Hermione Lee, for instance, is aghast at the "grim details" of the narrative and thus concludes: "The result is a serious, well-meant, gripping set of case-histories, but not a novel" ("At Spaghetti Junction," *The Observer*, May 30, 1982, p. 30). Of course, whether the "realities" of working-class existence can find a place in the novel as form is another matter, and requires further examination. In this instance, Barker clearly attempts to reproduce the storytelling of oral histories. The community is never conveyed by any one voice, *sui generis*, but by the concatenation of their layering. Thus, despite the claims that Barker's novel is "Lawrentian" (damning praise, to say the least), much of her technical expertise has correlatives outside the traditions of the English novel. See, for instance, Studs Terkel, ed. *Working* (New York: Avon, 1972); Zhang Xinxin and Sang Ye, eds. *Chinese Profiles*, trans. W. J. F. Jenner et al. (Beijing: Panda,

1986), reprinted and revised as *Chinese Lives* (New York: Pantheon, 1988). See also the importance of oral histories for Margot Badran's analysis of Egyptian feminism in Arina Angerman, et al. eds. *Current Issues in Women's History* (London: Routledge, 1989), pp. 153 – 170. Note, I am not suggesting that these works are formal determinants of Barker's work but that what she has called the "compound eye" approach has a strong resonance in oral history.

6. See Ken Worpole, "Expressionism and Working-Class Fiction," in *Dockers and Detectives* (London: Verso, 1983), pp. 77 – 93, and Tony Davies, "Unfinished Business: Realism and Working-Class Writing" in Jeremy Hawthorn, ed., *The British Working-Class Novel in the Twentieth Century* (London: Edward Arnold, 1984), pp. 125 – 136. Arguments concerning realism *per se* have been lively since the Lukacs/Brecht debates. A more recent analysis can be found in Catherine Belsey, *Critical Practice* (London: Methuen, 1980) especially Chapters Three and Four. For an overview of the pitfalls of realism for feminist writing see Toril Moi, *Sexual/Textual Politics* (London: Methuen, 1985), pp. 4 – 8. That Barker herself is not uncritical of the possibilities of realism may in part be measured by the dream sequences in *The Century's Daughter.* While it is true that the centered subjectivity of conventional realism may reproduce the integrated self of patriarchal ideology, *communities* of women are not in themselves unrepresentable in the realist mode.

7. Pat Barker, *Union Street* (London: Virago, 1982), p. 67. All further references will be indicated within the text.

8. There are obvious theoretical problems with "us and them" as a binary opposition, although one should note that these examples are not essentialist but strategic and historically specific.

9. The present essay is a shorter version of a critique of Pat Barker's fiction, which itself is part of a book-length manuscript, *The Dialogism of the Oppressed.* The "dialogism of the oppressed" refers to the ways in which marginalized writing dialogizes according to historically specific social situations: for instance, how its semantic positioning doubles in response to and as interventions against perceived cultural institutions of production and reception. Dialogism is a measure of difference and solidarity.

10. Williams used "structures of feeling" in different ways in his work, but here I refer principally to the explication in his *Marxism and Literature* (Oxford: Oxford University Press, 1977), pp. 128 – 135. While structures of feeling are not reducible to class identities, they may nevertheless semantically figure such identities, particularly in times of class "emergence." O'Connor argues that the concept of hegemony comes to replace earlier definitions of structures of feeling in Williams's work, but I would argue that this is true of only one element, namely "structure of feeling in dominance." See O'Connor, pp. 105–6 and pp. 114– 115.

11. Patricia Yaeger, "'Because A Fire Was In My Head': Eudora Welty and the Dialogic Imagination." *PMLA* 99 (1984), pp. 955–73.

12. See in particular Luce Irigaray, *This Sex Which Is Not One*, trans. Catherine Porter (Ithaca: Cornell University Press, 1985). The *impasse* is not the implied essentialism but an inability to theorize the material conditions of such language. For a materialist critique of Irigaray, see Toril Moi, *Sexual/Textual Politics* (London: Methuen, 1985), pp. 127 – 149. For a feminist-Bakhtinian reading of Irigaray's concept of specularity, see Anne Herrmann, *The Dialogic and Difference* (New York: Columbia University Press, 1989).

13. Robert Young, "Back to Bakhtin," *Cultural Critique* 2 (Winter, 85/86), pp. 71 – 92. This essay is useful for identifying some theoretical gaps not only in Bakhtin's work, but in contemporary Marxist reworkings of the same. The present essay is, among other things, an attempt to come to terms with some of these difficulties.

14. Irigaray's theoretical move here is only defensible to the degree to which *parler femme* describes a discursive process that is at once strategic and contingent. As noted above, while Irigaray does assert *parler femme* as process, she has yet to explain its concrete manifestations.

15. Bakhtin outlines the chief elements of double-voiced discourse in *Problems of Dostoevsky's Poetics*, ed. and trans. Caryl Emerson (Minneapolis: University of Minnesota Press, 1984), pp. 185 – 199. One of the chief advantages of Bakhtin's conception is that it allows analysis that does not depend on authorial intentionality as the locus of social meaning yet does not negate artistic agency. Barker's discourse is certainly oriented toward someone else's discourse within and without the putative "dialogues" of her fiction. The degree to which interlocutors are deobjectified in double-voiced discourse determines to a great degree the community identity conveyed: they "exist," as such, in their interaction.

16. Eileen Fairweather, "The Voices of Women," *New Statesman* 103 (May 14, 1982), pp. 21 – 23.

17. Isabel Scholes, "Old, Not Wise," *Times Literary Supplement* (Oct 17, 1986), p. 1168. Scholes describes herself as a "doubting reader" who wonders "if anyone could possibly have mattered less" [than Lisa]. This reader wonders whether such comments are the product of Barker's artistic failure or barely disguised class prejudice.

18. Paul Driver, "Liza Jarrett's Hard Life," *London Review of Books* 8 (December 4, 1986), p. 24. Such comments foreground the problems inherent in representing and/or analyzing working classes. Regarding fiction, for instance, one should ask just how often the "reality status" of consciously *bourgeois* fiction is questioned?

19. Reva Brown, "Review of *The Century's Daughter*," *British Book News*, December 1986, pp. 709 – 710.

20. Pat Barker, *The Century's Daughter* (London: Virago, 1986), p. 1. All further page references will appear within the text.

21. Lyn Pykett, "The Century's Daughters: Recent Women's Fiction and History," *Critical Quarterly* 29, 3 (Autumn, 1987), pp. 71 – 77. Pykett feels that Barker, like other feminist writers, is attempting to recuperate the past from a woman's perspective; yet I am arguing that it is much more an attempt to transform categories of historical knowledge.

22. See Cora Kaplan, *Sea Changes* (London: Verso, 1986), especially Chapter Seven. Many of the essays in this collection are brilliant both in their articulations and in their implications for socialist-feminist critique. Kaplan is unrelenting in her analysis of the productive interference of categories of class and gender.

23. For a fascinating analysis of the effective "presence" of servants in nineteenth-century bourgeois fiction, see Bruce Robbins' *The Servant's Hand* (New York: Columbia University Press, 1986). Barker, unlike Dickens for instance, is a lot less guarded about endorsing the servant's perspicacity.

24. See Mikhail Bakhtin, *The Dialogic Imagination*, ed. Michael Holquist, trans. Caryl Emerson and Michael Holquist (Austin: University of Texas Press, 1981), pp. 84 – 258. There is no space here to detail Bakhtin's complex history of chronotope in the novelization of discourse. What I am interested in, however, are the possibilities for reading memory through a specific set of time/ space relations, here provided by a working-class woman's narrative.

25. For more on the "nostalgia mode" see Fredric Jameson, "Postmodernism, or the Cultural Logic of Late Capitalism," *New Left Review* 146 (July/August 1984), pp. 66 – 68. While Jameson is rightly lauded for the insights provided on postmodernism in this essay, his notes on "real history" and "loss of the radical past" remain insistently masculinist. One could argue that masculinist versions of history are at stake in postmodern aesthetics according to Jameson. Too often it is *that* history which is recalled while women's history, as memory, is that which is lost.

26. Walter Benjamin, *Illuminations*, ed. Hannah Arendt, trans. Harry Zohn (New York: Schocken Books, 1969), p. 255.

Works Cited

Bakhtin, Mikhail. *Problems of Dostoevsky's Poetics*, ed. and trans. Caryl Emerson (Minneapolis: University of Minnesota Press, 1984).

_____. *The Dialogic Imagination*, ed. Michael Holquist. Trans. Caryl Emerson and Michael Holquist (Austin: University of Texas Press, 1981).

Barker, Pat. *Blow Your House Down* (London: Virago, 1984).

_____. *The Century's Daughter* (London: Virago, 1986).

_____. *The Man Who Wasn't There* (London: Virago, 1989).

————. *Union Street* (London: Virago, 1982).

Belsey, Catherine. *Critical Practice* (London: Methuen, 1980).

Benjamin, Walter. *Illuminations,* ed. Hannah Arendt, trans. Harry Zohn (New York: Schocken, 1969).

Davies, Tony. "Unfinished Business: Realism and Working-Class Writing" in Jeremy Hawthorn, ed. *The British Working-Class Novel in the Twentieth Century* (London: Edward Arnold, 1984): pp. 125 – 136.

de Lauretis, Teresa, ed. *Feminist Studies/Critical Studies* (Bloomington: Indiana University Press, 1986).

Driver, Paul. "Liza Jarrett's Hard Life," *London Review of Books* 8 (December 4, 1986), p. 24.

Herrmann, Anne. *The Dialogic and Difference* (New York: Columbia University Press, 1989).

Hitchcock, Peter. *Working-Class Fiction in Theory and Practice* (Ann Arbor: UMI Research Press, 1989).

Irigaray, Luce. *This Sex Which Is Not One,* trans. Catherine Porter (Ithaca: Cornell University Press, 1985).

Jameson, Fredric. "Postmodernism, or the Cultural Logic of Late Capitalism," *New Left Review* 146 (July/August 1984): pp. 66 – 68.

Kaplan, Cora. *Sea Changes* (London: Verso, 1986).

Lee, Hermione. "At Spaghetti Junction," *The Observer* (May 30, 1982), p. 30.

Moi, Toril. *Sexual/Textual Politics* (London: Methuen, 1985).

Newton, Judith, et al. *Sex and Class in Women's History* (London: Routledge, 1983).

Newton, Judith. "History as Usual?: Feminism and the 'New Historicism,'" *Cultural Critique* 9 (Spring 1988): 87 – 121.

O'Connor, Alan. *Raymond Williams: Writing, Culture, Politics* (New York: Blackwell, 1989).

Pykett, Lyn. "The Century's Daughters: Recent Women's Fiction and History," *Critical Quarterly,* 29, 3 (Autumn, 1987): 71 – 77.

Robbins, Bruce. *The Servant's Hand* (New York: Columbia University Press, 1986).

Scholes, Isabel. "Old, Not Wise," *Times Literary Supplement* (Oct 17, 1986): 1168.

Scott, Joan Wallach. *Gender and the Politics of History* (New York: Columbia University Press, 1988).

Vološinov, V. N. *Marxism and the Philosophy of Language,* trans. Ladislav Matejka and I. R. Titunik (New York: Seminar Press, 1978).

Williams, Raymond. *Marxism and Literature* (Oxford: Oxford University Press, 1977).

_____. *The Country and The City* (London: Paladin, 1975).

_____. *The English Novel,* (London: Paladin, 1974).

_____. "The Knowable Community in George Eliot's Novels," *Novel* 2 (1969): 255–68.

Worpole, Ken. *Dockers and Detectives* (London: Verso, 1983).

Yaeger, Patricia. "'Because A Fire Was In My Head': Eudora Welty and the Dialogic Imagination." *PMLA* 99 (1984), pp. 955–73.

Young, Robert. "Back to Bakhtin," *Cultural Critique* 2 (Winter 85/86): 71–92.

8

A Quote of Many Colors: Women and Masquerade in Donald Barthelme's Postmodern Parody Novels

Jaye Berman

In a publicity blurb for the 1985 reissue of *Parodies: An Anthology from Chaucer to Beerbohm — and After,* Veronica Geng, parodying traditional courtship ritual, declares that "if *Parodies* were a man, I'd ask it to marry me." *Parodies* is not a man, of course, but it is no wonder that Geng stamps it with a masculine identity, since approximately ninety-seven percent of its entries are written by men and an even higher percentage of the parodied literature is also by male authors. Although a much higher proportion of the parodies in this anthology are about women, female characters are most often depicted stereotypically as targets of male humor as in Max Beerbohm's "Scruts," a parody of Arnold Bennett's observations of the lives of the common people of his native North Staffordshire, whose heroine, a simple-minded stirrer of an inedible Christmas pudding, is described as "the incarnation of the adorably feminine" (Beerbohm, 181).

In the years following the first publication of this collection in 1960, the characterization of women in the essentially parodic writing of postmodern fiction, experimental fiction, or surfiction has become far more complex. In fact, the more active role of female characters in assisting the parodic function of postmodern literature has much to do with the interrogation of authority itself — achieved through hybridization, dialogism, and masquerade — characteristics that Mikhail Bakhtin identified with the carnival.

In a positive sense, masquerade involves any alteration of one's appearance for purposes of enhancing one's pleasure, power, or freedom. When, for example, in *Snow White,* Donald Barthelme's contemporary version of the fairy tale, Snow White's reading of revolutionary materials such as *Dissent, Liberation,* and the writings of Mao Tse Tung leads to her "wearing heavy blue bulky shapeless quilted People's Volunteers trousers rather than the tight tempting how-the-West-was-won trousers she formerly wore," she dresses in a way that simultaneously reflects and helps her to attain a new, expanding sense of identity (*Snow White,* 16). Her self-perception shifts from being just a "horsewife" to something hidden or forbidden; adopting the persona of a cultural revolutionary temporarily increases her sense of being alive. This is the trying on and testing out of new identities, the temporary release of suppressed identities, the role reversal and personality rehearsal that is proper to the liminal phase of ritual practice.

In postmodern literature the carnival fool, who acts as insincere impersonator of traditional values and mouthpiece of *ressentiment,* is more appropriately female because as an abject object, the anti-heroine is even further alienated from herself and her society than the anti-hero in his abject subjecthood. For the female character, the mask may not be removable; femininity itself is seen to be a role — as much for a woman as for a transvestite — requiring not only make-up, costumes, and well-rehearsed lines, but increasingly, even surgery, in order to be properly performed.

The female body, which has traditionally been both the object and subject of masquerade, is the obvious target of travestying parody, which uses language to reveal and conceal like a woman uses clothing. The emphasis on a woman's manipulation of her appearance as the hallmark of her femininity points to a crucial link between women and parody, particularly when the woman becomes aware of what psychoanalyst Joan Riviere concludes in "Womanliness as Masquerade": "Womanliness ... could be assumed and worn as a mask" (213).

What Barthelme presents in his parody of the newly liberated sixties woman, alternately respecting and rejecting the values with which she was raised, is a woman dressed in a costume more difficult to exchange than her trousers — the "dreck" language and enslaving ideology of her culture expressed by that language. There are several instances in the novel where a page is printed in large, boldly typefaced, capital letters as if meant to be proclaimed authoritatively in a stentorian voice. These pronouncements fall into two categories: 1) seemingly relevant statements about the Snow White fairy tale, and 2) seemingly irrelevant statements about various aspects of Western civilization: literature, religion, the "horsewife" in history, psychology, and philosophy. What these two categories have in common is that the authority who utters these truths is not identified, and the fragments of information do not add up to a full picture either of Snow White or of Western civilization.

The more baffling of these statements are those concerning Western civilization, since they seem irrelevant to the doings of Snow White and the dwarves. Although the sources of the statements are not identified, they all possess the authoritative tone of college textbooks, presenting a subjective interpretation as if it were objective fact, as in the following:

> THE SECOND GENERATION OF ENGLISH ROMANTICS INHERITED THE
> PROBLEMS OF THE FIRST, BUT COMPLICATED BY THE EVILS OF INDUS-
> TRIALISM AND POLITICAL REPRESSION. ULTIMATELY THEY FOUND AN
> ANSWER NOT IN SOCIETY BUT IN VARIOUS FORMS OF INDEPENDENCE
> FROM SOCIETY:
>   HEROISM
>   ART
>   SPIRITUAL TRANSCENDENCE   (*Snow White*, 24)

On the facing page, the reader is presented with a catalogue of what Snow White studied at Beaver College, including a course called *English Romantic Poets II: Shelley, Byron, Keats*. Similarly, a passage on the value the mind sets on erotic needs under various conditions may very well come from her *Theoretical Foundations of Psychology* textbook, the list of various aspects of "horsewifery" reads like an outline for the course Snow White took on the *Modern Woman, Her Privileges and Responsibilities*, and so on. The very name of the college, a slang term for the female genitals, implies criticism of this type of curriculum which ultimately reinforces traditional sex roles. The outline on the "horsewife," for example, emphasizes the views of those who advocate "horsewifery" as the proper "career" for women:

> VIEWS OF ST. AUGUSTINE
> VIEWS OF THE VENERABLE BEDE
> EMERSON ON THE AMERICAN HORSEWIFE ...
> ACCEPT ROLE, PSYCHOLOGIST URGES (*Snow White*, 61)

One way of making sense of these emphatic passages, then, is to read them as the language that constitutes her being. Snow White is *Snow White*, that is to say, she is textually composed. The repeated references to her skin white as snow and her hair black as ebony point to this identification. She does not read as a smooth continuum of cause and effect, however, but rather as a jumble of vague, half-remembered impressions: "THE HOUSE ... WALLS ... WHEN HE DOESN'T ... I'M NOT ... IN THE DARK ... SHOULDERS ... AFRAID ... THE WATER WAS COLD ... WANT TO KNOW ... EFFORTLESSLY" (*Snow*

White, 165) and the official views of her culture expressed in its official language: "IT WAS NOT UNTIL THE 19TH CENTURY THAT RUSSIA PRODUCED A LITERATURE WORTHY OF BECOMING PART OF THE WORLD'S CULTURAL HERITAGE" (*Snow White,* 143). That these two categories of statements do not correspond to one another points to the gulf between Snow White's female voice groping to express her inwardly felt experience as a woman and the authorized version of reality imposed from the patriarchal society without.

Snow White's attempts to liberate herself from the snares of her culture, via masquerade, fail because she remains imprisoned by its language and the cultural mythology that conventional language expresses. Despite her revolutionary reading and costuming, Snow White fails to address the most powerful myth of her culture, namely that some day her prince will come. Her wish for "'some words in the world that were not the words I always hear!'" indicates her fleeting awareness of a need for enacting a more radical transformation than the one she has undertaken, but she is still passively waiting for the words, like her prince, to come — she fails to realize that this new language is hers to create (*Snow White,* 6). Lulled into passivity by a false sense of destiny, she sits by the window day after day in a futile attempt to attract the attention of princely passers-by until all seven dwarves and even her author tire of her, and she is excised from the text via a mockery of transcendence.

In Barthelme's next novel, *The Dead Father,* a single female protagonist is replaced by two. When two female characters are brought together, dialogue ensues, and through dialogue these characters achieve a modicum of power — over the men and over each other — unobtainable by Snow White alone. The minimalist dialogues between Julie and Emma receive maximum emphasis in *The Dead Father,* distinguishing it from *Snow White* and also from those stories which reflect Barthelme's increased use of dialogue in his short fiction. That they are the verbal exchanges between the only two female characters in a book heavily populated by men would seem to further reduce their importance to and interference with the main plot.

But the Julie-Emma dialogues *are* important insofar as they provide a feminine cross-current which contributes to the counterpunctual dialogism of Barthelme's novel. Dialogism in the novel, according to Bakhtin, introduces a "semantic direction into the word which is diametrically opposed to its original direction ... the word becomes the arena of conflict between two voices" (Bakhtin, *Problems of Dostoevsky's Poetics,* 106). In this case, the arena of conflict is gender-based, male language versus female language.

Emma is herself a disruptive excess, appearing among the men out of nowhere and for no apparent reason. As a plot device, however, the feminine rivalry which Emma's appearance instigates provides a counterpart to the rivalry between the son-figure Thomas and the Dead Father. Seen together, these conflicts within each sex weave a social fabric strong enough to withstand the fraying created by the conflicts which flare up between the sexes. There is a certain passivity in the way the men accept their limitations in the eyes of the women and vice versa, whereas aggression characterizes the exchanges between Thomas and the Dead Father and also between Julie and Emma.

This mutual aggression is the dominant tone of the Julie-Emma dialogues, which at first glance appear as a list of clichés without particular relevance as the expression of either woman:

> Whose little girl are you?
> I get by, I get by.
> Time to go.
> Hoping this will reach you at a favorable moment.
> (*Dead Father*, 32)

Yet their first dialogue is surely a duel, a verbal parody of the physical "duel, Alexander vs. Sam" (*Dead Father*, 32), which immediately precedes it, and some individuation can be detected from their exchange. Emma's role is that of bold intruder on Julie's territory (Thomas, "the boss"), which threatens Julie's sense of personal power: "Who's the boss?," "He's not bad looking," "What's he like?," "Have you tried any of the others?" (*Dead Father*, 33 – 34). Julie vigorously defends her turf by presenting Emma with various threats: "Bad things can happen to people," "I can make it hot for you," "You don't know what you're getting into," "Wake up one dark night with a thumb in your eye" (*Dead Father*, 33 – 34).

Like Snow White, Emma and Julie oscillate between playing into the system (their rivalry with each other over the men) and a fleeting awareness that their competition over the men is a contest for what the men possess — power — and that a more constructive use of their energies would be to join forces in opposition to the men. Emma dryly remarks in the middle of her catfight with Julie, "Women together changing that which can and ought to be changed" (*Dead Father*, 34). Their sense of "sisterhood" is more pronounced when they are subjected to the Dead Father's account of a heroic exploit in which his penis miraculously saves the day:

A bumaree, said Julie, they have this way of
making you feel tiny and small.
They are good at it, said Emma.
We are only tidderly-push to the likes of them. .... It is obvious that
but for a twist of fate we and not they would be calling the tune, said
Julie.
It is obvious that but for a twist of fate the mode of the music would
be different, said Emma. Much different. (*Dead Father*, 51 – 52)

"The New Music" is, in fact, the title of an earlier version of *The Dead Father* that appeared as a short story in *The New Yorker*. Barthelme might have called it "The Vital Mother," since it consists of a dialogue between two stunted stalks of sons, reflecting on lives lived in the shadow of their mother, a powerful corn goddess. One of the brothers looks to "the new music" for salvation, but Barthelme is mocking in predictable postmodern fashion the transcendent power that the moderns placed in Art. Neither new language nor new music can bring renewal; rather, renewal brings about new forms. In Barthelme's fiction the growth of sons appears to be hopelessly stunted, but that of his anti-heroines depends on their recognition that the germinating seed lies within. Julie seems to want simple inversion of gender-based power relations, the type of scenario that Natalie Davis describes in "Women on Top." But Emma reads their situation more subtly and appears to understand that it is not so much a question of who is playing the tune as it is of what tune is being played. It is, indeed, the mode of the music that needs to change.

The last chapter of *The Dead Father* suggests that Emma and Julie ultimately remain trapped by the patriarchal culture in which they are situated despite their relative stature within it. Emma is last seen dabbing her eyes with a kerchief at the Dead Father's graveside. Julie is in the degrading situation of standing before the Dead Father with her skirt hiked up in order to expose her pubic hair, a parody of the golden fleece that Thomas held out as a reward for the Dead Father, to be conferred upon the completion of their "long and arduous and ... rather ill-managed journey" (*Dead Father*, 218). The joke that Thomas plays on the Dead Father is literally "on her," as is his hand, staking his claim on that which is paradoxically both the metonymic representation of Julie's womanliness and its disguise: "Thomas placed his hand on the Fleece, outside the skirt" (*Dead Father*, 220). If Emma and Julie are indeed trapped, it is (as it is with Snow White) because of "a failure of the imagination"; they "have not been able to imagine anything better" (*Snow White*, 59). As with Snow White, this failure of the imagination stems from a failure of the language, its lack of freshness, liveliness, and originality. Because their speech is a recycling of cliches produced by a patriarchal culture — "Whose little girl are you?" — its content cannot express their actual fears and desires. Their only recourse is to refashion the form of the language, fragment it, distort it, repeat and rearrange it, bend its rules as laid down by the Dead Father, a parody of authority figures — God, king, father — dominating thousands of years of Western civilization.

Yet the dialogism of the parodic writing — its awareness of competing definitions for the same thing — enables one to read the ending somewhat differently. It is unclear, for example, whether Emma is truly grieving for the Dead Father or whether she is merely masquerading as a mourner. The Dead Father's query as to whether the mourners are "hired or volunteers" throws into question the sincerity of her action (*Dead Father*, 217). Julie, too, may not be quite as much under Thomas's thumb as she appears. On the final page of the novel she marvels at the power of the Dead Father's still resonant voice and wonders aloud: "How does he do it?" (*Dead Father*, 220). Then, suddenly and significantly, she escapes Thomas's clutches, kneels beside the Dead Father, and clasps his hand. This last scene is Julie's attempt to have the Dead Father pass his power on to her directly rather than depend upon its being mediated through Thomas, his heir apparent. Thomas is out of the picture; the final moment belongs to Julie and the Dead Father holding hands, this despite the fact that throughout the book and up to the moment of his burial, Julie wouldn't allow the Dead Father to touch her. Those attempts at touching, however, were sexual in nature and only would have underscored her powerlessness. Now, she is the one who reaches out to touch him in recognition of his power and, perhaps, in order to receive his power. In a book that explicitly states that the power of the father will be denied to the son, whose "true task, as a son, is to ... become a paler, weaker version of him" (*Dead Father*, 179), there is an implicit suggestion that the daughter may be the heiress unapparent. The dying father cannot be reborn in the son as thousands of years of dying-and-reborn god myths would have it. Rather, the locus of rebirth is more fittingly "This where life lives," that is, the female body (*Dead Father*, 218). There is, nevertheless, something ludicrous if not monstrous in the notion of the father's voice issuing from Julie's body, and perhaps it is her desire to speak in another's voice rather than fortify her own that leaves her speechless.

In *Paradise*, Barthelme's subsequent and most recent novel, a third woman enters the frame, thus creating polylogue where once there was dialogue (Emma and Julie) and, before that, monologue

(Snow White). Simon, a middle-aged, Philadelphia architect on sabbatical, meets Anne, Dore, and Veronica in a carnivalesque setting—they are modeling lingerie in a New York bar — and impressed by their towering facades and anxious to play the hero, he invites the hapless trio to move into the cavernous apartment he has sublet for the year.

Like his parody of a patriarchal fairy tale in *Snow White* and his parody of a patriarchal myth in *The Dead Father,* Barthelme's parody of a male sexual fantasy is essentially, and even more obviously, a demonstration of the difference between male and female language. The voices of the women empower them in a way that their bodies cannot do; their voices make Simon self-consciously uncomfortable about his body, and he has numerous, anxious dreams in which clothes do not properly cover it.

Part of the topsy-turvy quality of the communal life of the women and Simon is that clothing does not seem particularly important to the women as a mode of disguise or self-expression, whereas Simon becomes obsessively concerned with costume. Anne, Dore, and Veronica only masquerade as a paid performance. Apart from the fashion show in the bar, the only other time that any one of the women is described as deliberately seductive occurs when Dore, in a white lace peignoir, asks Simon for $200.00 for her delinquent brother. Otherwise, they are always described as casually but not provocatively dressed in unisex jeans, t-shirts, and sweat clothes. But clothing really is not central to their modeling, either. When they model, their bodies are not used to display clothing; clothing is used to display their bodies. Costumes reveal more than they conceal, and the women find such exposure for pay degrading, a kind of prostitution. Their reaction to an offer to work the National Sprinkler Convention illustrates the point:

> "What if they gave us raincoats?"
> "It's not raincoats they want to see."
> "What if I said transparent plastic raincoats?" ...
> "Raincoats and body stockings."
> "No thrill in body stockings."
> "Let them use their vile imaginations."
> "I just feel like a body." (*Paradise*, 142)

Simon, the celebrator of their bodies, tries to cheer them up with an alternative view that only emphasizes their reification as commodities: "Look at it this way ... A body is a gift. A great body is a great gift" (*Paradise*, 142). The question is, however, to whom is the gift given — to the self who inhabits the body or to the spectator who looks at it?

For Simon to learn empathy, he must be unmasked in the Bakhtinian sense of having the mask of his "lofty pseudo intelligence" torn away through dialogic interaction with the women's apparent lack of intelligence. Their incomprehension of what Simon considers important, particularly their dismissive ignorance of history, is itself instructive.

The mindless chatter of the women teaches him what his history books left out, namely, their perceptions, their feelings, their humanity. Indeed, at several points in the course of the novel Simon describes his role in relation to the women as their listener — not confessor, analyst, or father figure — but simply, listener:

> When he asked himself what he was doing, living in a bare elegant almost unfurnished New York apartment with three young and beautiful women, Simon had to admit that he *did not know* what he was doing. He was, he supposed, listening. (*Paradise*, 59)
>
> The women would soon be gone. The best thing he could do was to listen to them. (*Paradise*, 187)

A relationship that begins with his god-like desire to refashion them in his image — he decides that the three of them should become architects — ends with Simon being the one who is changed by them. As a result of his total immersion in female language, Simon grows from being someone who, as his wife once charged, worries about the way women say things but not about what they mean into a sensitive, caring, and respectful listener.

But what Simon learns from the women is not the novel's most crucial lesson. That distinction belongs to the strength of community that the women create and express through a shared language that is other than patriarchy, other than monologue, but also, it must be noted, other than feminist discourse. They wear the slogans of textbook feminism as awkwardly as do Snow White, Emma, and Julie. Those prescriptions for change are not enough to effect change because they are expressed in a univocal mode that reflects male rather than female consciousness. It is not their radical reading that sends Anne, Veronica, and Dore through the door; rather, it is the imperative of change, spontaneity, and improvisation speaking through the very style of their speaking together that sets them, once again, in motion.

Snow White is ambivalently poised between the old and the new woman. Isolated from other women (even the wicked stepmother figure), an island in a sea of men, Snow White's dialogic battle takes place within, where the internalized voice of patriarchy speaks the words she always hears over and opposed to the fragments of what Bakhtin calls an internally persuasive voice struggling for a language in which to speak. Emma and Julie engage in externalized battles which reveal their ambivalence toward the patriarchal world in which they are inscribed. Their dialogic wordplay diffuses the power of the patriarchal voice, but that voice, the resonant monolog, is ultimately the voice of authority and desire that Julie inauthentically wants to wrest for herself. What distinguishes Anne, Dore, and Veronica from Emma and Julie is their solidarity; they are "sisterly most of the time," "very good to one another," and although there is occasional disharmony among them, they immediately pull together whenever they feel their community threatened from without, that is, by men (*Paradise*, 128). Unlike the other female characters in Barthelme's novels, they are able to establish a competing discourse that is truly competitive with patriarchal discourse because they are not competitive with each other. They share jobs, men, household tasks and decision-making fairly and equitably, and even though Anne does not want to leave Simon, she refuses his final proposal to stay because "it wouldn't be fair to the others" (*Paradise*, 203).

Barthelme's parody is a masquerade of language, where women struggle to find the internally persuasive voices that will effect "an unmasking of a non-functioning system," in this case, patriarchy (Hutcheon, *Narcissistic Narrative*, 50). In order to find that voice, a woman must try on and discard a variety of costumes, the "preliminary 'acting out' of the dilemmas of femininity" that Mary Russo sees in the hyperboles of masquerade and carnival (Russo, 225). But while these novels succeed in addressing the politics of gender through undressing, it is in what Victor Turner calls "the redressive phase of social dramas," that what is so threatening about women's voices — their dissatisfaction with men — emerges (Turner, 40). The emergence of this critique of patriarchy creates a state of emergency for the prevailing social order, exposing an unresolvable crisis which forestalls the reintegration that is the final phase of ritual practice. Without the stable norms that govern the rites of traditional societies, the final phase in liminoid, postmodern fiction more likely consists of "the social recognition and legitimization of irreparable schism between contesting parties" that Turner recognizes as an alternative to reintegration in the social drama (Turner, 41). This inability to resolve the schism may be one reason why Barthelme's novels do not really seem to end; rather, their final pages may be read as offering a temporary break in the battle, a moment of silence in the conversation during which costumes may be changed before the dialogue resumes.

Works Cited

Bakhtin, Mikhail. *The Dialogic Imagination.* Ed. Michael Holquist and trans. Holquist and Caryl Emerson. Austin: University of Texas Press, Slavic Series, 1981.

_____. *Problems of Dostoevsky's Poetics.* Ed. and trans. Caryl Emerson. Minneapolis: University of Minnesota Press, 1984.

_____. *Rabelais and His World.* 1968. Trans. Helene Iswolsky. Bloomington: Indiana University Press, 1984.

Barthelme, Donald. *The Dead Father.* New York: Pocket, 1975.

_____. *Paradise.* New York: G. P. Putnam, 1986.

_____. *Snow White.* New York: Atheneum, 1967.

Beerbohm, Max. "Scruts." *Parodies: An Anthology from Chaucer to Beerbohm — and After.* 1960. Ed. Dwight Macdonald. New York: Da Capo, 1985.

Bernstein, Michael Andre. "When the Carnival Turns Bitter: Preliminary Reflections Upon the Abject Hero." *Critical Inquiry* 10 (December 1983): 283–305.

Hutcheon, Linda. *Narcissistic Narrative: The Metafictional Paradox.* 1980. New York: Methuen, 1984.

_____. "The Politics of Postmodernism: Parody and History." *Cultural Critique* 5 (Winter 1986–87): 179–208.

_____. *A Theory of Parody: The Teachings of Twentieth-Century Art Forms.* New York: Methuen, 1985.

Irigaray, Luce. *This Sex Which Is Not One.* Trans. Catherine Porter with Carolyn Burke. Ithaca: Cornell University Press, 1985.

Riviere, Joan. "Womanliness as Masquerade." *Psychoanalysis and Female Sexuality.* Ed. Hendrik M. Ruitenbeek. New Haven College and University Press, 1966.

Russo, Mary. "Female Grotesques: Carnival and Theory." *Feminist Studies/Critical Studies.* Ed. Teresa de Lauretis. Bloomington: Indiana University Press, 1986. 213–229.

Turner, Victor. *Dramas, Fields, and Metaphors: Symbolic Action in Human Society.* Ithaca: Cornell University Press, 1974.

Van Gennep, Arnold. *Rites of Passage.* Trans. Monika V. Vizedom and Gabrielle L. Caffee. Chicago: University of Chicago Press, 1960.

9

"Witness [to] the Suffering of Women"[1]: Poverty and Sexual Transgression in Meridel Le Sueur's *Women on the Breadlines*

Susan Sipple

> During the depression, ... women and girls poured into the cities from the farms and ruined villages, looking for work. You never saw them on the soup lines. The city had no way to deal with the hungry women ... Many disappeared, took to the road, went east or west, were lost in the underground war against women. They are outside the economy, the statistics. You cannot even claim the bodies. (1–2)

In her 1977 introduction to *Women on the Breadlines*, Meridel Le Sueur painfully acknowledges that we know little about the hardships endured by poor, unemployed women during the Depression. The life experiences of those women were often lost—as the women themselves were lost — to depression, hunger, institutionalization, and death. In poverty, broken by the inequities of capitalism and sexism, poor women stood voiceless and invisible. But not always. In the four stories which make up *Women on the Breadlines*, stories gathered when Le Sueur lived and worked at the Workers Alliance in St. Paul (a Communist Front Organization designed to help the unemployed), women do find a common voice. What Le Sueur gives them is a language inspired by their similar struggles, one that reveals their suffering and makes them visible to those who do not share (and, in fact, often cause) their hardships.

Le Sueur acts as a "witness [to] the suffering of women" in the four stories in the collection (Le Sueur, *All Things*). "These are not stories, but epitaphs," Le Sueur writes in the introduction. They mark "the lives of women who in wars, depression or holocaust are at the bottom of the social strata, are trampled on, leave no statistic, no re-

135

cord, obituary or remembrance" (1). She transmits the voices of the women society finds threatening because their existence questions its power to support and control its members. The act of witnessing usurps the controlling power of the gaze in *Women on the Breadlines,* taking it from those who dominate and placing it with the poor, if only momentarily. The women themselves are made stronger when they begin to witness by testifying to the abuses of power wrought on their own bodies. As they come to realize that society's control over them is situated in its ability to make them silent, invisible, and obedient, they recognize the force in making others see them and listen to them. Individually, then communally, they begin to fight the "underground war against women," pitting gaze against gaze, voice against voice (Le Sueur, *Women,* 2). Witnessing is a subversive act in the war they fight, however, and as such it is dangerous. If they are too loud, too visible, if they are not complicit in hiding themselves, society threatens them through institutionalization, imprisonment, sterilization, or even starvation.

The Pre-Depression Hobo Woman and the Transient Woman of the 1930s

Prior to the 1930s, America had limited experience in dealing with the sort of women Le Sueur writes about: unemployed women, often homeless, who wandered the country or at least the city streets in search of employment and sustenance. Late nineteenth- and early twentieth-century American society saw few women who fit the category of the homeless wanderer — not necessarily because they did not exist, but because they were relatively few in number and, therefore, were easily ignored.[2] Pre-Depression America did pay some attention to the female hobo, the woman who tramped across the country by *choice,* seeking adventure as well as a job. Social workers who encountered them were so disturbed by their waywardness that some fought hard to put an end to female tramping. Because social workers and society itself considered women weak, moral, dependent, and naturally obedient, they assumed that women would find the hobo life repugnant. However, when they discovered that there were indeed women who chose the hobo lifestyle, they were shocked and convinced that these women must be aberrations, so unnatural did their actions seem.[3] As one writer of the time stated, "show me a 'lady hobo,' and I'll show you an angular-bodied, flint-eyed, masculine-minded travesty upon her sex" (Maxwell, 292). For the most part, however, hobo women could be ignored.

After the onset of the Depression, few women *chose* a life of sporadic employment and wandering. Wanderlust and the promise of unlimited job opportunities elsewhere motivated few transient women in the thirties; rather, they were thrust unwillingly onto the road when economic panic hit the nation. Many of those who were hardest hit by the Depression had been independent working women who had enjoyed some degree of job security before the crash, but who, after the onset of the Depression, were left destitute (Hahn, 63). Social workers began to call them "unattached": a woman "with no family or friend near enough to be of any practical aid" (Hahn, 63). Social workers may have understood the circumstances under which these women were living, yet still insisted that they adhere to the rules by maintaining order and the illusion of a middle-class life, an impossible task for the women who had been displaced from that class. Unattached women wanted to end their plight, yet fear of revealing their condition often forced them to stay away from the relief agencies designed to help them. Le Sueur notes that while breadlines existed to help feed the poor, few women took advantage of them: "Well, ... [the breadlines] were all men, and they would hoot at you. Here's a bunch of men for two blocks — if a woman joins them, or even a bunch of women, it would be a very exposed place for jokes and hoots and propositions and sexual approaches. Women just didn't go on them—even I didn't" (Le Sueur, "One Orange ... ", 19). Rather than face this humiliation, women starved. Later, because the standard social work policy of the time involved sending transient women back to their families, many of them avoided the agencies. Some women had escaped violent or repressive family situations to which they did not wish to return; some did not want to burden already struggling families; some retained a strong sense of pride and considered charity humiliating (Johnston, 30).

Unlike pre-Depression hobo women, unattached women in the thirties could not choose to exit and re-enter mainstream culture at will. Because they lacked choice, Depression-era transient women were unable, and sometimes even unwilling, to discard society's strict notions concerning womanhood. I would argue that because she had a sense of freedom, the pre-Depression hobo woman gained the power to use what might be called the weapons of the grotesque, of difference, in a more immediate way. Her resistance could be more powerful because she was completely conscious of the ways in which she was challenging mainstream society. As hobo Bertha Thompson suggests in *Boxcar Bertha: An Autobiography*, the "new order" (the unattached women of the 1930s) was different from the "old hard-boiled sister of the road who *chose* the road for adventure and freedom in living and loving" (254). Freedom from prescribed gender roles and from the constraints they placed on sexual desire and reproduction drove some women to choose the hobo life. They cast off society's definition of womanhood, but never discarded it completely. Instead, they kept it, made it a masquerade and a political weapon, and used it to discredit the patriarchy and to lend them power in their position in the subculture.[4]

The thirties woman may have found the possibility of sexual freedom when she slipped from her class position, but this liberation was often short-lived. Either she felt compelled to control her own actions because she had internalized society's dictums, or sexual control was overtly demanded of her. Because the thirties transient was forced outside official culture by the failure of a system she had once believed in and supported, her transformation from helpless victim to powerful transgressor was slower and more painful than it was for her hobo predecessors. She had to learn two things: that the economic structure of her society had failed and that, as a result, her identity within that structure had been erased. How could she be a respectable woman when she stood in opposition to official culture's definition of respectability? Yet, paradoxically, respectability and strict morality were still demanded of her. For these reasons, understanding that gender was not a coherent, seamless whole did not come quickly for transient women. Disowned by conventional morality, or at the very least disenfranchised, they began to feel a growing sense of anger and rebellion.

Social and Sexual Transgression in *Women on the Breadlines*

Le Sueur taps into the power of women's rage in "Women on the Breadlines," "Sequel to Love," "They Follow Us Girls," and "Salvation Home," stories she wrote for the leftist periodicals *The Anvil* and *New Masses* between 1932 and 1939. Later collected in *Women on the Breadlines*, these stories expose the ways society attempted to control women by controlling their bodies (by discouraging sexuality and prohibiting reproduction through compulsory sterilization, in particular). In addition, they reveal the ways Depression-era transient women came to use their bodies as transgressive representations against the culture that forced them into the position of the underclass. Bruised and scarred from years of work, childbearing, and abuse, sometimes pregnant, their bodies stand as signs of the failure of capitalism and patriarchal control.

The attempt to force women to act according to middle-class propriety can be read in *Women on the Breadlines,* especially when poor and transient women are told they must be well-groomed, well-mannered, and above all morally upstanding, and simultaneously, to suffer silently and be invisible. In "They Follow Us Girls," the story of a woman who is trailed by a relief agency spy, the narrator is painfully aware that her actions are continually monitored: "the dicks follow you and the police follow you tryin' to get some dirt on you so they can cut off the food from your mouth," she complains (14). The continual presence of the spy forces her to conform to the relief agency's moral standards. For many of the women in these stories, it is enough to know they are being observed, so internalized is their oppression: "I can't go anywhere," one woman says, "I'm scared" (15). She has come to believe in her own powerlessness without question, and willingly, though fearfully, conceals herself from the disapproving eyes of those who dominate. Others recognize society's power to force them to control themselves, and they resist that power or even use it against itself. For Le Sueur, what eventually makes these women different from those who have internalized their oppression is solidarity. Collectively, their anger and their power to react grow as they realize that the failed economy and the inflexibility of social control are to blame for their condition. Because they are being monitored, any subversive action they perform, no matter how slight, has the potential to effect change.

In Le Sueur's stories, however, the progression from silence to rebellion is slow. The narrator of the title story, "Women on the Breadlines," is continually confronted with women who, though they are often poor and starving, are too afraid to stand in a government breadline for fear they will overstep the boundaries of respectability. Instead, one woman Le Sueur describes "go[es] for weeks verging on starvation, crawling in some hole, going through the streets ashamed ... keeping the runs mended in her stockings, shut up in terror in her own misery, until she becomes too super-sensitive and timid to even ask for a job" (8). Herein lies the very insidiousness of this power. "Is there any place else in the world where a human being is supposed to go hungry amidst plenty without an outcry, without protest ... ?" Le Sueur asks (3).

In "Women on the Breadlines," written in 1932, Le Sueur's characters are largely unaware of the disruptive power they could possess and, in fact, leave that power largely unexplored in deference to the society which tells them to act demurely. Instead of seeking to usurp power in any overt way, they concentrate on survival. The narrator of the story tells of the women who spend their days at a free domestic employment bureau waiting "hour after hour, day after day" for a job that may never come. When work does come it is usually for the young, attractive ones, whose bodies do not yet show signs of having been ravaged. For those whose bodies do tell that tale, there is little hope for work. The narrator counts herself among these women who "work as hard as it is possible for a human being to work ... scrub for fourteen and fifteen hours a day, sleep only five hours or so, do this their whole lives, and never earn even one day of security, having always before them the pit of the future" (10).

The women in this first story exhibit incredible patience with a system that forces each of them into "being a slave without the security of a slave" (10). Their constant willingness to wait for work indicates that they have not yet come to realize how they have been used or used up, or that they have not found a strategy which will allow them to voice opposition to their plight or to make gains for themselves in ways other than those sanctioned by the system. They are, to a large extent, still bound by the morals and standards they adhered to before the Depression. Those who do seek help at the bureau "sit looking at the floor ... there is a kind of humiliation in it ... It's too terrible to see this animal terror in each other's eyes" (3). If their very existence is unacceptable, and if they are to any extent to blame for their condition, then they must remain as silent as possible, they reason. The fear of observation and punishment is clearest in the case of the women too timid to step foot in the employment bureau: "a woman will shut herself up in a room until it is taken away from her, and eat a cracker a day and be as quiet as a mouse so there are no social statistics concerning her" (8).

"Women on the Breadlines" is filled with subtle moments of protest, however. "Unattached" women fight hard to survive, yet their battle is continually thwarted by the poverty that surrounds them, and looking poor is equated with breaking the rules. "Try to get into the Y.W. without any money or looking down at heel," the narrator says. "Charities take care of very few and only those that are called 'deserving.' The lone girl is under suspicion by the virgin women who dispense charity" (7). Not only does this passage point out the competition between classes of women (a rivalry which in the early stories, at least, can deplete the power of women's subversion by undermining the possibility of a strong women's community), but it also suggests that while fear and humiliation keep transient women "respectable," there are those who resist respectability or who are incapable of achieving it. Women who have managed to maintain their status despite the Depression are "virgin women" — powerful, morally upstanding, good. Women who starve, letting their bodies waste away rather than suffer the humiliation of asking for government relief, women who look "down at heel," not necessarily out of overt rebelliousness, but because they do not have the energy or the money to look like anything but transients, these women are equated with immorality, sexual promiscuity, and powerlessness. Yet their very existence challenges the system and gives them some degree of power, for their bodies and their actions suggest the failure which society wants to keep hidden. Theirs may not be a conscious affront; nevertheless, they are still breaking the "rules."

For one of Le Sueur's characters, transgressive behavior which begins as a way to survive becomes (unconsciously, it is true) a way to call into question the very notion that women are passive, docile creatures. Ellen creates a spectacle by manipulating her ability to attract men, and her actions allow her to eat. When her hunger and the continual wait for employment finally become too much for her, Ellen breaks through the silence and decorum. Standing outside the back door of a restaurant, she kicks her legs into the air, "showing [them] so that the cook came out and gave her some food and some men gathered in the alley and threw a small coin on the ground for a look at her legs" (6). Without realizing it, Ellen reveals that femininity is nothing more than a social construct; it can be manipulated, used to a woman's advantage, put on and taken off at will. Her existence and actions show with glaring accuracy the inability of the system to create a stable, coherent view of itself. Some women, like Ellen, have only their bodies to sell in order to live. In forcing men to expose their desire by revealing them as voyeurs who will pay for a peek at her legs, Ellen survives a bit longer and demonstrates the limits and contradictions in gender roles.

Occasionally in "Women on the Breadlines," those who dominate also expose contradictions in their dealings with the poor. The narrator remembers how the woman in charge of the employment bureau at the Y.M.C.A responded to one transient woman's hysteria over the lack of work: "This woman told me ... that she could hardly bear the suffering she saw, hardly hear it, that she couldn't eat sometimes and had nightmares at night" (5). Her comments obviously suggest a degree of compassion towards the plight of the unemployed, even as they expose the institution's ability to tune out the suffering it sees and hears around it — that she could "hardly hear" the voices of the transient women she is supposed to help suggests that she has become immune to their problems. Sometimes their suffering disrupts her appetite or her sleep, yet she never acknowledges that the women she serves face starvation, sleeplessness, and homelessness continually. More often than not, though, she is able to ignore their pain. In

"Women on the Breadlines," then, in order to be seen, heard, and helped, transient women must overcome their fear and *force* others to see and hear them.

Throughout *Women on the Breadlines*, Le Sueur's characters become progressively aware of how society dictates sexual conduct and reproductive control. In the title story, women do not yet comprehend how they have been taught to internalize social control. Their refusal to become involved in intimate relationships, to marry, and to bear children, for example, is not simply a matter of personal choice. The narrator explains their feelings:

> The young ones know though. I don't want to marry. I don't want any children. So they all say. No children. No marriage. They arm themselves alone, keep up alone. The man is helpless now. He cannot provide. If he propagates he cannot take care of his young. The means are not in his hands. So they live alone. (9)

What sounds like choice, when read in the context of the stories where sexual and reproductive control is more blatant, is actually a response mandated by the economic crisis of the Depression and by the system's need to maintain order: if the poor reproduce, the number of people dependent on the state for aid would increase, putting even greater stress on the system. Yet, the seeds of reaction against the system are present even in this early story. The narrator voices the resentment poor women feel: "So we sit in this room like cattle, waiting for a nonexistent job, ... unable to work, unable to get food and lodging, unable to bear children—here we sit in this shame looking at the floor, worse than beasts at the slaughter" (9). Not until subsequent stories, however, do Le Sueur's characters learn that resentment can lead to anger, and anger to action.

In the second story in the volume, "Sequel to Love," sexual and reproductive control is more obvious than in the title story. The narrator, a woman in a mental institution, recalls the events that brought her there. Unmarried, pregnant and unemployed, with no money to have the abortion she initially wanted and tried to have, the narrator describes her decision to have her baby. Turning to the charities for help, she is told that she should eat nutritious food (useless advice, considering that any food is scarce). She describes her search for the baby's father, but short of finding her a bit of food, he can do little to help, for he is also a transient. Finally, when the time comes to deliver her baby, she turns to a home for unwed mothers run by the Salvation Army, and although she wants to, they will not let her keep her child.

Because she is poor and deemed unfit, they put her baby up for adoption. Eventually, she is placed in the mental institution, where she is faced with the reality that "they won't let me out of here if I don't get sterilized" (11). The young woman is continually visited by a social worker who tries to convince her to have the operation, arguing that she "like[s] men too much" (13). Through enforced sterilization, the authorities hope to curtail what they perceive as her immorality and, in addition, keep "undesirable" children from being conceived.

Each of the stories in *Women on the Breadlines* suggests society's inability to accept that transient women's bodies may also be mothers' bodies (or even bodies which experience sexual desire). That image stretches the limits of respectability, the very definition of motherhood as something pure and exalted, and turns it into something that must be controlled, even criminalized. Explicitly, in at least two of the stories, the moral and often legal force behind society's action is the eugenics movement. By 1938, twenty-nine states and one territory had eugenics laws on their statute books, and 28,000 sterilizations had been performed in the United States since the movement began in 1907 (Popenoe, 202). One critic suggests that "in some states [where] they have no sterilization laws some institutions occasionally sterilize on their own responsibility" (Brown, 141). Eugenicists believed that compulsory sterilization could protect subsequent generations from behavioral traits and physical defects they believed could be passed from parent to child. Therefore, they often encouraged sterilization for the "socially inadequate," a group which included "the mentally deficient, such as the morons and the idiots; the mentally diseased ... ; the dependents, such as the unemployed, the deaf, the deformed, and the blind; the delinquent, such as the wayward and the criminals; the degenerate ... ; and the infectious ... " (Landman, 162). With laws which included provisions like these, eugenicists tried to curtail reproduction in hopes of reducing the number of potentially dependent people. By controlling the growth and the actions of the underclass, they attempted to impede the strength of its opposition.

Society's desire to control poor women is continually apparent in "Sequel to Love." Sexual desire was abnormal in women, the consensus believed, and poor women were so abnormal that they had to be physically altered in order to assure their adherence to the rules. Any woman who acknowledged sexual desire had to be disciplined. However, in this story, the narrator's language reveals her resistance: "I like men. I ain't got any other pleasure but with men ... Why shouldn't I like men, why shouldn't a girl like a man?" (13). She understands that forced sterilization is a form of discipline and punishment for her sexual transgression. Furthermore, this woman uses her grotesqueness — her body which *does* feel desire and which *has* carried and given birth to a child outside of marriage and in a state of poverty — as a way to resist compliance. Without her agreement, the hospital can do nothing. As the story begins, we find that she has been in the institution for three weeks. She says, "I'd rather stay here in this hole with the cracked ones than have that done to me that's a sin and a crime. I can't be sleepin' hardly ever any night yet I'd stay right here than have that sin done to me because then I won't be in any pleasure with a man and that's all the pleasure I ever had. Workers ain't supposed to have any pleasure and now they're takin' that away because it ain't supposed to be doin' anybody any good and they're afraid I'll have another baby" (11). The narrator, though dejected, begins to feel anger at her situation. The system has taken everything from her: her job, her baby, her lover, her freedom, her "sanity" — and now it threatens to rob her of sexual pleasure and reproductive choice. Female sexuality fosters resistance by allowing women to control their own bodies. The first step in social control, therefore, is to bring women's bodies back under the system's rule. Through the invocation of standards of behavior, as well as through institutionalization and sterilization, women who pose a threat to those in power can be dominated, all in the name of social welfare and relief.

The narrator of "Sequel to Love" is saddened by her plight, but she is not without some slight power. While she may be called mad because she acts "immorally" and refuses to have the operation, she succeeds in forcing the institution to face its own lack of control by refusing to be sterilized, and she exposes culture's need to silence dissenting voices in order to maintain its masquerade of coherence. Her actions will not be as strong and effective as some of Le Sueur's characters, simply because she wages war on the system as an isolated individual, rather than as part of a collective. But the seeds of collectivity are present even in this story. She is isolated, but slowly she comes to realize that she may not be alone in her plight. By questioning the insanity of her fellow inmates, she begins to understand that mental institutions are not simply hospitals for the mentally ill; they are also places where rebellious women who dream of fulfilling their own desires and who are feared by the system can be stored away until the danger they pose is diffused. When she hears the other women in the institution "moanin'," she thinks, "I got to lay here every night, listenin' ... and thinkin' are they crazy ... " (13).

Like "Sequel to Love," "They Follow Us Girls" appeared in *The Anvil* in 1935, and like the women in the previous stories, its narrator has been without steady work for a long time. She has been scarred and abused, her hearing impaired from hanging out wash in the cold wind, one of the only jobs she was able to find, but which she has since lost. Now she works intermittently, trying to sustain herself on whatever wages she can earn and on the money she gets each month from the relief agency. As the story begins, the narrator suspects she is being followed by a relief agency spy — a woman hired "to get some dirt on you so they can cut off the food from your mouth" (14). She is paranoid at the thought of being followed and claims, "I've lost my happiness" (15). That she is under surveillance, then, is secondary to the fact that she has internalized the observer's gaze. She feels herself being monitored at all times, regardless of whether the spy is there, and her fear initially makes her follow the agency's rules.

As the narrator of the story comes to resent the fear and guilt she has been made to feel, she grasps the kind of control institutions hold over her. Like the narrator of the previous story, she can no longer do those things which brought her happiness; a relationship with a man, for instance, is out of the question:

> I can't get married now. I'm scared. I wouldn't get married now and have a baby. I would be scared. If they see you so much as look at a boy they say you are immoral and shouldn't be havin' any relief. If I had a baby at home with all the curtains drawn down tight and never went out maybe they wouldn't know anything about it ... I've lost my happiness. I can't be goin' around anymore at all. (15)

For this woman, the right to control her own body is the right to make alliances and to end the alienation that imprisons her. Without that right, she is trapped. If there is no one else to turn to and if women can be made to fear their own power as completely as this woman does, then they must adhere to the rules, or they will never survive. The narrator of this story understands the nature of control. Unlike the characters in "Women on the Breadlines," she knows that fear motivates her and that society manufactures that fear. Not until the end of the story does she learn how to resist it, but early on, at least, she understands the basis of her oppression.

"They Follow Us Girls" shows how women are taught that to survive they must participate in their own oppression. Anna Bradley, the "stool" who follows the narrator, is a well-known prostitute who does not make enough to survive, so she works for the agency, turning in other women in order to "get a few dollars a day" (15). The narrator comes to realize that Anna Bradley is a worker just as she is, that she wants nothing more than to survive, and that Anna performs this odious task in order to live. With the help of her left-leaning friend Mr. Hess, the narrator is able to progress from the frightened, solitary woman she is early in the story to a more confident, powerful, angry one at the end. Hess helps her to see the split between official culture and the transient subculture by stressing that the two groups speak different languages: "He says, you better come with your own people, he says, you better come down to the council with me, he says, with your own people, they're the only ones that care a tinker's damn about you, girl, your own people" (16). His words convince her because they offer her the chance to own her body and to control her future. Workers and her fellow poor will allow her to speak in her own rebellious voice.

In addition to revealing to the narrator the power of speaking out, Hess stresses the importance of collectivity and community. One person in solitude and isolation is unlikely to be strong enough to resist and effect lasting change, he tells her. Later, when she is reported to the relief agency and tricked into believing that they have some evidence of her immorality, her anger grows, and she realizes just how isolated she really is. She finds Hess and asks him who cares about the poor women on the streets: "All, he says ... All that feel the same, they are together. All, says Mr. Hess, that are followed and worked to the bone and hounded and bleed and murdered, says Mr. Hess. And I knew I was one of them" (18). By aligning herself with a subculture made up of others who have been scarred and abused by capitalism and by disassociating herself from a culture which demands that she cover her wounds and her desires, the narrator begins the process of empowerment. At this moment, she makes a commitment to organized resistance.

Whether in silent or outright rebellion, the women in *Women on the Breadlines* come to find strength in their difference. As poor people in a nation that tries hard to disown responsibility for poverty, and at times even ignores its existence, and as women who experience and enjoy sexuality and motherhood in a society which sees them as unfit and immoral, the women Le Sueur writes about do not fit the norm. "Salvation Home" is similar to "They Follow Us Girls" in that both tell the story of women who turn despair into action and alienation into the power of organization. In "Salvation Home," a young woman is held in a detention home filled with unwed mothers and mothers-to-be (it is hinted that they've committed crimes, but Le Sueur is vague on this point). The narrator knows she will be held in the home until she has had her child, and she continually faces involuntary sterilization.

The setting of this story, the home itself, stands as a microcosm of official culture, a place where poor and transient women are trapped and forced to conform, but where there are still undercurrents of resistance. The atmosphere is prison-like: bars and electric alarms on the windows, guards roaming the halls at night; long, tiring work details; and the enforced separation of mother and child. At night the women laugh and whisper among themselves, challenging the authority of the police matrons who demand silence. They pass secret notes to friends on the outside through girls who leave the home. In fact, note-passing becomes one of the most powerful ways to undermine the system because it allows contact with a community outside the home, one which gives the women inside the strength and the confidence to resist control. When the narrator receives a note from her friend Amelia, a member of the Workers Alliance, she finds the strength to endure: "Don't be afraid, baby," Amelia writes to her, "U are a maker now. U are going to have a good child ... Take hope, comrade ... Workers Alliance meet nex day frum this. Have child happy demand there be no misry for our peepl like we hev so we can hev our childs in gret city with sum joy" (21). Through childbirth, a woman gains one more weapon in the fight against society and its mission to halt the growth of the subculture through compulsory sterilization and adoption. With abundance comes an increase within the subculture, and such an increase could mean the development of a power that would be all the harder to diffuse. Amelia realizes that the power to sterilize women and to separate them from their children is a forceful one, but she also knows that poor women possess the power to create (as long as they can resist sterilization). They are "maker[s]," and their acts of creation whether in childbirth or in other forms of rebellion are disruptive. The possibility Amelia offers the narrator through community (that is, through joining the Workers Alliance) is the possibility of resistance with even greater zeal: she offers the chance for women to have children and to raise them in a misery-free environment.

The women in "Salvation Home" understand the restraints institutions place on them better than any of the other women in the collection, and they progress the farthest towards an organized resistance. For example, as they entertain themselves in the home, "the radio played 'I Love You Truly' and everyone laughed, and a girl who had one glass eye she lost in a munitions factory said, you son of a bitch if you loved me truly I wouldn't be here ... " (21). Three issues come together in this passage: first, women are at last fully aware that they bear the signs of the role capitalism played in causing their condition. The woman with the glass eye knows how dangerous the system can be. Second, in her admonishment of her lover, the speaker attacks romantic love, and implicitly, gender roles and their social construction. As an ideological force, romantic love prescribes actions which place women in passive, submissive roles. Yet this woman's sarcasm and anger concerning her experience with romance and its results — being pregnant, unmarried, and imprisoned — reveal her understanding of just how out of sync ideology is with her material existence. Finally, this passage conveys a sense of the growing anger against the system of patriarchal standards: the double standard, for example, which accepts a man's irresponsibility towards a woman, yet a woman who acts in ways deemed irresponsible is punished for her deeds. A woman like the one who speaks these words must be hidden away, for her very existence is disruptive.

By the end of "Salvation Home," Le Sueur's women have begun to overcome the fear and the shame so clearly present in the first story in the collection and present still in the following two stories. At the very end of the story, the narrator passes notes in the dark with a deaf woman named Alice who tells her about the Workers Alliance. Alice stresses the need for a community that would run counter to mainstream society: "We the common people, suffer together," she tells the narrator (22). When the narrator learns that the Workers Alliance is organizing women just like her, she feels a growing sense of excitement and power in the knowledge that she is a part of a community of women and of workers. And this knowledge ends in a mocking assertion of just how far these women have come in understanding their own disruptiveness, and how far they will be able to go: "She rolled over, the light went out, and I could hear her laughing. I began to laugh too" (22). The narrator no longer tries to suppress her laughter and disapproval of the system that has imprisoned her. She mocks it out loud, fearlessly. By the end of the story, it is clear that she will fight back by joining the Workers Alliance.

Meridel Le Sueur, *Women on the Breadlines,* and the Power of the Grotesque

Le Sueur's characters do fight the system, especially as they come to embody what Mary Russo, in her essay "Female Grotesques: Carnival and Theory," calls the power of carnival and the grotesque, a power which arises from the willingness to make a "spectacle" of oneself (213). By displaying what Russo calls their "open, protruding, extended, secreting bod[ies] ... of becoming, process, and change" (often through sexuality and pregnancy), women could protest the culture which positioned them as the underclass (219). Russo's appropriation of Bakhtinian theory is crucial to my reading, for she offers valuable insights into the ways in which the feminist scholar might introduce the social relations of gender into carnival theory. "There is a way," Russo suggests, "in which radical negation, silence, withdrawal, and invisibility, and the bold affirmations of feminine performance, imposture, and masquerade (purity and danger) have suggested cultural politics for women" (213). Carnival for the feminist, and indeed for Le Sueur's characters, becomes a period of transposed reality, in which official rules concerning the definition of womanhood are forced into suspension and interrogation, if only fleetingly.

The use of Bakhtinian theories of carnival, or of feminist appropriations of his theories, is problematic, I know, in discussing an economic and human tragedy like the Depression. For Bakhtin, carnival speaks of celebration, of transgressions that are liberatory and joyous. To suggest that there is something celebratory about the transgressions Le Sueur's women made during the Depression is inappropriate. Yet taken at their broadest, Bakhtin's notions about the freeing and empowering forces within a united community of the underclass during a period when official rules are unstable do allow for models which oppose bourgeois individualism. The women in Le Sueur's stories come to see the power in communal action. They learn to transgress the strict rules society sets for their behavior and to survive by using difference to their advantage in a time when few advantages were possible. By seeing them as grotesques, and by considering the Depression as a period when gender and class roles lost their strict boundaries, we can begin to understand how even their slightest transgressions lead toward larger social revolt.

To some extent, Le Sueur herself stands as the most powerful figure of the grotesque in these stories. Not only did her membership in the Communist Party place her outside mainstream society, but the very fact that she was a woman writing about *women's* oppression sometimes placed her at odds with the party itself. For instance, when *New Masses* published "Women on the Breadlines," they followed it with an editorial note pointing out that while the story had some good points, it had one flaw that set it at odds with their notions about the struggles of the unemployed woman:

> This presentation of the plight of the unemployed woman, able as it is, and informative, is defeatest in attitude, lacking in revolutionary spirit and direction which characterize the usual contribution to *New*

Masses. We feel it is our duty to add, that there is a place for the unemployed woman, as well as man, in the ranks of the Unemployed Councils and in all branches of the organized revolutionary movement ... ("Editorial Note," 7)

The party did not disbelieve the severity of women's lot during the Depression; rather, they argued with Le Sueur's decision to present it without providing an overt prescription for social change — in other words, without promoting membership in the Communist Party. Her decision to foreground *women's* struggles rather than only class struggles illustrates that one of her primary concerns was the quality of women's lives during the Depression.

Le Sueur's experiences as a woman writer in a publishing world dominated by men also marked her as different. "Males have been very, very abrasive to me," Le Sueur admitted in one interview. "Male editors, male critics — I didn't realize it until now when I don't have anything to do with them, or don't publish too much, but I just realize how much they've injured me ... " (Le Sueur, *West End,* 13). Like the women about whom she writes, Le Sueur experienced the power of men's control over her. And like the women in her stories, she fought back. She continues to write about women's lives because she understands that she is part of a community that must be represented. "They listen, especially the women," she says in the same interview. "Women audiences have changed my life ... My own audience has gotten born, the women I was writing for, are born!" (Le Sueur, *West End,* 13). By understanding her place in a community of women, Le Sueur herself seems to have found the power to overcome insecurity and to disrupt a publishing world dominated by men.

In her introduction to *Women on the Breadlines,* Le Sueur suggests that, in spite of all her work, the women she writes about become anonymous in life and in death, their bodies having lost the power of revolt. But despite that loss, their struggles to be heard and noticed were not in vain. In the introduction she says:

I was taught and made human by the strength and courage of these women, who, it seemed to me, received the entire and naked blow of oppression upon their bodies, as workers, child bearers, unpaid labor, lost and unnamed ... Of the women and girls who told me these stories, only one and myself are visible and alive. One had a lobotomy and doesn't know her name. One died in the snow. Several died of self-induced abortions, from T.B. and syphillis ... Many disappeared, took to the road, went east or west, were lost in the underground war against women. You cannot find or claim them, or recognize them to even say their names. They are outside the economy, the statistics. You cannot even claim the bodies. (1 – 2)

Their lives were hard, and perhaps their rebellion did not change the world in any socially noticeable way, but their narratives made Le Sueur courageous and strong, and through her efforts to record their stories, their lives help to empower others. By suggesting poor and transient women have the right to experience sexuality and motherhood, she questions the discrimination against women as sexual beings. Le Sueur says that their bodies are lost and cannot be reclaimed, that they are anonymous, but she forgets that her stories go far in reclaiming them.

While Le Sueur seems to question the lasting effectiveness of these women's actions, she ends her introduction with a suggestion which I read as a reaffirmation of the power of the grotesque: "In some future, more human society," she says, "there must be a monument, a park like at Lidice and Guernica, or for those exterminated in concentration camps — a monument here to [the transient women's] suffering, their anonymous deaths, to which we can take our children sunny afternoons to be sure that we never forget them" (2). What Le Sueur suggests is a concrete, eternal figure of the grotesque, one which would not be subject to attempts by official culture to diffuse its power but which would instead diffuse the power of that culture. And to a great degree, *Women on the Breadlines* does just that. For all the fear and pain transient women endured during the Depression, for all of the indelible marks of oppression their bodies bore, something more than just the memory of cruelty and agony survives. Their bodies, captured in the figurative concrete of Le Sueur's stories, become monuments, subversive symbols which will speak against official culture for as long as the stories are read.

Notes

1. The quotation by Le Sueur used in the title was part of an interview with her on the National Public Radio program, "All Things Considered," September 3, 1989.

2. I am not suggesting that the homeless, transient woman — the woman who did not choose her marginalization, but rather whose circumstances forced her outside the society in which she wanted to be included — was completely absent from American society before the Great Depression. My research, however, suggests that transient women of this type were far fewer in

number before the thirties than after, and so they did not pose a threat to society. According to Lynn Weiner in "Sisters of the Road: Women Transients and Tramps," an essay in *Walking to Work: Tramps in America, 1790–1935,* most pre-Depression transient women still retained the advantage of choice. They chose to live the transient life because the economic opportunities available to them demanded that they relocate quite often, not because of a massive failure in the economy.

3. For a more complete historical analysis of the ways in which both hobo and transient women survived in early twentieth-century America and for an analysis of how they were treated by mainstream society, see Lynn Weiner's essay, "Sisters of the Road: Women Transients and Tramps," in *Walking to Work: Tramps in America, 1790–1935.*

4. In *Boxcar Bertha: An Autobiography,* Bertha Thompson and Dr. Ben L. Reitman tell the story of a number of hobo women who manipulate society's idea of what it is to be female. One woman they discuss, for instance, declares it is "no trouble at all to get along on the road" (39). If she needs money, food, or drink, she simply goes "to one of the taverns and sit[s] down at a table and pretty soon someone will ask me to have a drink ... If no one pays any attention to me I ask the bartender if I can dance. That usually makes friends for me" (39). She used part of society's definition of womanhood — her ability to be attractive to men — as a tool, refusing to let it be a hindrance. Another hobo woman noted "it was easier for a woman to get along on the road if she was not too particular and she frankly considered her body as her working capital" (39). By using the conventions of official womanhood, hobo women gained advantages in the subculture and, perhaps more important, they exposed the instability of the patriarchy by exposing the ways in which femininity could be discarded at will.

Works Cited

Bakhtin, Mikhail. *Rabelais and His World.* Trans. Helene Iswolsky. Blooming-ton: Indiana University Press, 1984.

Brown, Mary. *An Introduction to Eugenics.* Boston: Chapman and Grimes, 1935. "Editorial Note," *New Masses* (January 1932): 7.

Hahn, Emily. "Women Without Work." *The New Republic* 75 (31 May 1933): 63–5.

Johnston, Marlise. "The Woman Out of Work." *Review of Reviews* 87 (February 1933): 30–32.

Landman, J. H. "Sterilization and Social Betterment." *Survey Graphics* 25 (March 1936): 162–63.

Le Sueur, Meridel. Interview. *All Things Considered.* Natl. Public Radio. 3 Sept. 1989.

Le Sueur, Meridel. Interview. *West End* 5.1 (Summer 1978): 8 – 14.

Le Sueur, Meridel. "One Orange for Christmas: An Interview with Meridel Le Sueur." With Nancy Jo Hoy. *Iowa Woman* (March 1987): 14 – 22.

Le Sueur, Meridel. *Women on the Breadlines.* Minneapolis: West End Press, 1977.

Maxwell, Cliff. "Lady Vagabonds." *Scribner's Magazine* 85 (March 1929): 288 – 92.

Popenoe, Paul. "Sterilization in Practice." *Survey* 74 (June 1938): 202 – 4.

Russo, Mary. "Female Grotesques: Carnival and Theory." *Feminist Studies/Critical Studies.* Ed. Teresa de Lauretis. Bloomington: Indiana University Press, 1986.

Thompson, Bertha and Dr. Ben L. Reitman. *Boxcar Bertha: An Autobiography.* New York: Amok Press, 1988.

Weiner, Lynn. "Sisters of the Road: Women Transients and Tramps." *Walking to Work: Tramps in America, 1790 – 1935.* Ed. Eric Monkkonen. Lincoln: University of Nebraska Press, 1984.

10

The Central Nervous System of America: The Writer as/in the Crowd of Joyce Carol Oates's *Wonderland*

Brenda O. Daly

As crowds of protesters converged in the streets to protest U. S. involvement in Vietnam during late 1969 and early 1970, Joyce Carol Oates was writing her fifth novel, *Wonderland,* a depiction of the U. S. from 1939 to 1970. Oates published two different versions of this novel. The first version, the 1971 hardcover edition, conforms to the practice of aesthetic unity, looping back to its point of origin, an act of patriarchal closure. This tragically closed circle illustrates a textual practice that mirrors a concept of the self — the self as an isolated, enclosed, competitive ego — in which such violence originates. Julia Kristeva describes such texts — those that mirror the bounded self — as "bounded texts,"[1] and in such works, regardless of genre, textual boundaries demarcate a romantic ego, isolated from community. Such a tragic/romantic ending describes Oates's initial edition of *Wonderland,* an ending in which the adolescent heroine is sacrificed to maintain textual unity and social stasis. Shelley represents an entire generation of young Americans sacrificed to a war maintained by official, "monologic," consciousness.[2] Jesse Vogel, Shelley's father and a famous brain surgeon, represents this monologic consciousness — he knows only one language, science — and Oates's first ending depicts Jesse as a contemporary King Lear carrying the dead body of his daughter as he grieves for this sacrifice to the (male) ego. In Oates's 1973 paperback edition of this novel, she rejects tragic closure, refusing to sacrifice the body (writing) to maintain the illusion of (vocal) unity. She replaces univocal closure with the ambivalence of dialogue.

"'I think you are the devil,'" says Shelley to her father, and he answers, "'Am I?'"[3] With this dialogue Oates divides her authorial self between both her characters, both father and daughter. She identifies herself as all her characters, as all the voices in *Wonderland*. I am not one, she announces as Whitman announced before her: I am the crowd. This vision of the self as not one, but rather as the many, moves beyond an old logic, the logic of either/or: either good or evil, either father or daughter, either voice or text. In her insistence upon the logic of both/and, Oates moves beyond binarism into dialogism, the logic of dreams and the creative process, the logic of carnival. From this point forward, particularly in novels of the 1970s, Oates will make increasingly explicit a writer's self-division into all the voices and texts absorbed by the hybrid novel. As Oates says, "Most novelists divide themselves up lavishly in their novels" (278).[4]

In this transitional novel — at least in the 1973 revision — Oates resists subordinating the voice of her adolescent heroine to achieve a unitary authorial voice, a voice usually assumed to be masculine. Oates identifies this monologic authorial voice with her hero, Jesse, a character in many ways a typical American male. Jesse's consciousness has been narrowed by his faith in scientific objectivity, a consciousness that often merely disguises a belief in masculine superiority. As Oates portrays Jesse, his objectivity is actually "realism," an anthropocentric illusion that denies the existence of the self, a self mistakenly defined as merely subjective. It is this self, Jesse's ghost self, that awakens him at night, this self that circles obsessively around the body of his daughter Shelley. In *Wonderland,* then, Oates explores the historical boundaries between "objective" and "subjective" modes of discourse — between science and romance — as they define personality, and as they construct categories of gender. Through her hero's obsession with the theory of homeostasis,[5] Oates examines those discourses that have shaped American culture, a culture that — while claiming to be democratic — has silenced the voices of women, children, and the poor. The novel begins on December 14, 1939, at the end of the Great Depression, moves through the period of the assassination of John Kennedy, and ends with protests against the war through the summer of 1970. The first of many of Oates's novels to focus upon extra-literary discourses, *Wonderland* opens during the Christmas season. The novel investigates this central epic in our culture whose mythical premises, hierarchical and anti-democratic, continue to shape our national consciousness.

Although a variety of discourses surface in *Wonderland*, Jesse remains deaf to the "Other," censoring the voices of music and poetry, the voices of women and children, the voices of memory and body. Oates herself was struggling with the contending voices and texts in U. S. culture, attempting to achieve a harmony — a unity — that would not censor such voices. According to Michael Holquist, it was a similar sense of "the world's overwhelming multiplicity that compelled Bakhtin to rethink strategies by which heterogeneity had been traditionally disguised as unity" (307).

In rejecting the convention of aesthetic unity, Oates resists such a false unity, but unlike Bakhtin, Oates recognizes not only hierarchies of class, but also hierarchies of gender as maintained by univocal closure. In the first edition of *Wonderland*, Oates had — as "Author, Man" — sacrificed the body of an adolescent girl to maintain traditional boundaries of text and self. Her revision makes a different argument, insisting upon a democratic chorus of voices. Oates does not explain her revision in these terms, but she did say, during an interview with *Newsweek* in 1971, that "with *Wonderland* I came to the end of a phase in my life, though I didn't know it," and she added that her collection, *Marriages and Infidelities,* published in 1972, "was a step in that direction."[6] This latter title, of course, suggests the logic of the double; to insist upon both marriages and infidelities is to speak duplicitously, as dreams speak. Not surprisingly, Oates insists that she dreamt her new ending.[7] In July 1973, she added this footnote to her essay, "Art: Therapy and Magic":

> Only once in my entire life did I very consciously — very intellectually — resist my intuition regarding something I wrote (the conclusion of one of my novels, *Wonderland*); with the result that, in deepest humility, I had to revise it after its appearance in the United States — causing the kind of confusion and inconvenience I dread. A mistake that will never be repeated.[8]

Indeed, this change in endings has created critical confusion, but at the same time the "mistake" has been instructive. By insisting upon obeying the logic of dreams — the collective unconscious, as Oates defines it, Oates resists privileging the intellect in which the boundaries of the ego reside, in which the monologic consciousness functions as tyrant. Instead, Oates moves toward dialogism, at once psychological and historical — having its roots in carnival, in folk festival, in crowds.[9]

The elements of carnival emerge in the grotesque realism of *Wonderland,* in images of tricksters and doubles. Oates's resistance to epic and scientific monologism is embodied in a trickster figure named Trick Monk, a scientist turned poet. Oates locates her voice in the struggle between Trick (romantic poet) and Jesse (science), represented as the rivalry between Trick and his colleague in medical school, Jesse Vogel. Through their competition for Helene, the daugh-

ter of a doctor whom both men worship, Oates explores the problem
of woman as written — woman as Alice inside Wonderland — and
woman as re-writing *Wonderland.* Situating the authorial "I" at once
inside and outside, Oates attempts to find a method of composition
and characterization which will illustrate her thesis: a "Song of Myself"
at once individual and communal, a female equally with the male, the
brain equally with the body. Individuality, as she says in her *Newsweek*
interview with Walter Clemons, is a myth:

> "I absolutely don't believe there is very much originality. I just see
> myself as standing in a very strong tradition and my debt to other
> writers is very obvious. I couldn't exist without them. I don't have
> much autonomous existence, nor does anyone. We are interconnected
> — it seems we are individual and separate, whereas in fact we're not."
> (73–74)

Oates shares with Bakhtin a belief that the "I" exists only through
dialogue, a minimal unit of two who are not sovereign egos, but rather
a consciousness at a particular historic moment whose choices, among
multiple discourses, do not indicate unity.

Oates, however, is more sensitive than Bakhtin to the problematic
relationship between women and language. Early in the novel she confronts the problem of woman-as-text, and this issue surfaces frequently. For example, in a letter to her father, dated December 1970,
Shelley Vogel asks Jesse, "How would you know the shape of your own
body then, if you couldn't read about other bodies?" (402). On December 14, 1939, when only a boy of fourteen, Jesse had explored this
question himself. Thus, the novel makes frequent references to Christmas, the central epic of our culture, but Oates gives this mythic, and
presumably timeless, discourse a specific historical and social context.
Somehow, Oates suggests, the shape of the body has been read, however unconsciously, through a myth that erases one's origins in the
body of a woman. Somehow, mythical and pornographic fantasies are
intimately related. The public celebration of Christmas is juxtaposed
with a private pornographic drawing of a woman's body which Jesse
sees above a toilet. Nauseated by a quarrel between his pregnant
mother and his worried father, Jesse excuses himself from Christmas
assembly. The voices of the school choir singing "Hark the Herald Angels Sing" echo in the background as Jesse glances above a vomit-filled
toilet. There he sees this drawing:

> a woman's body seen from the bottom up, the legs muscular and very
> long, spread apart, the head at the far end of the body small as a pea,

with eyes and eyelashes nevertheless drawn in very carefully so that they look real. Someone has added to the drawing with another, blunter pencil, making the body boxlike, the space between the legs shaded in to a hard black rectangle like a door. The arms have also been changed to walls and even the suggestion of brick added to them ... It is a mysterious drawing, two mysterious drawings, one on top of the other like a dream that fades into another dream, a nightmare conquered by another! (30–31)

This drawing graphically depicts the nightmarish underside — the repressed — of epic consciousness. Epic consciousness, by claiming that "man" is not of woman born, forgets the body, and the law of the father — a disembodied voice — inscribes itself as a trace: one dream fades into another as woman becomes the building material of culture. Jesse's initiation into this social order is violent: he comes close to being yet another son sacrificed to the father. He bears this wound, from his father's gun, for the rest of his life.

The same sacrificial morality occurs at the end of the novel when American children — whom Oates names "Angel," "St John," and "Noel" — become victims of a war-torn culture. Victimized as a child, Jesse becomes, in his turn, a victimizer. From a series of father surrogates, from "men of science," Jesse develops what Susan Griffin calls "the pornographic mind of our culture."[10] Like the grafitti artist, he learns to master his fear of "the enlarged space between the woman's legs," a space which, at the age of fourteen, he thinks of as "something you could walk into and lose yourself in, all that empty blackness" (31). Through his mastery, the graffiti artist enacts his revenge upon woman's power. Compulsively, binding his hysteria, the "masculine" mind denies the power of woman's womb by giving her a brain the size of a "pea." He views her body from outside, rather than from within, aggressively distorting the body with his pen. The second male artist, with his "blunter pencil," superimposes a building upon her body, establishing himself as woman's architect. Her body becomes his building material, his property. This widely shared view of woman denies her equality, denies her voice. As a scientist, Jesse learns to share this view of woman-as-nature, as desacralized matter under man's dominion.

Scientific discourse, as Julia Kristeva argues, accepts this epic logic: "Epic logic assumes a hierarchy within the structure of substance. Epic logic is therefore causal, that is, theological; it is a belief in the literal sense of the word."[11] But the binary mind insists upon unity, shifting its monotheism from God to the scientist, the "mind of man" as depicted in Mary Shelley's *Frankenstein*. Oates gives "Frankenstein" an American identity, transforming her hero — during a specific thirty-year period — from a monster created by Frankenstein into a duplicate of his creator. In Book One, Jesse moves from his grandfather's home — the only survivor of his father's murder-suicide — to an orphanage and, next, to the Pedersens. Adopted by Karl Pedersen, a doctor, Jesse takes on a new identity, this time becoming the creation of a "mad-scientist" who wants to mold Jesse in his own image. In this way Oates portrays the epic consciousness of both Willard Harte and Karl Pedersen who share a belief in their rightful authority over their families, regardless of their class. Both fathers also believe in individualism, each accepting credit or blame for their economic circumstances. Despite widespread economic failure, Willard Harte takes personal responsibility for his business failures, killing his entire family — as if their fate must be determined by him alone. Karl Pedersen has a similar view of the family, seeing himself "naturally" as the head, the final authority over his wife and children. When Jesse disobeys Pedersen, obeying Mrs. Pedersen's request for help in escaping her tyrannical husband, the law of the father speaks to Jesse in this note from Karl Pedersen:

> With this check and with this letter I pronounce you dead to me. You have no existence. You are nothing. You have betrayed the Pedersen family, which accepted and loved you as a son, and now you are eradicated by that family. Never try to contact us again. You are dead. You do not exist. (183–184)

The voices of Pedersen's wife and children have no power for the egocentric Pedersen who believes that his will must prevail even if it means that he must kill his son.

The title of the opening book of the novel, "Variations on an American Hymn," suggests Oates's desire to transform a sacrificial morality — like that practiced by Dr. Pedersen — into a celebration of the dreaming body, a consciousness which has been repressed, distorted into pornographic fantasies, in our culture. As the son of Willard Harte and, later, Karl Pedersen, Jesse learns nothing about a democratic dream; instead, he sees the mutilated bodies of the Hartes and the obese bodies of the Pedersens, victims of political/economic hierarchies. And in the flesh of Mrs. Pedersen, he also sees the nightmarish consequences of Dr. Pedersen's pornographic fantasies, a man who is "the head" of his family, as well as his community.

Dr. Pedersen literally holds the fate of the Pedersen family in his hands when, during their Christmas, the "good" man opens "The

Book of Fates," the family photo album. Throughout the years of her marriage, the album reveals, the once slender Mary Shirer—a doctor's daughter—has grown increasingly obese, as have her children, Hilda and Frederich. Oates's descriptions illustrate ambivalence; she is both satirical and sympathetic. Mrs. Pedersen appears in Jesse's doorway, a kindly woman, "who filled the doorway in a huge mint-green cotton house dress; on her feet were straw shoes with orange tassels and small brass mock bells on the toes" (161). And Dr. Pedersen appears, in a photo taken at an Elk's Club Halloween Party for Crippled Children, "enormous in a harlequin outfit, all rags and bells, holding a kind of scepter" (119). This carnivalesque description of the obese Pedersens identifies their religion: eating, consuming. It was "a ritual," complete with a table cloth "gleaming white, like an altar cloth" (91).

The balloon bodies of the Pedersens mirror the inflated ego of Dr. Pedersen, a man whose benevolent public persona disguises a secretly pornographic philosophy. Mrs. Pedersen exposes her husband's secrets to Jesse, in her words, but even more graphically, with her body. In despair, Mrs. Pedersen drinks. On one occasion, when she locks herself in the bathroom, Jesse helps to remove the door. He sees her body lying naked, an enormous body with "the head at the far end . . . too small for it" (157). Shortly after their marriage, Pedersen had locked her in the bedroom, forcing her to shave the hair off her body and to look at photos of dismembered bodies with pornographic captions. She tells Jesse:

> "He talks all the time about his public philosophy, but what about the secret one? Once a patient has come to him, he believes the patient is *his*. The patient's life is his. He owns the patient, he owns the disease, he owns everything. Oh, he's crazy. Ask him about these things. Just ask him. Not all his patients survive, you know. Ask him about the ones who die. His diagnoses are not always right. The great Dr. Pedersen has made mistakes. But he talks his patients into believing him so that they would rather die than go to another doctor, they have such faith in him, they get sicker and sicker and die, actually die, rather than call in another doctor . . . and he watches them die and won't bring in anyone else . . . right until the end he thinks he's right, he's unable to believe that he might be wrong." (171)

Yet Pedersen is a man so admired that he is even invited to give sermons at the Lutheran Church.

Pedersen adopts Jesse because, as an orphan, he will be more submissive to his will than his own children, who have grown ill from passive resistance to their father. At every meal they must report on

their intellectual achievements to their father, filling their love-starved
bodies with increasing quantities of food. Hilda feels her father's questions as "the body being addressed at its uppermost part, the head,"
and "she noticed how meekly the head nodded at the top of its squat
stem and the torso of the body leaned forward, eager and obedient, as
if prepared right now" to do her father's bidding (122). Having been
forced to become an extension of her father's ego, a human computer,
Hilda finally screams at him: *'You want to stuff me inside your mouth, I
know you . . . You want to press me into a ball and pop me into your mouth,
back where I came from. You want to eat us all up. . . . Father wants to kill me.
Eat me'* (140). According to psychoanalytic definition, Hilda would be
considered hysterical, but Oates emphasizes the truth of Hilda's accu-
sations, for Pedersen had earlier comforted her with these monoman-
iacal words: "You will have me inside you, in a way, even after I am
gone — inside you, carried around inside you" (133). Hilda recognizes
that there is no escape from her father's voice: 'He knew about the
tiny sac inside her, that elastic, magical emptiness that could never be
filled no matter how much she ate. It was the size of the universe"
(131). Later in the narrative Frederich will appear again, this time as
Trick Monk, a man whose poetry resembles Frederich's music. Although Jesse never sees his brother again, Oates has described Frederich as having a face "small for the rest of his body, prematurely
lined, with a mouth like his father, small and monkish" (92).

As a scientist, Trick is similarly monkish, sharing with Dr. Pedersen a disdain for the merely physical, an attitude disguising his fear
and hatred of the body, particularly the female body. Music or poetry
— the rhythmic discourses of the body — remain mysterious to Jesse
who has learned that they are not essential to his survival. As a scientist, it does not occur to Jesse to wonder, as his sister Hilda does, "Is
there a part of the soul that is not male or female?" (141). And Dr.
Pedersen informs him that even history is bunk, unimportant to a man
of science:

> "If you make claims about history and death and sickness and chaos
> I have no time for you. What can history tell us? It is all a joke! Ma-
> nure! We are not to be dragged down by the stupidities of the past.
> Hegel says, quite correctly: 'People and governments have never
> learned anything from history, or acted on principles deduced from
> it.' And so, what have we left . . . ? We have the health of the living
> organism. . . . I am striving, straining — ." (109)

Other people, "stupid crowds and herds, like animals," he explains,
are meant to die in wars, wars that stimulate economic growth. "It is

fate," he says; "What is war, Jesse? Is it death? Never! It is the very heartbeat of life — the last resources of life's energies!" (109). From Mrs. Pedersen, Jesse learns that the "good" doctor is working to design a germ bomb for the government of the United States.

Jesse learns his hatred of crowds from the egocentric Pedersen. Later, when Jesse encounters crowds of protesters as he searches for his daughter, Oates describes him as a man who "hated this formlessness. He was seized with a sudden hatred for it, almost nausea. He hated it, hated them. Hated the crowd in its joy in being trampled. Hated the noise. 'The communion,' which to Jesse, is merely 'anonymous garbage" (449). From this "mass consciousness" Jesse desires "a single figure, a single truth, a single human being at the center of this mob. A single eye that would see everyone, everything, and pronounce judgment upon it?" (449). The question Oates has posed here is the same question which, according to Michael Holquist, is always the "obsessive question at the heart of Bakhtin's thought" (307). It is "the mystery of the one and the many." Bakhtin would describe Jesse's mind as monologic. Oates portrays Jesse's "monologic" yearning as a search for a father-figure which, in this era, is manifest in a collective deification of science. Presumably a scientist free of social conflicts, amoral and objective, Jesse refuses to acknowledge self-doubt or confusion. He remains rigidly self-contained, making science his "single truth" and worshipping a series of scientists, his unacknowledged fathers: Drs. Pedersen, Cady, Perrault.

Oates portrays Jesse as fearful of crowds, while at the same time, she strives to transform the rhythms of the crowd into music. The tension becomes apparent as Jesse confronts the "communion" of the crowd, its "strange mass consciousness." He thinks of this carnivalesque phenomenon as "cancerous protoplasm":

> He had seen it many times through a microscope. Eating away its own boundaries, no limits to it, an inflammation seeding everywhere — to the spinal fluid, to the brain. How they surged in the chill open air of Chicago, roused as if by godly chimes — the bells of sunken churches, pealing and pulsating in a rhythm that people like Jesse could feel only remotely, being too old. It was a rhythm that beat in the loins of the young and showed in their faces. (448–449)

In contrast to the rhythms of the crowd, "a rhythm that beat in the loins," Oates gives us the voice of Dr. Pedersen, an arrogant individualist who sees crowds as fodder for war. Human beings, he has told Jesse, are fated to repeat war, "the very heartbeat of life." One might ask, as Pedersen does not, what point there is in healing individual bodies, bodies destined for dissolution in war. Pedersen's answer, of course, would be: for profit. This is not the "wisdom of the body" speaking, for the body has no "instinct" for death, but rather for life, for eros. It is rather the mind, narrowly defined as individual — as an isolated ego — that silences the body's wisdom.

In Book Two, "The Finite Passing of an Infinite Passion," Oates explores Pedersen's pornographic mind as it evolves during the turbulent period of the late fifties and into the sixties protests against social injustice. During these years — which include the assassination of President Kennedy, race and ghetto riots, and the Vietnam war — Jesse completes medical school and marries. His marriage and work seem to him apolitical although the news of Kennedy's death reaches him as he presents a paper on brain research. Those who lived through this period in American history will recall the image of Kennedy's shattered brain, a brain Jesse regards as "individual." Yet, at this time, Jesse buys a gun, which he later comes close to using against a young man. In 1963, his daughters are very young, and he wants to protect them. However, Jesse not only denies the sacredness of matter, he also ignores the promptings of his own body. Little dialogue occurs between his brain and body, and no dialogue occurs between Jesse and his wife. Like Dr. Pedersen, he names a doctor through his daughter, a courtship mocked by Trick Monk. Both men are seeking the love of Dr. Cady — an eminent scientist, a Nobel prize winner. Jesse is to win this contest, but his marriage to Dr. Cady's daughter without love leads him to fantasize adultery and, later, to sexualize his love for his daughter, Shelley. To dramatize Jesse's flight from the body — the hole in his consciousness — Oates introduces Trick Monk, a brilliant young medical student described in carnival terms, as "a young king and court jester, a clown with license to say anything" (206).

At the time of Trick's appearance, Jesse is engaged to a young woman, a nurse named Anne-Marie. Initially Jesse wants to tell her about his feelings, his arguments with professors:

> But he knew that she would not understand. He had no right to force her to understand. If he loved her he would guard her from such thoughts; if he loved her he would not bring her into himself, into his consciousness, but would allow her to remain herself. ... He had learned from the few novels he had read in his lifetime that love demanded rescue. He must rescue his beloved from danger, even the danger of himself. The story demanded that a male rescue a female from danger and he would be punished if he failed. (196)

As he joins the medical priesthood, he learns to share Trick Monk's preference for distance from the female body and, finally, he abandons

Anne-Marie. Trick, who voices thoughts for which Jesse has no vocabulary, "affected a horror of the body that was lyric and heavy, whimsical and grave: 'We in medicine,' he says, 'should go after the ultimate cure — the separation of the spirit from the flesh. Everything else is unsanitary nonsense'" (208). He mocks Jesse's desire to be of service to humanity.

Gradually, Jesse develops a similar disdain for the flesh although, for a time, he listens in horror as Trick shares his philosophy, beliefs remarkably similar to those of Dr. Pedersen. Trick says,

> "Did I ever tell you, Jesse, about my secret hopes for a career? It's a little late now, but I'm thinking of switching to ob. work; I'd like to be a great gynecologist; I'd like to take loving, gentle smears from the bodies of women, and examine them like this, in the solitude of a laboratory. I would be the most devoted and discreet of lovers and I would keep every secret." (210)

A man's body might fail him — surges of desire in a man's body make him vulnerable to failure — whereas the scientist may exercise complete control, entering a woman from a safe distance.

Trick voices Jesse's fear:

> " . . . I too would like to be invisible in this race of men, an instrument, a metallic model of an organ — for the real thing, the real organ, is apt to be disappointing, eh? Disappointing to a woman? Women are very demanding and very easily disappointed." (210)

Finally, however, Trick tells Jesse that he dreams of becoming a poet since "One kind of elimination is as good as another. Don't be a snob," he says, "because you're in love. Discharging in your beloved's body, discharging in her brain — which is more rewarding after all? I have a horror of germs" (211). The scientist, like the lyric poet, writes the bodies of women from anaesthetic, ascetic distance. Jesse learns a fear of "woman" — who once demanded rescue — for he might lose his power in "the center of her being, a socket of pure power that would suck him into it and charge him with its strength — asking nothing of him but the surrender and collapse of all his bones, the blacking-out of his consciousness" (215).

Jesse does not share Helene's feelings or her recognition that — in the bodies of animals — one can see what it means about "how we live and die." When Helene shared her fears of our "animal" fate,

> Jesse was astonished. He had wanted to comfort her, but how could he comfort such words? It hurt him to think that she should contem-

plate suffering like that, moving restlessly and independently of him, of his love for her, as if he had not the power to protect her ... Did she really think they must suffer like those animals? Her flesh and his flesh, flesh no more divine than that of the animals, doomed to the same bawdy fates. (246)

Jesse has censored his memory of the body just as he has censored his memory of his dying family — the Harte family. He has erased from consciousness his personal history, his memory of bleeding bodies torn by social forces. He doesn't recognize the communal implications, the tragedy, of the death of the Hartes. He doesn't share this memory with Helene; she never knows him intimately, nor does he know her in this way. His love for her is actually a love for her father, Dr. Cady — a man who occasionally uses "'unscientific' words like destiny, beauty, creation" (191). Marriage to Helene answers Jesse's question: "How to be that man without debasing himself" (228). Ambivalently, Oates both pities and parodies Jesse's childish father-worship. Trick, once again, voices Jesse's naive love for Cady, his god. Trick says,

> "A superior personality reduces me to Jell-O. In the presence of the great Benjamin Cady I provide an ashtray for him with my hands, automatically, unconsciously, and he taps his ashes out in my hands just as automatically, accepting me as an ashtray without even thinking about it." (202)

Jesse's "romantic" courtship of Helene, as Oates portrays it, will make his father-worship explicit.

Trick echoes the word "Jell-O" in a poem — a debased version of Whitman's "Song of Myself" — which he sends to Helene. Having been abandoned by his fathers — by Willard Harte, his grandfather Vogel, and Dr. Pedersen — Jesse will seek fulfillment of his communal yearnings, which have been perverted into a father-worship, through the body of Helene. Trick's poem demonstrates the loss of a democratic sense of community in the crevice between scientific and romantic discourse. The poem acknowledges what Jesse censors, his flight from his body, his hatred and fear of the vulnerable flesh. Trick begins with these words, a poem of self-hatred that distorts Whitman's celebration of the body:

> SONG OF MYSELF
> I am a vile jelly
> that grew wings
> and a bumpy facial structure

The phrase "vile jelly" — Cornwall's words as he stamps out Glouces-ter's eyes in the third act of *Lear* — illustrate the hatred of the body. The poem, though sent to Helene Cady, actually speaks of Trick's struggle with his love/hate for the "great" Dr. Cady. The struggle be-tween Trick and Jesse, like the struggle between Cornwall and Gloucester, alludes to the competition for the father's love, for the at-tention of a man who "automatically" uses Trick as an ashtray. The poem continues,

> beneath your bare feet
> I would subside again
> to jelly
> to joy (250–251).

By sending his poem to Helene, Trick makes a pathetic, though indi-rect, appeal to Cady for love, but this distortion of Whitman's "Song of Myself" emphasizes the romantic ego rather than the sacred body of the crowd.

Because Jesse hasn't the time to "imagine" Helene, she functions, as Pedersen's wife Mary had, as a point of contact between her father and her husband. "She floated between them, her father and her hus-band. They seemed to have no real consciousness of her except as a point of contact, an object, a beloved object" (264). Like Mary Shirer Pedersen, she finds that her father and her husband "did not seem to listen to her. They talked at her" (265–66). Years earlier, Jesse's adop-tive mother had told him that her sanity was being destroyed by male deafness to her voice. Yet Jesse had learned the harsh consequences of listening to a woman when Pedersen — in his anger — had abandoned him. Mrs. Pedersen had said,

> "He will be very angry. I know. But for years I've known I would have to leave him. It's a question of survival. My sanity. I tried to explain this to my father and to Reverend Wieden but they didn't under-stand; men don't understand, they don't see that I am a human being of my own, ... I am Mary Shirer ... I am still Mary Shirer." (164–65)

Jesse, too, learns a practiced deafness to women, a practice that nearly destroys his wife and daughter.

And just as women have no voices, the body has no wisdom, ac-cording to Dr. Perrault, another father-figure to Jesse. People would be better off without the distractions of the senses, Perrault believes. Panels of scientists will select the brains of brilliant men, and "resurrection" will become a fact in Perrault's heaven. Creation by male brains will replace creation in the womb. Like a contemporary Frankenstein, Perrault explains his vision:

> "We could not tolerate a prodigious brain losing its health because of a sentimental attachment to its body. We cling to our bodies even when they are diseased because they are all we have known. We are terrified at the thought of losing them. It's like the old terror of leaving one world and going to ... the next world. But, unlike that old cosmology, the new world — the new body — would always be superior to the old. Guaranteed. So resurrection would be real; you would wake up in paradise. The old body, the old earth: cast away for a true heaven. But first we must educate people out of the vicious sentimentality of loving the body, loving the personality, the personal self, the *soul,* that old illusion." (339)

At Perrault's dinner table, hearing these words, Helene becomes what Perrault would surely describe as "hysterical." She calls him a "killer," but Jesse, of course, believes Perrault. Jesse assumes that only his wife's pregnancy upsets her, but in Perrault's puritanical heaven, women would simply be eradicated and, presumably, children too, unless he believes that his brain-children — like disembodied angels — would provide a more satisfactory progeny. The logical outcome of centuries of misogyny — a modern scientific interpretation of epic cultural premises — is the complete destruction of "the old body, the old earth."

In Book Three of *Wonderland,* "Dreaming America," Oates will describe the nightmarish landscape of America as a mirror image of the consciousness of men like Perrault. In this way, she gives a contemporary historical and social context to Mary Shelley's rewriting of *Paradise Lost.* The allusion to the myth of Frankenstein is apparent in Oates's name for Jesse's daughter. Shelley becomes a projection screen for Jesse's ghost self — his body, his memories, his passion — a self that rises in the night to circle obsessively, incestuously about the body of his daughter. When Trick confesses that he has eaten a uterus, Oates suggests that this urge toward control is a compensatory activity, an urge to silence the body which reminds him of his vulnerability, his mortality.

Although the flight from the body is not exclusively a male problem — and Oates portrays Helene as frightened of motherhood and the body's music — the problem is far more severe for her husband. Oates describes Helene's fear of her body, during the early years of her marriage:

> She had been afraid to think about love, about loving a man, because
> it had seemed to her impossible, ugly, brutish. She had resisted think-
> ing about ... death. It was too ugly. She had grown up with a dislike
> of being touched, even by her parents ... Always she had feared her
> body. (267–68)

She stays in her loveless marriage not, as some women do, for economic
reasons — she has an independent source of income — but out of a fear
of living in her body. The experience of having children, initially so
frightening that she considers an abortion, gives Helene some bodily
sense of the wisdom of the body. Jesse, however, has no experience of
the body's wisdom. Finally, his oppressed, armored body rebels. He
meets a woman called "Reva Denk," and in pursuit of her he feels "a
lust that radiated out from his loins to make everything glow, the most
distant muscle, the bony structures behind his ears, the smallest toes
— everything, a festival of parts — glowing with certainty, with lust,
with love for that woman" (377). He does not, however, act upon this
love-lust, for he assumes — as Oates does not — that "lust" is evil, that
he must control himself. In an act of masochistic self-containment, he
cuts into his flesh with a razor that is like a "surgical instrument":

> He held the razor in place against his left cheek, and felt up and
> down the length of his body a sharp thrill of lust, so keen that he
> nearly doubled over ... but he did not drop the razor blade again;
> instead he held it firmly and stretched the skin of his left cheek down-
> ward with one hand ... And then lightly, timidly, he scraped the blade
> against his skin and blood spurted out at once. (378)

Finally, he digs the blade into "the tangle of pubic hair" and frees
himself.

It is a bizarre, but perfect fulfillment of Dr. Perrault's puritanical
belief: "Life is pain. Pain is life" (312). Jesse's attempt to live a "pure"
and impersonal existence, a life free of Reva Denk whose name
sounded "airy and then heavy as dirt" (316), finally confuses his love
for his daughter. In Book Three, Shelley writes, describing her father's
love, a love that drove her away:

> You were never home but when you came home you would sit at the
> edge of the pool and watch me swim, *oh I burned in the sunshine in the
> glare of your watching me; walking naked in front of any men now is no
> task, no risk for me, not after you.* (404)

Having been her father's possession, she readily becomes the property of a young man named "Noel," a man who parades her on a beach wearing only a sign: The Fetish.

Simply leaving home is no answer to Shelley's problem. Many men want to claim Shelley. Noel "owns" her, but unlike Shelley's possessive father, he willingly loans her out. In her new "family" — a community of war resisters, drug addicts, and other "criminals" — men have been sexually "liberated." Now they generously share "the fetish," their communal property. A "good" man, Jesse could not bear the thought that other men "could get at his daughter through the orifices of her body," and he pursues her like a lover "sick with yearning ... heartsick, lovesick" (437). While bringing her home from a detention center in Toledo — where her V.D. test was negative — Jesse's "other self had sprung out ... It had taken hold of Shelley and shaken her violently" (433). Afterward, lying in bed beside his wife,

> [He] felt the agitation of that other Dr. Vogel who prowled the house in the dark. He had to get up to join him. The other self, the ghost self, tugged at him and insisted that he get out of bed and come downstairs, where he could sit in the dark of the large, long living room, thinking of the night and of his daughter, sleeping upstairs, in a room almost directly above him. (433)

This self haunts Jesse. Shelley's flight is a form of resistance to the law of the father — all of the fathers — that seeks to fill a hole in their consciousness with the bodies of women.

Later, in Book Three, "Dreaming America," letters from Shelley to her father, as well as the voice of his wife Helene, break into the pattern of Jesse's quest for his daughter. Oates answers negatively the question of whether their voices will break into his quest-consciousness in the hardcover edition, and then — though tentatively — positively in the revised, paperback edition. The problem of composition, particularly of beginnings and endings, is therefore not only aesthetic, but ideological. Oates's departure from the conventions of univocal composition — her dismemberment of the authorial voice into the dialogic voices of a crowd of characters — marks a break with the bounded text. Many of Oates's arguments with the weight of tradition may be inferred, not only from the voice and the poetry of Trick Monk, but also from Shelley's letters. Shelley articulates the experience of a woman reading the texts that Oates has parodied in her own re-writing of Lewis Carroll's *Alice in Wonderland*. In a letter dated December 1970, Shelley writes:

When I was nine years old Grandfather Cady gave me a large illustrated copy of *Alice in Wonderland* and *Alice's Adventures Through the
Looking-Glass*. I sat with it up on the table before me, a big heavy
book, reading the paragraphs one by one and trying not to fall into
them and lose myself, trying not to feel terror, *it's only a book*; staring
at the drawings of this girl with the long, long neck and the straggly
hair and the wild, enlarged eyes, and the girl reduced to the size of a
mouse, sailing through the air dragged by the red queen's hand, sitting at the end of a banquet table while legs of mutton waddled down
toward her to eat her. I would close my eyes in a panic and feel you
dragging me through the air, feel my head coming loose with the
exertions of the wind and all the noise of Winnetka that was not said
out loud, screaming at the back of your head, the side of your face,
that noble face. Noel asked me what my worst terror was and I told
him, "A book falls down from a library shelf and comes open. It is a
very large book with a heavy binding. It falls onto me, knocking me
down, and then everything is very still — no one knows about it, the
book is not alive and has no will, it means no evil against me — and I
am lying there, paralyzed." (401)

The weight of tradition, of books, paralyzes a woman's will. Paralysis
of will has been defined as a symptom of hysteria, but this term falsely
names a disease of patriarchy resulting from centuries of injustice
against women.

"It's only a book," Shelley writes. It's only reading. Yet a woman
learns the shape of her body from books which empty a woman of the
right of authority, forcing her to mediate her experience through the
male mind. The shape of Hilda Pedersen's body, of her mother Mary
Shirer's body, of Helene's body, of Shelley's body — these are the results of woman's function as an object of exchange, a possession, a
fetish. Thus, the Christmas music which Jesse hears in the background
as he looks at the pornographic image of a woman's body — over a
toilet — is certainly an appropriate joining of sound and image, both
of which void the creative mind and independence of women.

Wonderland argues for a transformation of "the cosmos" as defined
by men like Vogel, Pedersen, Perrault, Cady and, by implication, Mil-
ton and Freud. It argues for a culture which listens to the voices of the
Hartes — the poor — and to the voices of women and children. It also
argues that in the "abyss of female silence" is meaning, the beauty of
the body, male and female. In the body of Jesse's daughter Oates illustrates the tragic consequences of patriarchy's oppression of women.
When Jesse finds Shelley, he sees her "face wasted, yellow, the lips
caked with a stale dried substance," a sick child whom he initially mis-

takes for a boy. Shelley explains that the shape of her body is meant to
protect her from him, from his possessive, x-ray mind:

> "I live here and this is my family here. Everything comes from them.
> Noel is my husband here — not you — never you — when I have a
> baby it will be for all of them here, and not you — Why did you come
> after me? I can't go back. I'm all dried out. I'm dried out. Look — "
> And she lifted the undershirt to show her chest — her shriveled little
> breasts, her ribs, the shock of her yellow skin. "It's all shut off, there's
> a curse on me to shut me off, my body, I don't know what happened
> — there is no blood and no baby either — the police have a radar
> machine that dries us all up —." (475)

As these children perceive it, they are being destroyed by their society,
a "radar machine that dries us all up." It would be easy to dismiss this
accusation, particularly this exaggerated — or "hysterical" — view of
the power of police. Yet these children have been forced to flee from
their fathers, whether to avoid being sacrificed to war or sacrificed to
sexual abuse, like Shelley, to their fathers.

The voices of women, of Shelley and Helene, call to Jesse to share
this pain, to free himself and them. "I am thinking of Christmas 1967,"
Shelley begins her December 1970 letter to Jesse, a letter that ends
with this plea:

> You walked out on us that night, Christmas night. You were gone all
> night. I don't want to think about where you walked, or why you left
> us like that, or why I sat at the top of the stairs waiting for you to
> come back, in secret, in the dark, afraid to go to bed.
> I want to be free.
>
> Love, Shelley (407).

Helene also remembers the Christmas Jesse had walked out on them,
but she can't put together the fragmented pieces of her husband's history. He has never told her this history, a history he assumes to be
merely personal, "subjective." He has no vocabulary for his feelings, as
if his brain — and the brains of his patients — have no connection to
their bodies. Oates places his consciousness — his disembodied mind
— in a social context, the tragic event of November 22, 1963, the death
of President Kennedy:

> Before two o'clock it had all happened and had become history: the
> motorcade in Dallas fired at, the President struck in the head, the
> President pronounced dead. Jesse felt again and again the impact of

those bullets in his own body; the head, the vulnerable head, the precious brain ... Why was it always this way, men dying, men dead? Why the exploded skull, the burst brain, why so many men in a procession that led to death? Dr. Vogel, sweating, could not understand it. (395)

This is the night that Jesse, trying not to think of Reva, wanting to protect his family from death — wanting to have dominion over death — turns the glare of his passion upon his innocent daughter, Shelley. The censorship of public passion — and the romanticizing of desire — characterizes the various discourses Oates has examined in *Wonderland*. Jesse, having no vocabulary for these realities, is a typically "innocent" American male.

Is this the reason, Oates asks in *Wonderland,* that men become killers? Does this denial of the body motivate the impulse toward mastery, a mastery aggressively imposed upon the bodies of women by the phallic pen? The second boy had drawn the woman's body — with her tiny head and giant body — as a house. Between her legs was a door, leading into an empty blackness, an abyss. In Jesse's search for his daughter, Oates implies, he may find the meaning in this hole in his consciousness, a puzzle he had tracked on the night of Christmas 1969, thirty years after his escape from a gun-toting father. He had left because "he had to hunt out something" (434). Circling the house like "an animal, a hunting animal,"

> Panic faded as his strength faded. He found that he had circled around his house, a circle that must have taken him five miles, the house remaining in its center, in the very center of his consciousness, his wife and daughters sleeping in the center, while snow fell in their sleep. (434)

At the center of this house is his daughter whose body he wants to contain, as Pedersen had contained his wife and children. Unless Jesse remembers his past, he will not find a way out of his circle; he will not hear the voices of women and children. For behind this nightmare of the wrath of fathers, whose love he seeks, is a memory of life in the womb, a nativity scene which reminds us of dependency, death, and organic identity. Jesse's search for Shelley leads him back to his old friend, Trick Monk. Trick has become a poet of the body, retitling a poem about the central nervous system, "Vietnam."

Again, it is the body of a woman that brings them together; this time, however, it is Shelley's body. "Remember the man you almost killed?" Shelley had written Jesse (451). Trick begs to be treated as an

equal — "'not in the world of reality, only in the world of poetry'" (456)
— and he shows Jesse a review of his poetry that describes "the increasing irony of the distance between the object *perceived* and the object *conceived* in American society" (456). The increasing distance
between science and poetry — between Jesse's "objective" and Trick's
"subjective" perception — makes Shelley an object of exchange, a shell
empty of meaning, a currency. Jesse begs Trick to listen to him, but
Trick fears him:

> "Dr. Vogel, my dear Jesse, you don't understand. You want to kill us.
> Don't kill us. Don't look at us like that," Monk said. He had begun to
> cry. "I can feel it in you, the desire to do something — to dissect us,
> or operate on us — to snip our nerves — to clean us out with a scour-
> ing pad." (457)

Jesse protests that he hadn't intended to kill Trick, that science doesn't
ask the death of poetry. As if to defend himself from the charge that
his poetry may be political in any way, Trick says that Nixon "is a kind
of hero to me ... he is a cult down here actually, America's attempt to
create the *Übermensch*" (456). In this pathetic appeal to Jesse, Trick
claims, contradictorily, that poetry does not exist "in the world of reality." These two discourses, old "enemies," are aspects of the same
brain, a feeling-thinking brain, a part of the body. Yet neither Jesse
nor Trick recognizes the relationship of their discourses to the communal body: "The Central Nervous System of America." They do not
hear each other, and no dialogue occurs between them.

Oates takes both Jesse and Helene into crowds where they may,
possibly, lose their narrow consciousness — their isolated individualism
— in a gigantic consciousness: Whitman's "En-Masse." To fill her emptiness, Helene goes to a shopping center called "Wonderland East," this
time to meet a man whom Oates calls, humorously, "Mannie." Her romantic interlude ends when they walk out into the street and hear the
rhythms of angry protestors. "'Take your fucking war and shove it!'" a
girl had shouted. Angrily, Helene had walked into the crowd of young
people, slapping a girl who seemed to be saying to her, *"It is over for you
... it is over, over over for you! For you!"* (424). This violence temporarily
frees her, but her freedom is not permanent — only "The Finite Passing of an Infinite Passion." Nevertheless, Oates points to the need for
passion to come out of the "romantic" rooms of private, personal history and into the street. In particular, the articulated anger of women,
of unfulfilled women — the "object" misconceived or misperceived —
must enter the carnival of public discourses.

Despite Oates's depiction of such anger — anger with the potential to change society — her first conclusion to the novel mirrors Jesse's effort to contain himself. Yet his self-containment, his self-mastery, is premised upon belief in a unified "I" — the "I" of the romantic ego. His denial of inter-relatedness results in the subordination of the voices of women upon whose bodies he projects his "feminine" aspects. This confusion of boundaries — a father's desire to keep inside himself what belongs outside — shapes the political realities of Yonge Street, the nightmarish landscape that Jesse enters in his search for his daughter. When Jesse leaves the United States to enter Canada, he gradually discards his individual identity. He buys new clothes that will give him anonymity in the crowd, leaving his old clothes, along with his identification papers, in a trash can. When he stops to buy a newspaper, he reads an underground newspaper, THE HOLE WITH A VOICE, that speaks for American children:

> The biggest headline was in black: NIXON PLANS MASS CON-CENTRATION CAMPS. Other stories dealt with FBI narcotics agents' activities, the "Most Wanted" list back in the United States, a communal picnic of draft dodgers and "freaks" that had evidently been broken up a few days before, and Prime Minister Trudeau, "Canadian puppet of imperialistic war-mongering nations." Inside, a smudgy cartoon showed a middle-aged, flabby man holding a gun to the head of a long-haired child, presumably his own son. *We all die for our country*, the caption said. (467)

In Jesse's quest for his daughter, Oates must decide if he will again compulsively bind his hysteria, symptomatically expressed in his fear and hatred of the crowd, or if her hero will break this homeostatic pattern. In order to resist this compulsion, Oates implies, Jesse must learn to read dialogically, that is, poetically. He must examine boundaries that seem fixed in order to free himself and Shelley. Once again, Jesse sees a representation of a womb in a toilet on Yonge Street (young/Jung street). This time, however, "At the very center of the little womb was an eye, elaborately inked in" (466). In contrast to the artist at the beginning of the novel, this artist places the "I" — the eye — within the womb. Does this shift in vision suggest that the artist recognizes himself in/as the body of the crowd? Or does it imply that Jesse seeks control even of the womb, as do other father-figures in the novel? Oates's ambivalence allows for either interpretation, the one tragic, the other open: an image of the cosmic womb, an abyss out of which children, and the future, emerge. Which future Oates engenders depends on Jesse, who must move beyond his belief in homeostasis and his emotional paralysis.

Although Jesse, as a scientist, has been obsessed with the theory of homeostasis, he has not investigated the multiple discourses that have shaped his consciousness. A neurosurgeon who operates on the human brain, he has not fully explored relationships among language, memory, and consciousness. The binary divisions of mind and matter, self and society, culture and consciousness, remain a mystery to him. Oates, of course, is preoccupied with these issues, exploring the theory of homeostasis in a cultural context — political, economic, religious, familial. Jesse first reads and (monologically) recites a history of this theory to please his adoptive father, Dr. Pedersen. Speaking in complete sentences, as Pedersen requires, Jesse begins with Hippocrates:

> "Hippocrates believed that disease could be cured by natural powers within the living organism. He believed that there is an active opposition to abnormality as soon as the condition begins. In 1877, the German physiologist, Pfluger, said that the cause of every need of a living being is also the cause of the satisfaction of the need. The Belgian physiologist, Fredericq, said in 1885 that the living being is an agency of such sort that each disturbing influence induces by itself the calling forth of compensatory activity to neutralize or repair the disturbance. The higher in the scale of living beings, the more perfect and the more complicated the regulatory agencies become. (107)

Such a definition of the organism ignores history — whether that of the individual organism or larger units into which the various species organize themselves — and also ignores the problem of language.

For Oates, of course, the problem of language is primary, as it is for Bakhtin. Holquist explains that Bakhtin's homeostatic theory of communication — in which the relation of mind to world is seen as a dialogic continuum — was based upon the research of a behavioral scientist, Aleksky Alekseevich Ukhtomsky. Bakhtin learned, by attending one of Ukhtomsky's public lectures, according to Holquist, that "the central nervous system was in its essence rhythmical; it translated the random, uncoordinated impulses (noise) the body experienced on its surface into a smoothly functioning unity (music) within the various systems of the body" (316–317). The mind/brain mediates, translating what it hears and sees in a process of constant listening and answering. In the carnivalesque crowds — whether this crowd appears on the streets or in texts — both Oates and Bakhtin see society's central nervous system: a social body analogous to the individual body. Given this revised homeostatic vision — self as organism, self within social organism — the old boundaries between self and society, between matter and mind, are transformed. It is the poet, Trick Monk, who comes closest to this vision when he simply retitles an old poem on the central nervous system, "Vietnam."

Oates underscores the social aspects of homeostasis when, in the midst of the obese Pedersen family, Jesse continues his recitation:

> In *The Wisdom of the Body*, the American physiologist, Walter Cannon, quotes the French physiologist Charles Richet: *The living being is stable. It must be so in order not to be destroyed, dissolved, or disintegrated by the colossal forces, often adverse, which surround it. By an apparent contradiction it maintains its stability only if it is excitable and capable of modifying itself according to external stimuli and adjusting its response to the stimulation. It is stable because it is modifiable — the slight instability is the necessary condition for the true stability of the organism.* (107)

To view the organism as stable is to deny the organic processes of birth and death, a process that affects the family, for example, as adolescents grow and leave home. To insist upon stases in these natural processes is to become grotesque, a rigidity easily caricatured, but at the same time, painfully destructive for those oppressed by such thinking. Like many families, the entire Pedersen family lives according to this static model, controlled by Dr. Pedersen, the "head," the monologic intellect. Such control is deadly and an intellectual error. Oates makes Jesse's desire for control explicit when Jesse, after one of Dr. Cady's poetic lectures in medical school, asks himself, "Isn't the great lesson of science *control*? The lesson of homeostasis and cybernetics: *control?*" (195). This desire for control, if not recognized as contrary to genuine objectivity, impedes scientific investigation. As Evelyn Fox Keller argues, "So long as thought has not become conscious of itself, it is prey to perpetual confusions between objective and subjective, between the real and the ostensible."[12] As Eileen Teper Bender points out, Oates has stated in a critical essay that "'wherever one encounters the Aristotelian-Freudian ideal of homeostasis, in opposition to the Oriental or Jungian ideals of integration of opposites, one is likely to encounter a secret detestation of the feminine'" (55).[13] Bender also argues that family "homeostasis" — a word employed by R. D. Laing — is ultimately violent. It is a stasis maintained at the expense of natural growth.

Shelley Vogel, like many other youngsters in this novel, is leaving home to escape such control; nevertheless, in the first edition of *Wonderland*, Oates — like her hero — maintains control over the voices of

women and children. The Vietnam War is symptomatic of this homeostatic violence in the social body. Oates depicts this violence at the
end of the 1971 edition when Jesse, having failed to integrate his "feminine" aspects, tracks his daughter to a fence. Unlike the young Jesse
— who was strong enough to leap a fence to escape his violent father
— Shelley is too weak. She dies as Cordelia dies: in the arms of her
ego-bounded father. "The fence will not give," Oates repeats in a preface to the 1971 edition. By 1973, the fences have given, and Oates has
reconceptualized the self: the questor is transformed into the crowd.
In the poem prefacing the novel, and signed by Trick Monk, Oates
articulates the dialogic relationship of these eyes — the multiple "I" of
the crowd — a heteroglossia of voices that her hero must learn to hear
if society is to be transformed. This process of creative rebirth is called
"Wonderland." Oates/Trick writes:

> the eye widens
> the iris becomes an eye
> intestines shape themselves fine as silk
> I make my way up through marrow
> through my own heavy blood
> my eyes eager as thumbs
> entering my own history like a tear
> balanced on the outermost edge
> of the eyelid. (10)

Neither scientist nor artist controls this mysterious process, a process
envisioned here as an evolution of consciousness *within* the social
womb.

Notes

1. I am indebted to Kristeva for this distinction between the "bounded"
(or univocal) text and the dialogic text. Kristeva, of course, owes this distinction to Mikhail Bakhtin.

2. See Bakhtin's "Epic and Novel."

3. *Wonderland* (Greenwich, Conn.: Fawcett, 1973). I quote only from this
paperback edition, except where indicated. The hardcover edition was published by Vanguard in 1971.

4. See "The Hostile Sun: The Poetry of D. H. Lawrence." In the same
footnote Oates also says that Lawrence "imaginatively divided himself into the
characters in his stories, both male and female."

5. Bakhtin is equally obsessed with the theory of homeostasis, as Michael Holquist argues in "Answering as Authoring: Mikhail Bakhtin's Trans-Linguistics."

6. *Newsweek*, 11 December 1971, p. 77.

7. Personal interview at the College English Association Conference, Detroit, 23 April 1973.

8. *American Journal* 1 (3 July 1973), 20.

9. Bakhtin makes this point most effectively in *Rabelais and His World*. Bakhtin insists, as Oates does in *Wonderland*, that "this is not the body and its physiology in the modern sense of these words, because it is not individualized. The material bodily principle is contained not in the biologic individual, not in the bourgeois ego, but in the people, a people who are continually growing and renewed" (19). The grotesque realism of *Wonderland* may have enabled Oates to move beyond the "family romance" — in which eating disorders such as *bulemia* and *anorexia nervosa* are often situated — into the communal, or social body. Even the title of Oates's collection of criticism, *New Heaven, New Earth* (1974), announces this discovery of the collective or social body. As Bakhtin says, "Earth is an element that devours, swallows up (the grave, the womb) and at the same time an element of birth, of renascence (the maternal breasts). Such is the meaning of 'upward' and 'downward' in their cosmic aspect" (21), and such is the understanding that readers of Rabelais, in the sixteenth century, would have assumed. In the celebration of this body, one discovers cosmic laughter.

10. See *Pornography and Silence: Culture's Revenge Against Nature*.

11. "Word, Dialogue, and Novel," p. 78. Although in this essay Kristeva does not link carnivalesque resistance to epic hierarchies to the maternal body, her final essay in this volume, "Place Names," argues for unconscious associations of space, laughter, and the maternal body. Significantly, at a session called "The Social Body" at the conference on "Women's Bodies, Women's Voices," two therapists described how bulemics, through an attachment to the body of the therapeutic group (women only), learn to care for their individual bodies. (University of Iowa, April 1988).

12. See "Feminism and Science." Keller has developed this argument in *Reflections on Gender and Science* (New Haven: Yale University Press, 1985).

13. The question naturally arises: is Bakhtin's preoccupation with this theory an indication of his "secret detestation of the feminine"? Wayne Booth has argued that in his defense of Rabelais, Bakhtin betrays "sexist" attitudes. See "Freedom of Interpretation: Bakhtin and the Challenge of Feminist Criticism." My own view, at present, is that Bakhtin is ambivalent, as in his description of carnivalesque celebration of the social body as both a "degeneration" and a "renewal."

Works Cited

Bakhtin, M. M. *The Dialogic Imagination: Four Essays.* Ed. Caryl Emerson and Michael Holquist. Austin: University of Texas Press, 1981.

———. *Rabelais and His World.* Trans. Helene Iswolsky. Bloomington: Indiana University Press, 1984.

Bender, Eileen Teper. *Joyce Carol Oates, Artist in Residence.* Bloomington: Indiana University Press, 1987.

Booth, Wayne. "Freedom of Interpretation: Bakhtin and the Challenge of Feminist Criticism" in *Critical Inquiry* 9, 1 (September 1982): 45 – 76.

Griffin, Susan. *Pornography and Silence: Culture's Revenge Against Nature.* New York: Harper and Row, 1981.

Holquist, Michael. "Answering as Authoring: Mikhail Bakhtin's Trans-Linguistics" in *Critical Inquiry* 10, 2 (December 1983): 307 – 19.

Keller, Evelyn Fox. "Feminism and Science" in *Feminist Theory: A Critique of Ideology.* Ed. Nannerl O. Keohane. Chicago: University of Chicago Press, 1982.

Kristeva, Julia. *Desire in Language: A Semiotic Approach to Literature and Art.* Ed. Leon S. Roudiez. Trans. Thomas Gora, Alice Jardine, and Leon Roudiez. New York: Columbia University Press, 1980.

Oates, Joyce Carol. "Art: Therapy and Magic" in *American Journal* 1 (3 July 1973).

———. "The Hostile Sun: The Poetry of D.H. Lawrence" in *New Heaven, New Earth: The Visionary Experience in Literature.* New York: Fawcett, 1974.

———. *Wonderland.* Greenwich, CT: Fawcett, 1973.

11

Language and Gender in Transit: Feminist Extensions of Bakhtin

Sheryl Stevenson

Tracing an Orlando-like figure through shifting guises of femininity and masculinity, Brigid Brophy's *In Transit* lends support to Sandra Gilbert's idea that modernist writers envision gender identities as transiently assumed roles, "costumes of the mind" (393). An Anglo-Irish inconoclast with decidedly modernist affiliations, Brophy operates in the tradition of Woolf and Joyce, particularly in using parody to unsettle inherited notions of gender.[1] But her 1969 novel places a distinctive emphasis on connections between gender and language, which Brophy reinforces by exploiting conventions of allegory. *In Transit* thus concentrates its actions in a single symbolic setting, an international airport, which distills the highly mixed, transient quality of modern culture. As a representative citizen of such a culture, the novel's dubious Everyman (or woman) is barraged by languages and surrounded by gaudy images of social unrest: a student revolution, a lesbian putsch, an assault by parachuting nuns — each aimed at the Control Tower of masculine authority. This environment of intense linguistic and social conflict seems fraught with occupational hazards, especially apparent in the dual disease or paired afflictions which utterly undo Brophy's protagonist: "linguistic leprosy," a deterioration of the character's language, and gender-amnesia, the ultimate identity crisis.

By suggesting that individual identity is tied to language, and by presenting both in an unstable condition, *In Transit* draws attention to a juncture between feminist studies of gender and Mikhail Bakhtin's theory of language. Like Bakhtin, Brophy emphasizes that human consciousness is a social phenomenon, constituted by widely shared, ideologically charged discourses. Yet by concentrating on the social na-

181

ture of *gender* identity, her novel also anticipates a major focus of the seventies and eighties feminist scholarship.[2] Feminism and dialogism meet and illuminate each other in Brophy's text.

   Devices of modernist fiction facilitate this mutual exchange between feminism and Bakhtin, by making language, as Brophy's narrative itself proclaims, "one of the hero(in)es immolated throughout these pages."[3] This ritualized sacrifice takes place in the novel's exuberantly fantastic, allegorical plot, as Language plays the part of the female victim relished by pornography. Yet the mutilation of language also occurs in portmanteau words, multilingual puns, stylistic parodies, and a disjunctive narrative structure, shifting from an initial first-person narrative to various third-person accounts mixed with "authorial" digressions. Paying explicit tribute to Joyce ("the old pun gent himself" [36]), Brophy's self-consciously modernist narrative graphically renders the mutability of language which Bakhtin stresses, while also highlighting the problematics of gender explored by contemporary feminists. The following discussion will therefore approach Bakhtin's theory of language through parallels in Brophy, while moving toward connections *In Transit* makes among language, gender, and the novel itself as an art form. Brophy's synthesis of these three areas suggest extensions of Bakhtin's ideas in two directions he has been criticized for not considering: modernist fiction and feminist issues (see Hayman; and Booth, Russo, Yaeger).

   A path into Bakhtin's theory can be charted through qualities he ascribes to language — as dialogic, ideological, "heteroglot," and antisystematic. These qualities take startling, wacky forms as *In Transit* defamiliarizes this subject which literally becomes one of the text's "hero(in)es."

   Brophy embodies her concept of language in an allegorical dream-quest undertaken by the novel's initial first-person narrator and protagonist, later identified as Evelyn Hilary O'Rooley (nicknamed "Pat"). The plot springs from the protagonist-narrator's decision to forego flight and remain "in transit," in the unrooted, culturally mixed state which the narrator presents as the twentieth-century frame of mind (22 – 23). Encompassed by a Babel-like confusion of tongues, the narrator dramatizes how languages pervade the subjective consciousness. These languages are, first of all, the national tongues which mix and collide within the narrator's perceptions and punning thoughts. Yet the airport's environment of many languages seems itself symbolic of proliferating forms of discourse which the narrator ingests — magazines, TV, postcards, signs, as well as various literary forms. (For example, the airport's public address system broadcasts a wildly camp, gender-inverted Italian opera, appropriately named for the airline, *Al-italia*.) A hodgepodge of voices, the first-person narrative conveys a psyche so permeated by social discourses that it seems, as Bakhtin says, a *"borderline"* phenomenon, merging self and society and so having "extraterritorial status."[4] In both Bakhtin and Brophy this metaphor of extraterritoriality (of being in transit, between states) reflects a notion of language as the constituting element of a radically social psyche.

Peculiar features of Brophy's protagonist-narrator further fill out her novel's Bakhtinian conception of language. The decision "to live in in-transit" (28) marks one such peculiarity. This move is apparently motivated by egalitarian "internationalism," a radical *linguistic* politics summed up in the narrator's citizenship oath: "I adopt the international airport idiom for my native" (28). Pat O'Rooley seems predisposed to this "ideological gesture," having been transported as a child from Ireland to England and hence deprived of a "native language" (28, 29). "Extraterritoriality" is George Steiner's term for this condition, a lack of "at-homeness" in any national tongue which he sees as characteristic of multilingual artists like Nabokov and Beckett (11, 5). Bakhtin finds a similar "linguistic consciousness" endemic to multilingual *cultures,* where contact with alternative languages breeds a disease with any one formulation (*DI*, 60). An emblematic citizen of the twentieth century, Brophy's deracinated narrator seems to embody Bakhtin's idea and, indeed, claims that in the airport (an internationally mixed, modern culture) "no one is native. We are all in transients" (29).

Along with acute awareness of languages and their limits, the first-person narrative reveals a second eccentricity in Brophy's protagonist: obsessive concern with locating and addressing various interlocutors. This obsession is articulated in the novel's opening paragraphs, as the narrator focuses not on Barthes's characteristic question, "Who is speaking?" (*S/Z*, 41), but on the question of the addressee of the narrative discourse:

> Ce qui m'étonnait c'était qu'it was my French that disintegrated first.
>
> Thus I expounded my affliction, an instant after I noticed its onset. My words went, of course, unvoiced . . .
>
> Obviously, it wasn't myself I was informing I had contracted linguistic leprosy. I'd already known for a good split second.
>
> I was addressing the imaginary interlocutor who is entertained, I surmise, by all self-conscious beings — short of, possibly, the dumb and, probably, infants (in the radical sense of the word). (11)

If we take the protagonist-narrator as a representative figure, then the novel suggests that inner speech as well as spoken discourse is always directed to someone, even if the interlocutor is ultimately imagined, a projection. *In Transit* plays up this idea when the narrator briefly takes the p.a. system as an interlocutor:

> The phantom faces of the interlocutor are less troubling than the question of *where* he is. I am beset by an insidious compulsion to locate him ...
>
> The problem was the more acute because I was alone in a concourse of people. After a moment I noticed that my situation had driven me to think my thoughts to the public-address system, which had, for the last hour, been addressing me — inter aliens — with commands (couched as requests), admonitions (a tumble of negative subjunctives) and simple brief loud-hails, not one of which had I elected to act on. (12)

Brophy's extremely other-oriented protagonist closely resembles Dostoevsky's narrator in "Notes from Underground," as analyzed by Bakhtin: "The discourse of the Underground Man is entirely a discourse-address. To speak, for him means to address someone" (*PDP*, 236). Both apparent monologuists are actually dialoguists, revealing one of the ways in which all discourse is "dialogic": "every word is directed toward an *answer* and cannot escape the profound influence of the answering word that it anticipates" (*DI*, 280).

Dostoevsky's Underground Man begins his narrative in this way: "I am a sick man ... I am a spiteful man. I am an unpleasant man. I think my liver is diseased. However, I don't know beans about my disease, and I am not sure what is bothering me" (3; Dostoevsky's ellipsis). Similarly, *In Transit* immediately confronts us with a diseased narrator, but in this case the sickness is one of language, "linguistic leprosy," the third oddity of Brophy's peculiar Everyone. The narrator thus complains of foreign tongues atrophying and "fall[ing] off" (12), like the fingers and toes which can be lost through leprosy. Yet the narrative mixes and compares Greek, Latin, Gaelic, Italian, and French, commenting on the "idiomsyncrasy" (40) of each. Gripped by "compunsion" (35), Brophy's intensely multilingual protagonist-narrator playfully illustrates the "crossing" of languages which Bakhtin sees as fundamental to their evolution (*MPL*, 76). Exaggerating this condition of languages within the narrator's consciousness, *In Transit* dramatizes how language itself is "in transit" — ever in a process of change as languages mix, mutate, "die."

I see this idea fleshed out in Brophy's comic Story of Oc—that is, "O" with a "c" or "ch" added. Providing a great example of female parody-pornography, the narrative incorporates substantial excerpts of a porno-novel, purchased by Pat from the airport bookstall and entitled, "L'HISTOIRE DE LA LANGUE D'OC" (which is translated, "THE STORY OF OC'S TONGUE" [98]). As a student at a girls' school of pleasure, the bondage fanatic Oc undergoes various exquisite tortures, during which she finally dies. Along the way, in an offhand reference, the narrative reminds us that the *langue d'oc* was the language of Southern France, replaced by the northern *langue d'oïl* (the alternative terms referring to each area's pronunciation of the word for "yes" [129]). In Brophy's kinky allegory, the porn-heroine Oc represents the specific, transient language—subject to a process of mutilation and death which parallels the narrator's linguistic leprosy. The novel then makes this parallel explicit when the first-person narrator goes through a scene of linguistic torture (216–18), a dismemberment of the narrative's language, which is sandwiched between the final binding of Och and the announcement of her death (214, 222).

The parallel stories of Oc and Pat foreground the radically transient status of language and of human consciousness, while also pointing toward ties between changes in each. As a masochist whose name recalls inter-language conflict, the mutable Oc/Och illuminates Bakhtin's notion of language as "a continuous process of becoming" (*MPL*, 81), a dynamic struggle of tongues. On one level, this conflict occurs between "centripetal" and "centrifugal" tendencies in language (*DI*, 270–73). Hence, groups and institutions seeking political and ideological centralization posit a "correct," unifying language, which is constantly undermined by heterogeneous social usage (or "heteroglossia"), the ceaseless stratification of any national language by countless social groups, each of which has a "language" of its own, with meanings and inflections reflecting the group's world view (*DI*, 270–73; 290–91). As each word is imbued with values and associations, fraught with conflicting connotations acquired in the course of "its socially charged life," the word itself "exists in continuous generation and change" (*DI*, 293; *MPL*, 157). Bakhtin's "anti-linguistics," as Susan Stewart calls it, thus presents language as antisystematic, "ideologically saturated" (*DI*, 271), and ever in transit.

Matching Brophy's paired transients, Oc and Pat, Bakhtin sees human consciousness as strongly tied to the shifting languages (and ideologies) of society: "Language lights up the inner personality and its consciousness; language creates them ... Personality is itself generated through language."[5] Brophy joins Bakhtin in stressing that the

subjective consciousness is formed in a responsive, dialogic relationship with the words and world views of others.[6] To see how *In Transit*
brings out the implications of this position for current gender theory,
we need to consider the ultimate peculiarity of Brophy's protagonist,
the uncertain gender of Evelyn Hilary O'Rooley. By studying this final
trait in some detail, we can see how the novel ties the formation of
gender identity to a larger process of linguistic and cultural change.

Following Pat's decision to put off departure and stay in the Transit Lounge, the narrative discourse is filled with enthusiastic apos-
trophes, elaborating the benefits and egalitarian politics of choosing a
nonstatic, nondefined state of becoming. But while Pat O'Rooley gaily
rejects "arbitrary" categories (27), like those of nation and class, which
artificially limit human self-definition, the state of in-transience also
seems to entail loss of gender distinctions: in other words, the narrator
can no longer remember whether he or she is male or female (69).

From this point, the novel's fragmented, zany plot highlights Pat's
romance-quest in seach of a fixed sense of gender identity. While virtually the whole of *In Transit* can be seen as a series of parodic discourses, some of the most marked and swiftly changing parodies occur
after the onset of Pat's gender-amnesia. Pursuing Pat in his/her shifting sense of gender, the narrative indicates each shift with a new parody. Two examples can suggest how each parodied discourse is imbued
with conceptions of masculinity or femininity which Pat tries on and is
tested by — romance adventures in which the styles Pat takes on are
tested notions of gender.

When first convinced of being female, Patricia descends into the
airport's basement, a "lesbian underworld" of female porters (128),
and then is whisked onto the panel of a television game show, *WHAT'S
MY KINK?* Addressed as a man, under the intense glare of public
attention, Pat faces the moment when the cameras will focus on him?
her? with an accession to the language of popular adventure stories:

> Time ponderously raced: a count-down of seconds passed at fever-
> speed and yet in the detail of slow-motion. This was an experience of
> time with enlarged pores.
>
> When the moment came, would he/she be able to utter a syllable?
>
> It was a clenching pressure of dread, in which a soul might crack:
> and he publicly exposed ... A count-down of seconds, it was, until
> the very second when this individual, Pat, should have one second to
> make or mar: and if it was a second of shame, there was no revoking
> it, ever. (134 – 35)

Given the implicit macho of this passage, it is hardly surprising that at the crucial (reiterated, expanded) *second,* "Pat resolved to be Patrick" and "coolly and decisively" fires his winning answer (135).

In a later sequence, when Pat decides she is instead a lesbian, her choice of an exclusively female self-definition is reflected by the narrative, which mimics the super-"feminine" genre of popular romance. A woman of quiet dignity, pop-romance heroine Patricia is approached and wooed by an aristocratic stranger, an aging Byronic roué equipped with military bearing and a face distinguished by a duelling scar (145). Queenly Patricia rejects this self-confessed "Don Juan," yet as she accompanies him to his departure gate her fears of his possible death in flight are expressed in a sentimental, metaphor-enriched style which presumably expresses her chastely "feminine" sense of self (that is, as a lesbian). This wacky parody undermines, even as it exposes, assumptions about men and women which saturate the gush of popular romance, with its darkly attractive, sexualized males and vascillatingly attracted, sentimental females. The sexual ideology implicit here — one of absolute differences between the sexes — is exploded by the scene's camp termination:

> "Kiss my hand," she said, letting fall the separate words like queen's pearls or tears.
>
> "My dear," he said, letting the tones of a roué cynic curl the edges of his words like autumn-leaf mustachios tobacco-cured in an irony against himself, "I know we are said not to live in a permissive society. But I would not risk exposing you to the comment and disapproval which, I very strongly suspect, would ensue were a middle-aged man to be seen, in so public a place as this, to kiss the hand, be it never so beautiful, of a boy." (148)

This scene exemplifies a pattern of the novel's gender adventures, since from this encounter "Patricia" (now in quotes, a gay male) spins off to try out another distinct, yet finally inadequate, conception of his masculinity (or "her" femininity). In this unsettling of the protagonist's gender identity, Pat's story resembles Joyce's Nighttown episode in *Ulysses,* which takes Bloom through fantasized metamorphoses of himself, as he experiences the ambiguities of his gender, the multiformity of his desires.[7] And Pat's quest also recalls another fantasy-shaped underworld descent, that of Lewis Carroll's Alice. Changing sex as often as Alice changes size, Pat undergoes a series of Wonderland transformations, which can be explained as fantasies and which mainly differ from Alice's similar dream-quest for self-definition in

that Pat, unlike Alice, does not become a queen (of either sex). Trying
on numerous styles of manliness or femininity — like that of Slim, the
sleazy detective, or Oruleus, the Spenserian knight — Pat seems im-
pelled by the limits of each gender-conception and each parodied discourse to move on to another style, another conception, in a never
completed process. Hence, at the novel's close, Patricia's and Patrick's
simultaneous but contrasting deaths are depicted in adjacent columns,
a vast improvement on John Fowles's double-ending of *The French Lieu-
tenant's Woman* in that it exhibits even more clearly the ambiguous,
indeed contradictory, nature of the protagonist.

Commenting on this aspect of *In Transit*, David Lodge suggests
that contradiction is a primary structural principle of postmodern novels, which often focus on "sexually ambivalent" characters or other
central, unresolved paradoxes (229). While Lodge's perspective is illuminating, his brief analysis seems to miss a crucial effect of Brophy's
unresolved representations of gender. Rather than simply presenting a
metaphysical paradox (Pat is and is not male, is and is not female), her
parodies draw attention to the process of self-definition through language, and more specifically, through widely shared discourses. By
shifting styles with every fleeting notion of Pat's gender, the narrative
implies that Pat O'Rooley can only become "feminine" or "masculine"
through transient cultural conceptions, expressed in specific, often
contradictory, texts or discourses. The problem of gender becomes a
matter of cultural change and social (rather than metaphysical) contradiction. Brophy's androgynous protagonist then represents something
more than a Freudian-based conception, indicating the ubiquity of human sexual desire and the ability of people to identify with models of
either sex (psychoanalytic tenets which *In Transit* flaunts with much
glee).[8] Going further, much like Virginia Woolf's *Orlando*, Brophy's
novel ties notions of masculinity and femininity to specific periods and
discourses, implying that the individual's sense of his or her gender —
and of what constitutes femininity or masculinity — will alter along
with broader shifts in intellectual and literary fashion.[9]

While clearly linked to other modernist explorations of gender,
Brophy's novel also intersects with more recent feminist studies from
diverse disciplinary perspectives. Since the early seventies, anthropol-
ogists have increasingly focused on "meanings" or "interpretations" of
sexuality and gender, which they trace to highly specific factors of society and culture.[10] Linguistics further specifies the role of language in
the social formation of gender identity. Sally McConnell-Ginet explains
this thrust of linguistics: "The major challenge that feminist scholarship on language poses is to explain how there could be any interaction

at all between language and an individual's thought, on the one hand, and the social and cultural contexts in which language is used, on the other" (4). In meeting this challenge, feminist inquiry has spurred linguistics itself toward what can be seen as a Bakhtinian view of language, turning from emphasis on universal structures toward study of conflicting, and possibly liberating, language use: "Indeterminacy and multiple meanings are not the exception but important features of linguistic systems that underlie the role of language in changing society, culture, and personal consciousness" (McConnell-Ginet, 21).

The role of ideologically charged language in shaping both social institutions and individual consciousness has especially been central to feminist studies of gender influenced by French historian Michel Foucault. Rosalind Coward, for example, stresses the value of Foucault's *History of Sexuality* in showing how sexuality and identity are "discursively constructed" (281–85). Offering more resistance to Foucault (by way of Bakhtin), historian Carroll Smith-Rosenberg details the place of nineteenth-century women's writing on prostitution and gender. Foucault lies behind Smith-Rosenberg's notion that "[w]e construct our sense of self out of words" which are themselves "cultural constructs" (35). Yet she agrees with other feminist historians who "challenge Foucault's understanding of the constraining force of 'discourse'" (37). Wishing to complicate his model by accounting for women's transformations of dominant discourses, Smith-Rosenberg uses Bakhtin's idea that society's languages tend toward diversity and disruption as well as unification and hegemony. Film theorist Teresa de Lauretis makes a similar move in her assertion that "the construction of gender" takes place not only in the media, schools, and courts, but also "in avant-garde artistic practices and radical theories," including feminism (3). Hence this construction is "also affected by its deconstruction" through competing, alternative discourses (3).

Repeatedly approaching gender as "construct," "interpretation," "discourse," or "representation," contemporary feminist scholarship suggests both the constructing role and the disruptive possibilities of language. Feminist inquiry can further benefit from connections Bakhtin makes between the heterogeneity of language and specific literary forms: the novel, carnivalesque discourse, and parody. American scholars have widely admired and discussed Bakhtin's view that the novel's multiplicity of discourses and styles presents a dialogue between ways of conceiving the world, an aesthetic representation of the many-voiced, "dialogic" nature of language itself, which undermines any singular, monologic "truth."[11] "Centrifugal" dialogism opposes "centripetal" monologism in literature as well as in language, as Bakh-

tin finds the epic and poetry tending toward a restrictive, unified viewpoint while the novel heroically promotes creative diversity (*DI*, 272 –
73).

How can the novel's many-voiced dialogism contribute to the construction (and deconstruction) of gender? *In Transit* illuminates this
question by combining conceptions of language and the novel which,
like Bakhtin's, highlight the decentralizing tendencies of each. The
antisystematic nature of language especially emerges in exchanges between "Och" and a linguistics professor, who act out the "centrifugal"
and "centripetal" roles that Bakhtin ascribes to language and modern
linguistics (a recurring theme of "Discourse in the Novel" and *Marxism
and the Philosophy of Language*). While the highly rational linguist resists
radical changes, Och is essentially anarchic, as she suggests in the following comments:

> "To be absolutely frank, what I should most like to resemble is a small
> but powerful and concentrated bomb. My ambition is to explode and
> shatter the rules ... "

> "And yet for all my creative energy I feel impotent," Och sadly said.
> "I can't find anyone who will teach me the rules. So how can I make
> sure of breaking them?" (193)

The kind of bomb Och wishes to emulate does, however, explode,
starting an avalanche of printed matter from the airport bookstand,
during which Linguistics tries (with dubious success) to teach Language its rules:

> O'Rooley and the professor at once linked themselves into a protec-
> tive canopy over Och; and so it was about their two heads alone that
> a gently, scarcely more than ticklingly absurd world began to cave in.
> A soft fall of newsprint bombed them, a structural collapse not vio-
> lent but slipshod.

> The professor was most heavily struck by blunders of form, especially
> the formula "he was x, y and had a z."

> "Well, tell me the rule, then," Och implored, tugging from under-
> neath at the professor's raincoat.

> "'X, y and z,'" the professor began to explain, "can legitimately be
> thus strung together only if you suspend them from one verb ... "

> She was cut off by a large fall of things this big and persons not that
> bad ... "It should be 'so big' or 'thus big' or 'as big as this,'" she was
> panting when she was almost done for by the editorial of the *Evening
> Standard* of 6 June, 1968, which spoke of "every mass media." (208 –
> 09)

Though O'Rooley joins the professor in trying to shield language from "error," he suggests that they may be "swimming against the grain of the living language" (210). Within Pat's livingly mixed "Irishidiomism" (210), Brophy incorporates one of Bakhtin's favorite phrases, "living" language.[12] This interesection between the views and even phrases of Brophy and Bakhtin points to their mutual conception of language as a dynamic, conflictive process rather than a restrictive, internalized system. For both, the rule-bound system is overwhelmed by anarchic usages, which include (in Brophy's zany scene) William Faulkner's novels — a final onslaught of deviance which is fatal to the system-protecting linguist.

Brophy's allegory aligns the syntactically deviant, experimental novel — here represented by Faulkner — with the "erring," centrifugal impulses of language itself. It is not surprising, then, that *In Transit* renders this dynamism of language not only in the comic explosion of printed "errors," but also in its own narrative discourse. Increasingly fragmented by parodies, interpolated texts, diagrams, and "authorial" digressions, the modernistic narrative graphically conveys an "in transit" protagonist, dissolving into a series of voices and possible selves.

Yet *In Transit* also explicitly considers how fiction might contribute to this dynamic condition of both self and language. Just as Bakhtin foregrounds the novel's dialogic potential through contrasts with epic and poetry, so Brophy juxtaposes Pat O'Rooley's reader-response evaluations of several literary forms. Where the dialogic-monologic polarity serves as Bakhtin's touchstone, erotic pleasure functions in *In Transit*, as in Barthes's *Pleasure of the Text*, to assess various experiences of reading. Calling upon erotic analogues, Brophy's protagonist thus finds that the unsatisfying characterization within mystery novels leads the reader into "lust-hunting-down the characters who are increasingly not there," yielding an experience similar to that of pornography, a "literary masturbation" (44, 103).

Distinctive characterization results in Pat's greater pleasure from *Alitalia*, Brophy's parodic representative of the "furthest-fetched of all forms of fiction": "Sweet monster opera, I am in your whirlpool kiss. You have sucked me deep into your contralto throat, drawn me down into identification with your characters by your sheer liquid expressiveness of their emotions" (54). Printed in dual columns (Italian text, English translation), with "transvocites" (Frank Kermode's term for the work's male sopranos and female baritone [415]), this parody-opera stresses the implausible characters audiences can be led to identify with, the fictions of identity to which readers are drawn. Yet because of the opera's tonality (because its hero Orestes is "bereaved in tune" [57]), the narrator can be whirled and pulled to extremes, and still be

left reassured — self-assured and reinforced. *Alitalia* is not, in other
words, one of those musical compositions the narrator earlier defends:
"Not that it's unfairplay to play on our expectations of key and, instead
of playing in key, dispense with it. The object is to unstring us: one of
the psycho-tortures self-inflicted, by way of pleasure, in masophisti-
cated societies" (51). Instead of masochistic "psycho-torture," *Alitalia*
produces a self-complacent "euphoria" in Pat O'Rooley (61). Brophy's
screwy opera thus illustrates, oddly enough, Barthes's tame "text of
pleasure": "the text that contents, fills, grants euphoria; the text that
comes from culture and does not break with it, is linked to a *comforta-
ble* practice of reading" (14). By implicitly opposing her tonal opera
with music that "unstring[s] us," Brophy matches Barthes's greater ad-
miration for the "text of bliss," "the text that imposes a state of loss,
the text that discomforts . . . , unsettles the reader's historical, cultural,
psychological assumptions, the consistency of his tastes, values, memories, brings to a crisis his relation with language" (14).

  In Transit forthrightly discusses and pursues such discomforting
effects through a series of "interludes," entitled variantly "Interludi-
brium," "Interlugubre," "INTERLEWD," "INTERLOO" (64, 69, 83,
99, 112, 159, 214). In these digressions, the reader is directly addressed
by an authorial first-person narrator, who signs one such "Open-Let-
ter" (64) with the initials "(p.p.B.B.)" over "E.H.(P.)O'R.," a playful
identification of Brophy with her "HERO," as Leslie A. Dock observes,
noting the anagram formed by the protagonist's initials (304). Foregrounding techniques and ambiguities of the narrative's "machinery"
(64), these ludic addresses seek to unstring both reader and writer by
calling into question the status of each. Hence in one such interjection
(just after the onset of Pat's gender-amnesia), the authorial narrator
asserts that "relations between us are by no means so straightforward"
as some may assume:

> Suppose for the sake of argument that I am a fictitious character or
> at least one who appears so to you. I have invited from you a certain
> temporary identification. I am prepared to be taken over, possessed,
> by you. In your own eyes, I don't doubt, you are a very real part of
> the real world. But please remember that, to me it is you who are the
> fictitious — the, indeed, entirely notional — character. To be engulfed
> by you into an identification must be like being nibbled at, ticklingly,
> by a void. I have to summon my weightiest resources of gravity to
> take you seriously. I don't even know, for example, what sex you are.
> (70–71)

  Through its interludes, *In Transit* presents the novel itself as a dialogue between writer and reader (Kermode calls Brophy's work "a phe-

nomenological fantasia" [414]). Yet this dialogue takes place "inter aliens" — between mutually unknown, hence mutually "fictitious," participants. The protagonist-narrator's weird interlocution with the public address system thus becomes a model for the dialogic text, illuminating Bakhtin's ideas by dramatizing how the reader's and writer's interlocutor is always a fiction. Further, these interludes teasingly flaunt uncertainties of gender identity by reinforcing ties between "Brigid Brophy," as a fictitious character in her own novel, and Patricia-Patrick, potential selves the author explores and (in their simultaneous deaths) abandons, with the summary comment "Explicit fiction."[13] If this inconclusive ending leaves "Brigid Brophy's" gender both fictitious and unresolved, a similar effect is achieved by the authorial narrator's final address to the reader as "both of You" (230), imputing an analogous androgyny, or at least ambiguity, to the reader. This last authorial address is then followed by the word "FIN," inscribed on the fin of a fish. Foreclosing closure with a typical verbal-ideographic pun, the novel invites the reader to pursue the implications of "both of You" toward an ambiguous, unfixed gender identity, a fictitious, multiple self which each individual authors as "Brophy" has, dialogically, in response to the words of others, the discourses of society.[14]

Bakhtin emphasizes the novel's devices for representing an unsettled dialogue between ideas and voices, along with a many-voiced, "dialogic" consciousness (*PDP*, 271). *In Transit* conveys this dialogism and multiplicity by drawing on specific devices of *modernist* fiction. As the narrative disintegrates into a multitude of texts, set apart by point of view, style, spacing, typography, and inserted diagrams, the novel fully exploits possibilities of the printed word for rendering distinct languages and viewpoints. Hence, it is appropriate that, besides language, Brophy's other proclaimed "unsung, unstrung heroine" is "Miss Print" (142). Yet through the ambiguity of this pun, *In Transit* sings (or is it unsings?) both the printed text and its tendency toward error, exemplified by *L'histoire de la Langue d'Oc*, the sole novel lengthily examined within Brophy's novel. Filled with misprints and ambiguous cases of possible error (100 – 01, 141 – 43), *Oc* is made even more unstable when Pat detaches one of its pages, causing the loss of a paired page that apparently would have been critical in his/her "sexegesis" (143). The repeated direction "Déchirez" (137, 141, 143) then reiterates the entropic, tear-out status of the material text, countering any notion that written language affords an escape from transience or an exegetical key to gender.

In Transit highlights the mutability of texts, languages, conceptions of gender, and individual identities. In Brophy's allegory of interacting transients, language appears as a disruptive element, not a prison-house; rather than determining gender identity, it offers a surplus of conflicting meanings for femininity and masculinity. This conception of language — a meeting ground between Bakhtin and feminism — spawns the parodies of Brophy's novel. As they juxtapose numerous "official" and popular versions of woman and man, these parodies convey a carnivalesque stance toward the "social construction of gender," as a limited, highly conflictual, shifting process. Dramatizing how gender is socially determined and indeterminate, historically situated and fluid, *In Transit* richly illustrates the novel's power in promoting an open-ended "sexegesis."

Notes

1. Brophy's iconoclasm can be seen in *Fifty Works of English and American Literature We Could Do Without*. For evidence of her affiliations with modernist writers, see *Prancing Novelist*, a critical biography of Firbank, and *The Adventures of God in His Search for the Black Girl*, an admiring parody of Shaw in which G. B. S. himself appears.

2. See, for example, Herbert's recent *PMLA* article; Greene and Kahn's overview essay; and the feminist studies discussed later in my essay.

3. *In Transit*, 214. Subsequent references to this work will be included parenthetically in the text. Unless otherwise noted, all citations concerning Brophy refer to *In Transit* and will be indicated by page number only.

4. *Marxism and the Philosophy of Language*, 26, 39. Subsequent references to Bakhtin's works will be included parenthetically in the text, using the following abbreviations: *DI* (*The Dialogic Imagination*), *MPL* (*Marxism and the Philosophy of Language*), *PDP* (*Problems of Dostoevsky's Poetics*). I have followed current practice in attributing *Marxism and the Philosophy of Language* and *Freudianism: A Marxist Critique* to Bakhtin, even though problems with these attributions keep me aware of Bakhtin's indeterminacies (see Todorov, 6 – 11; Bruss and Titunik; and Clark and Holquist, 146 – 70).

5. *MPL*, 153. Coming even closer to Brophy's pairing of Pat and Oc, Bakhtin also writes that the "personality is generated *along with* language" (153; emphasis added). Emerson concentrates on this juncture between linguistics and psychology in Bakhtin's thought, while Morson memorably paraphrases Bakhtin's conception: "We *are* the voices that inhabit us" (232). For succinct statements concerning the "ideological" nature of consciousness, see *Freudianism*, 24; and *MPL*, 12.

6. In *Speech Genres*, Bakhtin discusses how "the unique speech experience of each individual" — by which he seems to mean inner speech, along with spoken and written discourse — "is shaped and developed in continuous and constant interaction with others' individual utterances" (89).

7. I am indebted to Kenner's reading of Joyce.

8. In an interview, Brophy suggests that behind her novel's presentation of gender lies "a simple Freudian recognition of the basic bisexuality of everybody," along with a belief in "the mental interchangeability of the sexes" (159).

9. In a passage which particularly could be applied to *In Transit*, Gilbert describes Orlando's sex-change as "simply a shift in fashion (so that Woolf associates it with shifts in literary style, shifts in historical styles, changing modalities of all kinds which remind us that, like Orlando, all is in flux ...)" (405).

10. The quoted phrases appear in overviews by Ortner and Whitehead (1) and Rosaldo and Lamphere (5), discussing this direction in anthropological studies.

11. My encapsulation of Bakhtin's theory of the novel — as presented particularly in "Discourse in the Novel" and *Problems of Dostoevsky's Poetics* — has been informed by the work of many scholars I have already cited (especially Emerson, Clark, Holquist, Yaeger, and Booth).

12. For examples of the phrase "living language" (and its variants "the living utterance," word, or speech), see *MPL*, 71, 81; *DI*, 276.

13. This reading of the novel is developed at some length by Dock, 304 – 15.

14. I am drawing on Holquist's essay, particularly pages 315 – 18, in which he presents this concept of "authoring" a self as a major implication of Bakhtin's work.

Works Cited

Bakhtin, M. M. *The Dialogic Imagination: Four Essays*. Trans. Caryl Emerson and Michael Holquist. Ed. Michael Holquist. Austin: University of Texas Press, 1981.

————. "Discourse in the Novel." In *Dialogic*, 259 – 422.

———— [V. N. Vološinov]. *Freudianism: A Marxist Critique*. Trans. I. R. Titunik. Ed. Titunik and Neal H. Bruss. New York: Academic, 1976.

————. *Marxism and the Philosophy of Language*. Trans. Ladislav Matejka and I. R. Titunik. New York: Seminar, 1973.

———— [Mikhail]. *Problems of Dostoevsky's Poetics*. Trans. and ed. Caryl Emerson. Minneapolis: University of Minnesota Press, 1984.

———— [M. M.] *Speech Genres and Other Late Essays*. Trans. Vern W. McGee. Ed. Caryl Emerson and Michael Holquist. Austin: University of Texas Press, 1986.

Barthes, Roland. *The Pleasure of the Text.* Trans. Richard Miller. New York: Hill and Wang, 1975.

———. *S/Z.* Trans. Richard Miller. New York: Hill and Wang, 1974.

Booth, Wayne C. "Freedom of Interpretation: Bakhtin and the Challenge of Feminist Criticism." *Critical Inquiry* 9 (1982): 45 – 76.

Borker, Ruth. "Anthropology: Social and Cultural Perspectives." *Women and Language in Literature and Society.* Ed. Sally McConnell-Ginet, Ruth Borker, and Nelly Furman. New York: Praeger, 1980: 26 – 44.

Brophy, Brigid. *The Adventures of God in His Search for the Black Girl.* Boston: Little, Brown, 1974.

———. "An Interview with Brigid Brophy." *Contemporary Literature* 17 (1976): 151 – 70.

———. *In Transit: An Heroi-Cyclic Novel.* London: Macdonald, 1969.

———. *Prancing Novelist: A Defense of Fiction in the Form of a Critical Biography in Praise of Ronald Firbank.* New York: Barnes & Noble, 1973.

Brophy, Brigid, Michael Levey, and Charles Osborne. *Fifty Works of English and American Literature We Could Do Without.* New York: Stein and Day, 1968.

Bruss, Neal H., and I. R. Titunik. Preface. *Freudianism: A Marxist Critique.* By V. N. Vološinov. Trans. Titunik. Ed. Titunik and Bruss. New York: Academic, 1976. vii – xiv.

Clark, Katerina, and Michael Holquist. *Mikhail Bakhtin.* Cambridge, MA: Belknap Press of Harvard University Press, 1984.

Coward, Rosalind. *Patriarchal Precedents: Sexuality and Social Relations.* London: Routledge & Kegan Paul, 1983.

De Lauretis, Teresa. *Technologies of Gender: Essays on Theory, Film, and Fiction.* Bloomington: Indiana University Press, 1987.

Dock, Leslie A. "Brigid Brophy, Artist in the Baroque." Dissertation. University of Wisconsin-Madison, 1976.

Dostoevsky, Fyodor. *Notes from Underground* and *The Grand Inquisitor.* Trans. Ralph E. Matlaw. New York: Dutton, 1960.

Emerson, Caryl. "The Outer Word and Inner Speech: Bakhtin, Vygotsky, and the Internalization of Language." *Critical Inquiry* 10 (1983): 245 – 64.

Gilbert, Sandra M. "Costumes of the Mind: Transvestism as Metaphor in Modern Literature." *Critical Inquiry* 7 (1980): 391 – 417. (Rpt. in *Writing and Sexual Difference.* Ed. Elizabeth Abel. Chicago: University of Chicago Press, 1982. 193 – 219.)

Greene, Gayle, and Coppélia Kahn. "Feminist Scholarship and the Social Construction of Woman." *Making a Difference: Feminist Literary Criticism.* Ed. Greene and Kahn. New York: Methuen, 1985.

Hayman, David. "Bakhtin's Progress." Rev. of *The Dialogic Imagination. Novel* 16 (1983): 173–77.

Herbert, T. Walter, Jr. "Nathaniel Hawthorne, Una Hawthorne, and *The Scarlet Letter:* Interactive Selfhoods and the Cultural Construction of Gender." *PMLA* 103 (1988): 285–97.

Holquist, Michael. "Answering as Authoring: Mikhail Bakhtin's Trans-Linguistics." *Critical Inquiry* 10 (1983): 307–19.

Kenner, Hugh. "Circe." *James Joyce's* Ulysses: *Critical Essays.* Ed. Clive Hart and David Hayman. Berkeley: University of California Press, 1974. 341–62.

Kermode, Frank. "Sterne Measures." Rev. of *In Transit. Listener* 25 Sept. 1969: 414–15.

Lodge, David. *The Modes of Modern Writing: Metaphor, Metonymy, and the Typology of Modern Literature.* Ithaca: Cornell University Press, 1977.

McConnell-Ginet, Sally. "Linguistics and the Feminist Challenge." *Women and Language in Literature and Society.* Ed. Sally McConnell-Ginet, Ruth Borker, and Nelly Furman. New York: Praeger, 1980. 3–25.

Morson, Gary Saul. "Who Speaks for Bakhtin?: A Dialogic Introduction." *Critical Inquiry* 10 (1983): 225–43.

Ortner, Sherry B., and Harriet Whitehead. "Introduction: Accounting for Sexual Meanings." *Sexual Meanings: The Cultural Construction of Gender and Sexuality.* Ed. Ortner and Whitehead. Cambridge, England: Cambridge University Press, 1981. 1–27.

Rosaldo, Michelle Zimbalist, and Louise Lamphere. Introduction. *Woman, Culture, and Society.* Ed. Rosaldo and Lamphere. Stanford: Stanford University Press, 1974. 1–15.

Russo, Mary. "Female Grotesques: Carnival and Theory." *Feminist Studies/Critical Studies.* Ed. Teresa de Lauretis. Theories of Contemporary Culture 8. Bloomington: Indiana University Press, 1986. 213–29.

Smith-Rosenberg, Carroll. "Writing History: Language, Class, and Gender." *Feminist Studies/Critical Studies.* Ed. Teresa de Lauretis. Theories of Contemporary Culture 8. Bloomington: Indiana University Press, 1986. 31–54.

Steiner, George. "Extraterritorial." *Tri-Quarterly* 17 (1970): 119–27. Rpt. in *Extraterritorial: Papers on Literature and the Language Revolution.* New York: Atheneum, 1971. 3–11.

Stewart, Susan. "Shouts on the Street: Bakhtin's Anti-Linguistics." *Critical Inquiry* 10 (1983): 265–81.

Todorov, Tzvetan. *Mikhail Bakhtin: The Dialogical Principle.* Trans. Wlad Godzich. Theory and History of Literature 13. Minneapolis: University of Minnesota Press, 1984.

Yaeger, Patricia. "'Because a Fire Was in My Head': Eudora Welty and the Dialogic Imagination." *PMLA* 99 (1984): 955–73.

12

Subject, Voice, and Women in Some Contemporary Black American Women's Writing[1]

Mary O'Connor

> You black, you pore, you ugly, you a woman. Goddam, he say, you nothing at all. (Walker, 187)

This nothingness — constituted by all that is the negative of society's values in race, class, and gender — may be seen as a place of origin for not only Alice Walker's *The Color Purple* but for much black feminist writing. It is a nothingness imposed from without, an entity defined by the patriarchal and white world of power and wealth. Many feminist books begin with male voices embedded in the words of whatever women narrators, characters, or authors are speaking, but this male language is also the condition against which the books fight. If all plot entails conflict, some rupture in a more-or-less stable structure, then that conflict in these books is the fight against the domination of male voices in an attempt to inundate them with viable alternatives.

I do not use the term "voices" loosely here, but as a technical term to refer to language as it exists in a historical context. The linguistic theories of Mikhail Bakhtin are helpful for a feminist analysis of literature precisely because they insist on the historical nature of utterances rather than the mechanical definitions of the structuralist's *langue*. Despite Bakhtin's own limitations in considering gender or race in his discussion of voices, his statements such as "I hear *voices* in everything and the dialogic relationships between them" stand against any formalist a-historical analysis of literature (Shukman, 4). The works of the Bakhtin circle — Vološinov's *Marxism and the Philosophy of Language*, Bakhtin and Medvedev's *The Formal Method in Literary Scholarship*, Bakhtin's *Problems of Dostoevsky's Poetics* and the essays in *The Dialogic Imagination* — have consistently argued for an understanding of the social context of discourse in any linguistic or literary analysis. Feminist critics have turned to the Bakhtin circle for just this reason: "the dialogic, because of its asystemic nature and its insistence on the social significance of discourse, is a term that embraces both a comparative and an ideological interrogation of literary practices" (Herrmann, 4).[2]

An argument might be made that many contemporary books written by black women are so compelling to women readers because they return us to the bourgeois illusion that art can be a place of truth, some metaphysical space of visions and retreat. This feeling of solidarity eases the pain, offering some compensatory world of connectedness. Many of the writers even believe in the ultimate truth of a spiritual life, if not filled with a traditional male God, at least with the spirits of their grandmothers. Both connectedness and spiritual life can be seen as modes of revolution when placed in the context of a life of isolation and physical brutality. Books such as Alice Walker's *The Color Purple*, Gloria Naylor's *The Women of Brewster Place*, and Ntozake Shange's *for colored girls who have considered suicide/when the rainbow is enuf*, work through and towards moments of connectedness, of love between women, but they do so not as some utopian world of escape. I would rather argue, as Susan Willis has done, that utopian space can offer revolutionary possibilities for change ("Eruptions," 279 – 80). Walker's, Naylor's, and Shange's texts figure women whose "stories" are "ferret[ed] out," to use Shange's expression, from the silence of their burrows until the many voices that have been producing these women are sung and debated. There is always a composite voice, whether it is the seven women in Shange who gather their "half-notes scattered/without rhythm," or Naylor's sequence of women living in the tenements of Brewster Place telling their stories. In every case the voices struggle with names and stereotyping, with silence and screams.[3]

Women's literature has been motivated by the imperative to know who we are and how to act on that knowledge, but our liberation comes belatedly as we discover that the "wholeness" of men is indeed a fabrication, constructed by the ideologies or superstructure of a certain economic base. Freedom in this poststructuralist world must come from analyzing and subverting all constructed identities, especially those which place us in an exploited position. Women must still deconstruct the patriarchal image of ourselves as silent, submissive, and an object of pleasure or possession, but problems arise when we start to construct our own identity.

These issues have been debated in feminist literary theory — whether it is our job to establish a new identity, unified and strong,

based on personal experience that is not dependent on male dominance, or to forego this Romantic illusion and look for an identity that
is based on the fluid process of history. Cora Kaplan

> would rather see subjectivity as always in process and contradiction,
> even female subjectivity, structured, divided and denigrated through
> the matrices of sexual difference. I see this understanding as part of
> a more optimistic political scenario than the ones I have been part of,
> one that can and ought to lead to a politics which will no longer over-
> value control, rationality and individual power, and which, instead,
> tries to understand human desire, struggle and agency as they are
> mobilized through a more complicated, less finished and less heroic
> psychic schema (181).

With this premise in mind I have turned, in part, to the theories
of Bakhtin for a methodological context. His position, it may be argued, is a critique of the transcendental subject, offering in its place a
theory of co-existent subject positions which we take up in relation to
the various discourses that are active in our world. His *dialogism,* which
is "a struggle among socio-linguistic points of view, not an intra-lan-
guage struggle between individual will or logical contradictions" (*DI,*
273), takes into account the various determining and producing historical factors in our lives and at the same time allows for the idea of an
active response on the part of the subject to these various discourses
and other subject positions. Thus, his theories do away with the need
for the cogito or unified self which we have come to see as an illusory
construct. They allow for a model of intersecting ideologies, in other
words, a connection with history in society, as well as a model of con-
necting with others. Finally, they allow for process and change. This
last category is supported by his theory of the carnivalesque where
cultural productions, whether a festival in the street or a literary text,
can present us with an image of the overthrow of authority.

It might be fruitful to compare, for instance, Gloria Naylor's resolution in *The Women of Brewster Place* to what Susan Willis sees as the
"eruptions of funk" in the work of Toni Morrison, eruptions that produce alternative social worlds, often a household of three women
(278). Naylor is in no way sentimental about the reality of communities, male or female. In many ways Willis's arguments are similar to
those of Bakhtin, as the lower bodily stratum or the grotesque in
Bakhtin's terms may be translated into eruptions of funk. In his theory as well as in that of Willis's analyses of Morrison, the evocations of
the grotesque, the portrayal of otherness, can produce a moment of
utopian vision which relativizes the authoritative norm and thus produces the possibility of change.

The more voices that are ferreted out, the more discourses that a woman can find herself an intersection of, the freer she is from one dominating voice, from one stereotypical and sexist position. The male voices are heard, but contended, in these books. Although consciousness may seem to be the ultimate goal — one single definition of self by which to live — this self must be one in constant transition because it is always in dialogue with other personalities who represent other social forces. The self produced for the moment must necessarily redo itself in its next encounter. In the moment of so-called knowing itself in language, it must revise that knowledge because one's language is always handed down and always addressed to another. "The word in written discourse," as Díaz-Diocaretz has argued, "is part of an ideological argument, in a constant process of transferral, since the word does not forget where it has been and can never wholly free itself from the context of which it has been a part" ("Sieving," 120, on Bakhtin, *Dostoevsky,* 167). Depending on the structure and ethos of the text, the conclusion or closure will be more or less ironic, more or less utopian. Even if, as in *The Color Purple,* the fairy-tale structure (Lupton, 409) risks the bathos of a happy-ever-after ending, we are made aware of the struggle throughout the novel by the battle of words with words.[4]

The struggle may be seen in relation to what Showalter and others have called the "poetics of the Other" (Showalter, 184) or what Wayne Booth has called the double-voiced discourse of feminist texts (Booth, 45 – 76). But it must also be seen in relation to the sense of double-voicedness in black culture theorized as early as 1903 in W. E. B. DuBois's *Souls of Black Folk:*

> After the Egyptian and Indian, the Greek and Roman, the Teuton and Mongolian, the Negro is a sort of seventh son, born with a veil, and gifted with second-sight in this American world, — a world which yields him no true self-consciousness, but only lets him see himself through the revelation of the other world. It is a peculiar sensation, this double-consciousness, this sense of always looking at one's self through the eyes of others, of measuring one's soul by the tape of a world that looks on in amused contempt and pity. One ever feels his two-ness, — an American, a Negro; two souls, two thoughts, two unreconciled strivings; two warring ideals in one dark body, whose dogged strength alone keeps it from being torn asunder. (3)

With variations, this "double-consciousness appears again in Ralph Ellison's "double-vision" (132) and, significantly, in Henry Louis Gates, Jr.'s "two-toned discourse," inspired in part by Bakhtinian theory ("Criticism," 4; *Signifying,* 51).

My use of Bakhtin's dialogism might best be illustrated by an example he gives in "Discourse in the Novel" of one whose language is for the most part not dialogized: the peasant. In speaking of the process by which a peasant might develop a dialogic awareness of language (with apologies for a simplification of the real peasant's life), he emphasizes the process of confrontation and relativization of any given set of languages. His theory of dialogism and the example of the peasant offer possibilities for a feminist analysis of literary texts:

> Thus an illiterate peasant, miles away from any urban center, naively immersed in an unmoving and for him unshakable everyday world, nevertheless lived in several language systems: he prayed to God in one language (Church Slavonic), sang songs in another, spoke to his family in a third and, when he began to dictate petitions to the local authorities through a scribe, he tried speaking yet a fourth language (the official-literate language, "paper" language). All these are *different languages*, even from the point of view of abstract socio-dialectological markers. But these languages were not dialogically coordinated in the linguistic consciousness of the peasant; he passed from one to the other without thinking, automatically: each was indisputably in its own place, and the place of each was indisputable. He was not yet able to regard one language (and the verbal world corresponding to it) through the eyes of another language (that is, the language of everyday life and the everyday world with the language of prayer or song, or vice versa).
>
> As soon as a critical interanimation of languages began to occur in the consciousness of our peasant, as soon as it became clear that these were not only various different languages but even internally variegated languages, that the ideological systems and approaches to the world that were indissolubly connected with these languages contradicted each other and in no way could live in peace and quiet with one another — then the inviolability and predetermined quality of these languages came to an end, and the necessity of actively choosing one's orientation among them began. (*DI*, 295–6)

Walker's *The Color Purple* could well be plotted by the heroine's growing awareness of the languages that surround her. My feminist analysis is interested in the voices that are thereby made relative and thus changeable and those that help to initiate change and in what direction. Walker is able to convey this juxtaposition and evaluation of languages in an early scene where Celie's stepfather is trying to marry her off. Celie recounts the scene, since the book is made up of a series of letters written by her to God or to her sister Nettie, and letters from Nettie to Celie.

Well, He say, real slow, I can't let you have Nettie ... But I can let you
have Celie ... She ain't fresh tho, but I spect you know that. She
spoiled. Twice. But you don't need a fresh woman no how. I got a
fresh one in there myself and she sick all the time. He spit, over the
railing. The children git on her nerve, she not much of a cook. And
she big already.

Mr. — he don't say nothing. I stop crying I'm so surprise.

She ugly. He say. But she ain't no stranger to hard work. And she
clean. And God done fixed her. You can do everything just like you
want to and she ain't gonna make you feed it or clothe it.

Mr. — still don't say nothing. I take out the picture of Shug Avery. I
look into her eyes. Her eyes say Yeah, it *bees* that way sometime.

Fact is, he say, I got to git rid of her. She too old to be living here at
home. And she a bad influence on my other girls. She'd come with
her own linen. She can take that cow she raise down there back of the
crib. But Nettie you flat out can't have. Not now. Not never.

Mr. — finally speak. Clearing his throat. I ain't never really look at
that one, he say.

Well, next time you come you can look at her. She ugly. Don't even
look like she kin to Nettie. But she'll make the better wife. She ain't
smart either, and I'll just be fair, you have to watch her or she'll give
away everything you own. But she can work like a man.

Mr. — say How old she is?

He say, She near twenty. And another thing — she tell lies. (17 – 18)

Celie's voice would seem to be absent from this account of the
male voices around her. But at two points we find an intersection of
other positions: Celie's "I stop crying. I'm so surprise" and Shug
Avery's "Yeah, it *bees* that way some time." On the one hand, Celie's
surprise signals the reader to shift perspective, to stand outside what is
being said. On the other hand, Shug's "it *bees* that way," a quotation
that Celie imagines the face on a photograph to be saying, stands with
Celie, both enlightening her as to the ways of the world — the world
that she is still learning about and experiencing in all its horrors — and
at the same time standing with her as some form of reassurance: this
is the way the world is and I'm still here to talk about it. The voice is
both specifically Shug Avery's — the woman who will provide Celie with
an emancipatory discourse — and, more generally, the discourse of a
popular tradition — a communal voice of black women.[5] As readers,
we are meant to choose and assess with Celie.

Henry Louis Gates, in his revealing analysis of *The Color Purple*, points out that, in fact, the only voice we hear is Celie's own, since all is written in the epistolary form: "There is no true mimesis . . . , only diegesis . . . the opposition between them has collapsed" (*Signifying*, 249). I want to argue that even within the diegetic mode of letter writing, the other person's voice is heard either as reported speech or as dialogized borrowed speech. What is remarkable in *The Color Purple* is this movement from a juxtaposition of languages to a dialogized evaluation of them.

The at-first seemingly monological appropriation of the male discourse about women is thus slowly undermined by the text so that when Albert (the Mr. — , of this quotation, who does eventually marry Celie) later tells her she is nothing but "pore, black and a woman," she is able to respond, taking his word and supplementing them, transforming them into her own affirmation:

> I'm pore, I'm black, I may be ugly and can't cook, a voice say to everything listening. *But I'm here.*
>
> Amen, say Shug. Amen, amen. (187, my emphasis)

The nothing, then, is transformed and defeated by existence, by *I'm here*, and by her saying, *"I'm here."*[6] I am, therefore I am not nothing, or *not* an object to be bartered, possessed, exploited, and abused. The fact of her presence resists formulations and implies a reality beyond the labels of one man's discourse. A further discourse, that of Shug's "amen" repeated three times, echoes Celie's claim, but not entirely in a monological way. The fact of another's speech affirms the existence of two subjects. As Herrmann argues, Bakhtin's dialogic allows for "the recognition of the other not as object but as 'an/other' subject" (6). Furthermore, the fact of Celie's *saying* "I'm here" confirms her position as a subject in discourse, fully acknowledged and active in dialogic relation to others. I am, therefore I speak, and you better listen, listen to all my voices, all the other voices I've found to contradict you with. In fact, Albert has tried to reduce her to nothing because she has used language against him by cursing him: "You can't curse nobody . . . you nothing at all" (187).

The beginning of the novel establishes the link between existence, speech, and freedom. The novel opens with Alphonso (the stepfather)'s exhortation to Celie — his prohibition quoted in italics which stands on its own before Celie's first letter. It is the only sentence in this epistolary novel outside the letter form:

You better not tell nobody but God. It'd kill your mammy. (11)

Once again male speech is at the origins of Celie's speech — the origin
of the novel. Her body, her actions, the existence of the child inside
her, are at this point to be denied. If spoken, they are a threat to the
existence of someone Celie loves, her mammy. Speaking would be an
act of murder, a matricide. But ironically enough, Alphonso gives her
one way out: "don't tell nobody *but God*" (my italics) — perhaps the
result of some dialogical residue of his Christian culture. Celie picks
up the idea, and although she is too ashamed of her life to talk to God,
to face that person, she can, through the mediation of pen and paper,
write to God. And so her words begin with "Dear God."

Celie has more than a trace of her white Christian heritage in her
speech. Her first letter continues, "I am fourteen years old. ~~I am~~ I have
always been a good girl. Maybe you can give me a sign letting me know
what is happening to me" (11). She presents her qualifications — her
age and the fact that she has always been a "good girl," suggesting she
is talking to an ideal authority by whose rules she has lived her life: in
other words, to the white male God. But the "I am" is ironically
crossed out, and instead we get a story: "Last spring after little Lucious
come ... " So, with existence denied, she can still turn to writing, to
her letters, and through them she will eventually reclaim her "I am."
Narrative, thus, is produced by the displaced, repressed, or absent
being. As Gates has argued, Celie from "an erased presence ... writes
herself into being" (*Signifying*, 243).

The male voices that forbid her to speak and demand that she be
a good girl will be overthrown. The ideal male authority — the white
God himself — will be transformed through counter-voices into a multiplicity of voices. Once Celie has worked her way toward some awareness of her exploitation, she is able to say to her friend Shug:

What God do for me? I ast.

She say, Celie! Like she shock. He gave you life, good health, and a
good woman that loves you to death.

Yeah, I say, and he give me a lynched daddy, a crazy mama, a lowdown dog of a step pa and a sister I probably won't ever see again.
Anyhow, I say, the God I been praying and writing to is a man. And
act just like all the other mens I know. Trifling, forgitful and
lowdown.

She say, Miss Celie, You better hush. God might hear you.

> Let 'im hear me, I say. If he ever listened to poor colored women the world would be a different place, I can tell you. ... [He] just sit up there glorying in being deaf, I reckon. (175–6)

Here God himself is monological—deaf to the languages of "poor colored women." Ultimately the other voices will drown out the monological male voice of God until God is transformed into "everything that is or ever was or will be." Celie writes:

> Still, it is like Shug say, You have to git man off your eyeball, before you can see anything a'tall.

> Man corrupt everything, say Shug. He on you box of grits, in you head, and all over the radio. He try to make you think he everywhere. Soon as you think he everywhere, you think he God. But he ain't. Whenever you trying to pray, and man plop himself on the other end of it, tell him to git lost, say Shug. Conjure up flowers, wind, water, a big rock. (179)

Celie's sister Nettie on the other side of the Atlantic, in her highly ambiguous role as a black Christian missionary doing the work of white people among the black tribes of Africa, has to work through a similar displacement especially of a white European God. When she tries to mix the two discourses—black and white, European and African—she inevitably is forced to give up one, or both, be it the photographs of Livingston, Stanley or Christ, or the African tribe's scarification of faces, or the Olinka men who begin to sound like "Pa back home."

If Celie starts her letters in silence, in silent confessions to a white male God because he's the only one she, at this point in time, has to take "along" (26), she eventually shifts her addressee to Nettie, her lost sister, and it might be argued that the lost sister, the other woman, is the only true receiver of Celie's tale. "I don't even look at mens" writes Celie. "I look at women, tho, cause I'm not scared of them" (15). She escapes the patriarchal voice dominating her by means of the voices of other women and the connection she feels with these women. An alternative to her exploitation by men does show up within the first few pages of the novel—the photograph of Shug Avery, the beautiful cabaret singer and Albert's lover. The photograph introduces Celie to another world of wealth (furs and motorcars) and triumph (Shug stands with her foot on someone else's car), while still maintaining an element of Celie's own experience (Shug's eyes are sad). Celie is immediately riveted into silent action:

> An now when I dream, I dream of Shug Avery. She be dress to kill,
> whirling and laughing. (16)

The dream eventually turns into reality as Shug becomes her mentor
and her lover. From Shug, Celie learns to stand up and fight, to enjoy
her body, to be economically self-sufficient, and to create her gender-
free God.

The connection with women, even to the extent of sexual love between them, has a privileged place in the novel. It weaves through the
book in ascending power as the domination of men over Celie dimin-
ishes, and as Celie's own self-awareness and sense of identity grow. One
climactic moment occurs when Celie tells Albert she's leaving him:

> What will people say, you running off to Memphis like you don't have
> a house to look after?
>
> Shug say, Albert. Try to think like you got some sense. Why any
> woman give a shit what people think is a mystery to me.
>
> Well, say Grady, trying to bring light. A woman can't git a man if
> peoples talk.
>
> Shug look at me and us giggle. Then us laugh sure nuff. Then
> Squeak start to laugh. Then Sofia. All us laugh and laugh.
>
> Shug say, Ain't they something? Us say um *hum,* and slap the table,
> wipe the water from our eyes. (182)

The carnivalesque joke here is that Celie has found emotional and sexual satisfaction beyond the world of men. The last thing she wants is to
"git a man."

Celie will also achieve economic self-sufficiency. Her designing
and sewing lead her into both the world of the artist and the world of
economic production. It has been argued that Walker risks "mimicking
the values of the dominant [capitalist] culture" (Lupton, 414); rather,
she is trying to produce a combination of artist creation and cottage
industry. The extent of her enterprise so far includes two women who
work and talk with her. One of the most moving passages in the book
describes Celie's designing of pants for various characters — she designs each pair of pants for a specific individual to serve her or his
work in life:

> I start to make pants for Jack. They have to be camel. And soft and
> strong. And they have to have big pockets so he can keep a lot of
> children's things. Marbles and string and pennies and rocks. And

they have to be washable and they have to fit closer round the leg than Shug's so he can run if he need to snatch a child out of the way of something. And they have to be something he can lay back in when he hold Odessa in front of the fire. (191–2)

The pleasure the reader derives here is from Celie's success, but also her inventiveness, her clear unchecked creativity which is not self-centered but directed outward.

Celie's last letter is addressed to "Dear God. Dear stars, dear trees, dear sky, dear peoples. Dear Everything. Dear God" (249). With Nettie's return, no more letters are necessary. It is implied that speech will replace writing as the two sisters will be able to commune, to share their "stories" face to face as they live them. The ending finally defeats narration because it solves the problem of silence, the "Don't tell nobody" of the opening. There is an attempt to establish a de-gendered community centered around Celie and her sister. The villain step-pa is killed off (although he only dies in his sleep); Albert is "converted" and can be seen sitting on the porch sewing with Celie, the two of them smoking their pipes and Albert listening to Celie's tales, finding her such good company; Adam, Celie's son, has scarred his face to match his Olinka bride's; some of the women wear pants; and some of the men wear dresses (even though these are called robes); the family structure, which up till now had proven disastrous for all the characters, is now reconstituted in this new household of husband and wife, lesbian lovers, adulterous lovers, and grown children who now have birth mother, adoptive father, aunt and stepmother all under the same roof. The book ends with a Fourth of July party, not celebrating the birth of a Nation, but the freedom of its slaves:

White people busy celebrating they independence from England July 4th ... so most black folks don't have to work. Us can spend the day celebrating each other. (250)

The racist problems are not solved in this book, although there is a suggestion that Sophia has established something with her former white ward. The socio-economic world outside this small black community of friends and relatives has not changed except that a few black women now have a house, work, love, and an income. But within the community all differences have been dispersed in a fairy-tale ending. We have indeed moved beyond Bakhtin's world of dialogism into his world of the community, an ideal social state where "aggressive intercutting of discourses" is no longer necessary (Godzich, Oct. 1).

At the end of *The Women of Brewster Place,* Naylor brings women together cooking and partying, but her resolution comes within the very real confines of a racist, sexist, and class-conscious society. The question here is how to survive. The party is a block party, a first step towards establishing this tenement community and pressuring the landlord for better living conditions. Nevertheless, the narrator's conclusion retains some irony: the tenements deteriorate and the inhabitants move on to yet another Brewster Place — even if it is not called that — to encounter more of the same. Again the economic world of production and exploitation is not changed. The novel at its end only claims to have given us the existence and persistence of these women, the "I'm here" of *The Color Purple.* However, empowerment has come to the novel's characters through solidarity and the telling of their tales. The author stands behind the "colored daughters" who will dream on, who survive, now and with the addition of this book, not always in silence. Once again, the key to persistence comes from a kind of narrative, this time figured in the novel as dreaming. The dreams, however, are not intimations of a transcendent presence as much as they are modes of producing a self that is not oppressed.

The women are framed by the street itself, its history of corruption and decay. Within this context they struggle to survive as human entities, as something more than biological specimens of a decaying world. When, in Mattie Michael's last dream, the women tear the brick wall down at the end of Brewster Place, that is, demolish the deterministic structure that has entombed them in a naturalist's world of exploitation, poverty and brutality, we know this action is a metaphor for breaking out of that deterministic world. The women, working on an entirely unconscious and collective impulse, start to throw the bricks out into the avenue. The carnivalesque scene of chairs and barbecues, umbrellas and spiked high heels going at the wall and being hurled at the windows of the station wagons and Datsuns outside, expresses the violence and at the same time the confines of these women's experience. The violence that has been done to them by the "normal" bourgeois world of Datsuns (those people who have profitted by the exclusion, the blocking out of view, of Brewster Place from the main avenue) is now literally thrown back at them in this parody of a revolution. This is not a travesty; the women are in no way demeaned by their activity. Rather, their material conditions erupt out of silence and are made known. Their contrast with the norm allows for a momentary vision of change.

Nevertheless, despite the collectivity and the carnival spirit, the scene does not ultimately undo the memory of staring into these same bricks with Lorraine while she goes insane during her rape one story earlier. The violence lingers as both a violence done to these women and one that necessarily erupts in reaction. To claim their own, to define themselves as something other than the discourse imposed on them by patriarchy or capitalism, they must rally their high heels and their barbecues in violent combat. Their actions as actual political revolution must be seen on one level as impotent gestures — there is no takeover of municipal power. Like the medieval carnivals that inspired Bakhtin's theories, this revolutionary gesture is only temporary and the old order will be resumed — a new Brewster Place will be built and the women will continue to suffer. But the vision has taken place and indeed has threatened those outsiders, figured in the taxi driver who races away from the "riot in this street" (187).

There is another moment earlier in the novel which does perhaps balance the horror of Lorraine's rape. Ciel, a young woman, has lost both her children, one through an abortion her husband forced her to have, the other through an accident while her husband tells her in another room that he is leaving her. Ciel goes dead; she cannot mourn and is killing herself by not eating:

> Mattie stood in the doorway, and an involuntary shudder went through her when she saw Ciel's eyes. Dear God, she thought, she's dying, and right in front of our faces.
>
> "Merciful Father, no!" she bellowed. There was no prayer, no bended knee or sackcloth supplication in those words, but a blasphemous fireball that shot forth and went smashing against the gates of heaven, raging and kicking, demanding to be heard.
>
> "No! No! No!" Like a black Brahman cow, desperate to protect her young, she surged into the room, pushing the neighbor woman and the others out of her way. She approached the bed with her lips clamped shut in such force that the muscles in her jaw and the back of her neck began to ache.
>
> She sat on the edge of the bed and enfolded the tissue-thin body in her huge ebony arms. And she rocked. Ciel's body was so hot it burned Mattie when she first touched her, but she held on and rocked. Back and forth, back and forth — she had Ciel so tightly she could feel her young breast flatten against the buttons of her dress. The black mammoth gripped so firmly that the slightest increase of pressure would have cracked the girl's spine. But she rocked.
>
> And somewhere from the bowels of her being came a moan from Ciel, so high at first it couldn't be heard by anyone there, but the yard dogs began an unholy howling. And Mattie rocked. And then,

> agonizingly slow, it broke its way through the parched lips in a spa-
> ghetti-thin column of air that could be faintly heard in the frozen
> room.
>
> Ciel moaned. Mattie rocked. Propelled by the sound, Mattie rocked
> her out of that bed, out of that room, into a blue vastness just under-
> neath the sun and above time. She rocked her over Aegean seas so
> clean they shone like crystal, so clear the fresh blood of sacrificed
> babies torn from their mother's arms and given to Neptune could be
> seen like pink froth on the water. She rocked her on and on, past
> Dachau, where soul-gutted Jewish mothers swept their children's en-
> trails off laboratory floors. They flew past the spilled brains of Sene-
> galese infants whose mothers had dashed them on the wooden sides
> of slave ships. And she rocked on. (102 – 103)

The chapter continues on for two more pages until finally Ciel can cry
and fall asleep. The love, bodily warmth, and blasphemous fireball of
the older woman eventually exorcize the deadness and the silence. Mattie's "No! No! No!", like Shug Avery's "Amen, Amen, Amen," affirms
existence rejecting in its repetitions the voices that stand against it.
The "blasphemous fireball" exorcises the silence until an inaudible
moan is eeked out.

The book leaves us finally with these connected and now vocal
colored daughters. The author can write that the street only "dies
when the odors of hope, despair, lust, and caring are wiped out by the
seasonal winds ... " (192). Instead of the death of the street, the last
line of the book is "So Brewster Place still waits to die." The book ends
with the ongoing life of the women despite the fact they have all been
evicted:

> But the colored daughters of Brewster, spread over the canvas of
> time, still wake up with their dreams misted on the edge of a yawn.
> They get up and pin those dreams to wet laundry hung out to dry,
> they're mixed with a pinch of salt and thrown into pots of soup, and
> they're diapered around babies. They ebb and flow, ebb and flow, but
> never disappear. (192)

As I have noted, these dreams play an important role in the novel. As
figures of desire they embody all that is not defined by discourse directed against them and as such put that discourse into question. From
the acknowledgements and the epigraph through each story a dream
is figured right up to the final revolution in Mattie's dream. With the
end of that chapter, Etta wakes up Mattie: "Woman, you still in bed?
Don't you know what day it is? We're gonna have a party" (189).

Ntozake Shange, in her preface to *for colored girls who have considered suicide,* also displaces her authority to speak of the play's origins in a women's group, in performance, and in dance workshops. She describes the evolution of the work in terms of an interplay between actors and audience, or between the different actors, between writers and environment. The thrust of the book was to clarify "our lives — & the lives of our mothers, daughters, & grandmothers — as women" (xiv), but the process is achieved through a presentation and intersection of various different voices — a process, in other words, essentially dialogical, as the play presents us with seven different women and their stories. The goal is not to establish all women as equal or as identical, but to present the uniqueness and, as in *The Color Purple* and *Brewster Place,* the connectedness of women. The play opens with the women running in from separate exits, freezing in postures of distress. When one woman tries to call to the others there is no response: they are silent, separate, and in pain. The opening poem, "dark phrases of womanhood," presents the problem to be solved by the play. As yet, woman is only "half-notes scattered/without rhythm," and this is partly because she has the prohibition, as in *The Color Purple,* not to speak: "don't tell nobody don't tell a soul/she's dancin on beer cans & shingles" (1–2). This separateness continues as some women reject others, parodying one dancing, or refusing to dance, but gradually as the stories unfold, as difference and similarity are established, they begin to dance together until the end when they can "enter into a closed tight circle" (67).

The ending of *for colored girls* comes close to a utopian world of love and connectedness as the seven women sing their "song of joy": "i found god in myself/& i loved her," but the last line with its present progressive tense ("& this is for colored girls who have considered suicide/but *are movin* to the ends of their own rainbows" [my italics]) suggests that the struggle continues well after the dance. As the title implies, the play is made up of two impulses: one toward suicide and the other toward hope. By the end of the play women have sung the song of their body, dancing, poetry and love of women, but the various stories, including Beau Willie's story where a mad husband drops his two children from the fifth-story window, leave us with no doubt that the inevitable confrontation with despair will continue. The voices speak back to the numerable irresponsible lovers, rapists, or bearers of privilege and accepted morality, but we are reminded of fatal consequences of silence in the abortion poem or most dramatically when Crystal's lack of voice takes her children from her:

> i stood by beau in the window/with naomi reachin for me/& kwame
> screamin mommy mommy from the fifth story/but i cd only whisper/
> & he dropped em. (63)

This story calls for a period of mourning, a process of soothing and
healing perhaps comparable to Mattie's rocking of Ciel, and indeed
the play ends with a communal song that takes the women up through
the pain.

In another context, the poem called "toussaint," while being a
story of a young black girl who in 1955 was forced to attend integrated
schools and live in an integrated neighborhood, is also about history
and the position of the subject in it. The child's sense of reality is
ironically first evoked when she *reads* about Toussaint L'Ouverture.
Her voice of rebellion must pass through her imaginary historical
friend, while her identity is only fully articulated when she finds her
voice and place in history. At each stage the historical context is crucial:
the time of the revolutionary in Haiti and the time of the young girl in
America. While Toussaint is one who "didnt low no white man to tell
him nothin/no napolean/not maximillien/not robespierre" (27), the
young girl has to figure out "how to remove white girls from my hop-
scotch games/& etc ... 1955 was not a good year for lil blk girls"
(28–9).

Having found a young black boy called Toussaint Jones who
"waznt too different/from" the slave hero, she moves into her own historical moment fully conscious of her position and her desire to change
it:

> toussaint jones waz awright wit me
> no tellin what all spirits we cd move
> down by the river
> st. louis 1955 (32)

The poem ends with this signature of place and date.

What I have been calling a play is actually a series of poems,
which in turn are stories, memoirs, or exhortations. Within these
stories are multiple voices heard and debated. Even the dances that
punctuate the stories offer other voices which have helped to constitute
the subjects of these poems, songs by Martha and the Vandellas or the
Dells. Shange is able to introduce the various voices without appropriating them all, without making them all hers.

Without having ferreted out all the voices, male and female, for
these works, the project is remarkably clear. The Bakhtinian dialogism

is not a strict binary opposition between, for instance, the marginal woman's voice and the central dominant male voice. It is rather, in these books, the exploration and activating of the unvoiced exiled world of women — that other place in all its variety. It defines and redefines the subject with multiple heroines, multiple stories, themselves in constant struggle to ferret out the voices of the past and present, be it Martha and the Vandellas, Toussaint l'Ouverture, or the spirits of their grandmothers. If there is any trace of idealism left, I would say it is in the persistent call for love between women, a love seen as a healing of the wounds created in our patriarchal world. Perhaps this is the new ethos of our age — a carnivalesque one in as much as the fact that this love has been forbidden by the male authority and is seen as a premise for changing the world, for turning it upside down.

Notes

1. An original version of this paper, entitled "Feminist Dialogics and Contemporary Black American Women Writers," was read at the International Bakhtin Conference, Hebrew University of Jerusalem, 15 June 1987.

2. See also Bauer, Carby [*Reconstructing*], Díaz-Diocaretz, Finke, and Yaeger.

3. For a broader discussion of the struggle with naming, see Benston, 151 – 72.

4. In revising this paper, I have had the benefit of King-Kok Cheung's insights into *The Color Purple:* "Despite the excruciating process of change [Celie has] endured," she argues, the "text conveys a sense of triumph that is due . . . less to the happy ending itself than to the way the final stage is negotiated, to the means by which a voice truly one's own is fostered" (172). Although I would take issue with the voice that "is truly one's own," Cheung's emphasis on the process of negotiating success is crucial.

5. See Hazel V. Carby's analysis of the lyrics of Afro-American women's blues.

6. Cheung makes a similar point (168).

Works Cited

Bakhtin, Mikhail. *The Dialogic Imagination: Four Essays.* Ed. Michael Holquist. Trans. Caryl Emerson and Michael Holquist. Austin: Texas University Press, 1981.

————. *Esthétique de la création verbale.* Trans. Alfreda Aucouturier. Paris: Gallimard, 1984.

————. *Rabelais and his World.* Trans. H. Iswolsky. Cambridge, Mass.: MIT Press, 1968.

Bakhtin, Mikhail and P. N. Medvedev. *The Formal Method in Literary Scholarship: A Critical Introduction to Sociological Poetics.* Trans. Albert J. Wehrle. 1978; Cambridge, Mass.: Harvard University Press, 1985.

Bauer, Dale. *Feminist Dialogics: A Theory of Failed Community.* Albany, NY: State University of New York Press, 1988.

Benston, Kimberly W. "I Yam What I Am: The Topos of (Un)naming in Afro-American Literature." In *Black Literature and Literary Theory.* Ed. Henry Louis Gates, Jr. New York: Methuen, 1984. 151–72.

Booth, Wayne C. "Freedom of Interpretation: Bakhtin and the Challenge of Feminist Criticism." *Critical Inquiry* 9 (1982): 45–76.

Carby, Hazel V. "It Jus Be's Dat Way Sometime: The Sexual Politics of Women's Blues." *Radical America* 20 (1986): 9–22.

————. *Reconstructing Womanhood: The Emergence of the Afro-American Woman Novelist.* New York: Oxford University Press, 1987.

Cheung, King-Kok. "'Don't Tell': Imposed Silences in *The Color Purple* and *The Woman Warrior.*" *PMLA* 103 (1988): 162–74.

Díaz-Diocaretz, Myriam. "Black North American Women Poets in the Semiotics of Culture." In *Women, Feminist Identity and Society in the 1980s.* Ed. M. Díaz-Diocaretz and I. M. Zaval. Amsterdam: John Benjamins, 1985, 37–60.

————. "Sieving the Matriheritage of the Sociotext." In *The Difference Within: Feminism and Critical Theory.* Ed. Elizabeth Meese and Alice Parker. Amsterdam: John Benjamins, 1988.

DuBois, W. E. B. *The Souls of Black Folk: Essays and Sketches.* Chicago: A. C. McClurg, 1918.

Ellison, Ralph. *Shadow and Act.* New York: Random House, 1964.

Finke, Laurie. "The Rhetoric of Marginality: Why I Do Feminist Theory." *Tulsa Studies in Women's Literature* 5 (1986): 251–72.

Gates, Henry Louis, Jr. "Criticism in the Jungle." In his *Black Literature and Literary Theory.* New York: Methuen, 1984. 1–24.

————. *The Signifying Monkey: A Theory of Afro-American Literary Criticism.* New York: Oxford University Press, 1988.

Godzich, Wlad. Seminar. Comparative Literature 1400L: The Critical Theory of Bakhtin and his Circle. 1987–88. University of Toronto.

Herrmann, Anne. *The Dialogic and Difference: "An/Other Woman" in Virginia Woolf and Christa Wolf.* New York: Columbia University Press, 1989.

Kaplan, Cora. "Speaking/Writing/Feminism. In *On Gender and Writing.* Ed. Michelene Wandor. London: Routledge and Kegan Paul, 1983. Rpt. in *Feminist Literary Theory: A Reader.* Ed. Mary Eagleton. Oxford: Basil Blackwell, 1986.

Lupton, Mary Jane. "Clothes and Closure in Three Novels by Black Women." *Black American Literature Forum* 20 (1986): 409–21.

Naylor, Gloria. *The Women of Brewster Place.* 1982; Harmondsworth: Penguin, 1983.

Shange, Ntozake. *For colored girls who have considered suicide/when the rainbow is enuf.* 1977. New York: Bantam, 1980.

Showalter, Elaine. "The Other Bostonians: Gender and Literary Study." *Yale Journal of Criticism* (1988): 179–87.

Shukman, Ann, ed. *Bakhtin School Papers.* Somerton, Oxford: RPT Publications, 1983.

Vološinov, V. N. *Marxism and the Philosophy of Language.* Trans. L. Matejka and I. R. Titunik. New York: Seminar Press, 1973.

Walker, Alice. *The Color Purple.* New York: Pocket Books, 1982.

Willis, Susan. "Eruptions of 'Funk': Historicizing Toni Morrison." In *Black Literature and Literary Theory.* Ed. Henry Louis Gates, Jr. New York: Methuen, 1984. 163–83.

———. *Specifying: Black Women Writing the American Experience.* Madison: University of Wisconsin Press, 1987.

Yaeger, Patricia. *Honey-Mad Women: Emancipatory Strategies in Women's Writing.* New York: Columbia University Press, 1988.

13

Problems of Gordimer's Poetics: Dialogue in *Burger's Daughter*

Louise Yelin

Burger's Daughter, set in South Africa between 1948, the year the first Afrikaner government took office, and 1976, the year of the Soweto students' school boycott, self-consciously examines language and politics in the world it represents. The novel's title identifies its protagonist, Rosa Burger, as someone's daughter. The name *Burger* evokes the bourgeoisie, although the Burger in question, Rosa's father Lionel, is a white leader of the South African Communist Party (SACP) and an activist in the struggle against apartheid. Burger may have named his daughter after Rosa Luxemburg; *Die Burger* is also a leading Afrikaans newspaper. The novel sets Rosa Burger's personal history and quest for self-definition against the events that comprise the recent history of South Africa, events that involve Rosa's parents and their comrades in the movement, including Rosa herself. At the same time, *Burger's Daughter* dramatizes the ways that social, political, and ideological conflicts are played out in language and replayed in such texts as *Crime and Punishment* and *The Story of an African Farm.*

Mikhail Bakhtin's sociolinguistic approach to the novel, in describing the ways that novelistic discourse parodies, carnivalizes, dialogizes, or otherwise reaccentuates both the social languages and dialects that comprise a specific language-world and other prior or adjacent literary texts, helps in the reading of novels like *Burger's Daughter.*[1] In addition, it enables, indeed forces, us to address the contention of different voices and of diverse and conflicting subject positions that constitute both *Burger's Daughter* and Burger's daughter.[2] More important, it helps to conceptualize the relation between the novel and the discursive matrix in which it is written and which it rewrites. But if Bakhtin's theory helps us to read *Burger's Daughter,* Gordimer also refines our reading of Bakhtin and, therefore, our sense of what a feminist dialogical criticism might accomplish. For, writing as a white, English-speaking South African woman engaged in the struggle against apartheid, Gordimer enters the dialogue between women and patriarchal cultural hegemony and the dialogue between colonial or postcolonial "margins" and (the) European "center." Writing about a white, English-speaking South African woman, she delineates the situation of white opponents of apartheid in the 1970s. In giving Rosa Burger the complex lines of political filiation implied in her name, Gordimer asks whether the discourse of classical Marxism, as represented in the novel most prominently by Lionel Burger, or the (European) novel of ideas, as practiced by Fyodor Dostoevsky and theorized by Bakhtin, can adequately convey the significance of racial and gender politics in contemporary South Africa.

In the essay that follows, I place Gordimer and Bakhtin in dialogue. Part I considers the self-consciously dialogic narrative discourse of *Burger's Daughter*. In part II, the differences made by race, place, gender, and history in Gordimer's rewriting of episodes in *Crime and Punishment* and *The Story of an African Farm* are discussed. In part III, Gordimer's treatment of *dialogue* is examined. While showing how Bakhtin illuminates *Burger's Daughter*, I argue that *Burger's Daughter* makes visible terms like *race* and *gender* occluded in Bakhtin's work, exposes the andro- and ethnocentricity of his writings, and, most important, refines Bakhtin's conception of *dialogue* as opposition by simultaneously analyzing and speaking out against the complicity of European and patriarchal cultural traditions in the maintenance and legitimation of apartheid.

Here I Stand

Burger's Daughter begins in 1962 with a description of a group of people standing outside a prison waiting to bring parcels to the inmates who are only later revealed as those detained for their participation in the struggle against the regime. Among the group is the novel's protagonist, Rosa Burger, identified first as "a schoolgirl in a brown and yellow uniform" and subsequently as "Lionel Burger's daughter ... fourteen years old, bringing an eiderdown quilt and hot-water bottle for her mother" and then given a name and a rather detailed description of her physical appearance (9 – 10). The three ways that Rosa Burger is designated in this sequence seem initially to be synonymous or complementary ways of describing the same person, but the three designations — schoolgirl, Lionel Burger's daughter, Rosa Burger — actually represent the relationship of a perceiver or narrator and the persons/things described: How Rosa is seen depends on who is seeing her and from where, and the who and the where are not neutral terms but politically charged, like everything else in this novel about a country where "society *is* the political situation" and where "politics is character" ("A Writer in SA," 23).

The language-world represented in *Burger's Daughter* is a universe of discourse constituted by the intersection and stratification of the languages, dialects, and speech genres of typical social groups: social heteroglossia, or, more properly, given that in South Africa, English contends with Afrikaans for domination over the speakers of indigenous languages, partial heteroglossia.[3] Throughout the novel, the terms that designate Rosa represent the various perspectives, the ideologically charged rhetorics, of different groups in English-speaking South African society. Among these are, to name just a few, a headmistress's school report; fragments of a biography of Lionel Burger by a journalist sympathetic to his cause; surveillance reports for the Bureau of State Security; the speeches and leaflets of the Soweto students; and Lionel Burger's speech at his trial for treason. Stephen Clingman notes (186ff) that Gordimer takes Burger's speech from the one that Bram Fischer, a leader of the SACP and the model for Lionel Burger, actually delivered at his trial. This speech, as Clingman points out, is only one of numerous quotations from actual historical documents. The strategy of quotation gives voice to texts and opinions such as the Soweto student's leaflets and the writings of Fischer and Joe Slovo, a prominent member of the SACP and the African National Congress (ANC), banned or otherwise publicly unavailable in South Africa. Clingman describes Gordimer's strategy of unattributed quotation as a "textual collage ... with a distinct logic ... that goes beyond pure formalism" (187). But he elides the distinction between quotation, whether attributed or not, and what Bakhtin identifies as "represented language" (DN, 358) and V. N. Vološinov calls "reported speech" (115 – 21 and passim). In the latter, Vološinov says, we can discern two tendencies in the "authorial context surrounding the reported speech ... that of commenting and that of retorting" (118 – 19). Gordimer's presentation of Burger's oration from the dock bristles with the tension between "reported speech and reporting context" (119) — that is, the novel into which the speech is inserted — and between implied comment and retort, whether by Rosa or an omniscient narrative voice:

"A change of social control in compatibility with the change in methods of production — known in Marxist language as 'revolution' — in this I saw the answer to the racialism that was destroying our country then and — believe me! believe me! — is destroying it even more surely and systematically now. I could not turn away from that tragedy. I cannot now. I took up then the pursuit of the end to racialism and injustice that I have continued and shall continue as long as I live. I say with Luther: Here I stand. *Ich kann nicht anders.*" (26)

Gordimer's extraordinary sense of the dialogic contention of ideology in language makes us simultaneously hear Burger's speech as the spontaneous, eloquent, and moving discourse of enlightened Marxist humanism and, in the context of South Africa for a first-world reader, as a rather tired piece of Communist Party rhetoric: that is, as an exemplary instance of double-voiced discourse directed both toward the referent — in this case, justice or injustice — and toward someone else's word.

To return to the novel's opening sequence: the "schoolgirl in uniform" is produced by a journalistic view of the anti-apartheid movement, one that purports to "humanize" it by packaging it for consumers of the mass media. Lionel Burger's daughter is Rosa seen by those she calls "the faithful," the activists in the struggle against apartheid and her parents' comrades in the SACP. The faithful have their own language or dialect, their own narratives of the novel's events. One of these, an account of Rosa's participation in the movement, is given just after the opening sequence. In this account, Communist Party rhetoric appears as a hodgepodge of contending cliches that present Rosa as a heroine at once revolutionary and domestic: "Already she had taken on her mother's role in the household, giving loving support to her father, who was all too soon to be detained as well. On that day he had put others' plight before his own" (12). This passage indicates the continuing hegemony of bourgeois-patriarchal ideology and points to a contradiction that defines Rosa, a contradiction between feminism (Rosa's liberation as a woman) and the struggle for justice in South Africa. But while the repetition of domestic cliches might appear to discredit the faithful, they are, in fact, a leading voice among white South African opponents of apartheid in the 1950s and '60s. Here, as in the presentation of Burger's speech, Gordimer's deployment of multi-voiced discourse is a strategy both narrative and political, for it enables her — and hence encourages the reader — to be critical of Communist pieties or communist doctrine and at the same time to endorse the work of individual communists and of the SACP in the struggle to end apartheid.

Burger's Daughter plays off a third-person narrative that attempts to name, capture, or represent — to contain — a social totality against the more personal first-person narration of the protagonist. Rosa's narrative emerges in part as a response to the question posed by the opening sequence, a question she also asks herself: *"When they saw me outside the prison, what did they see?"* (13). Rosa embraces narrative complexity and indeterminacy and eschews authority over her own narrative. More important, the construction of her narrative reinforces the novel's dialogic paradigm of discourse, for the division of *Burger's Daughter* into three parts is governed not by changes in the third-person narrators but by changes in Rosa recorded as a sequence of shifts in her narratees: lover, surrogate mother, father.[4] I have argued elsewhere (Exiled, 401 – 08) that this sequence reverses the conventional trajectory of the *bildungsroman* which in both male and female versions takes its protagonist away from mother and father. In addition, the strategy of marking the significant changes in Rosa's life as changes in the person to whom she tells her story also suggests that identity, like discourse, is constructed in/by the relationship of speaker and addressee. As Rosa puts it, using her father's words, "Life must be in need of a conduit towards meaning, which posited: outside self. That's where the tension that makes it possible to live lay, for him; between self and others; between the present and creation of something called the future" (86). *Dialogue* in *Burger's Daughter*, as Don Bialostosky points out (Response, 4 – 5), is associated with "unfinalizability" — an unresolvable tension between conflicting possibilities, narratives, accounts of Rosa's life. But Gordimer neither identifies *dialogue* with indeterminacy nor equates it with carnivalesque transgression or play. *Burger's Daughter* insists on moral responsibility, both in its plot — the end of the novel endorses Rosa's return to anti-apartheid work — and in its revision of *Crime and Punishment* and *The Story of an African Farm.*

II: The Curse of Pathos

In *Burger's Daughter*, Gordimer rewrites, or writes against, the horse-beating episode in *Crime and Punishment* and an analogous incident in *The Story of an African Farm*. Specifically, Gordimer borrows and in turn revises Olive Schreiner's critique of race and gender in order to emphasize race and gender issues ignored by Dostoevsky and Bakhtin alike. This rewriting thus exposes the ways that such Bakhtinian concepts as *dialogue*, *polyphony*, and *carnival* may elide the masculine or the European with the universal and occlude differences of race, place, and gender.

The horse-beating episode in *Crime and Punishment* is actually a dream. It begins when Raskolnikov, wandering about St. Petersburg in the process of deciding whether to kill Alyona Ivanovna, goes to a tavern, drinks a glass of vodka, and falls asleep at the side of the road. He soon dreams that he is a child again, "walking one holiday with his father outside the town" (Part I, ch. 5, p. 46). The boy — throughout the narration of the dream, Raskolnikov is referred to as "the boy" — watches in horror as a drunken peasant, spurred on by his friends and by a crowd of jeering onlookers, beats his horse to death. This dream, along with the echoes of it that occur later in the novel and the proleptic images of it earlier on, vividly dramatizes the psychic conflicts of Raskolnikov, conflicts that literally discompose his mind. But the manifest content of the dream also evokes the poverty, drunkenness, and brutality and the disruption of familial norms, forms, and values that characterize the social world of *Crime and Punishment,* a world whose contours Raskolnikov is apparently powerless to alter. The narration of this dream exemplifies what Bakhtin describes as Dostoevsky's polyphony: The dream orchestrates the perspectives of the narrator, Raskolnikov (the dreamer), the boy (Raskolnikov in the dream), the peasant Mikolka, the horse, and the onlookers who carnivalize the scene. The polyphonic narration produces in the reader a set of conflicting feelings — including a particularly disturbing feeling of titillation evoked by the jeering, cheering onlookers — like the ones Raskolnikov experiences.[5]

Gordimer's rewriting of this episode reworks the material of Raskolnikov's dream in a way that focuses our attention on the South African setting of the novel.[6] Some time after Lionel Burger dies in prison, Rosa decides to leave South Africa, to "defect" from "Lionel's country" (210, 264). Her decision is a highly complicated and attenuated response to two events she witnesses. First, she sees a white man, a tramp, dead on a park bench; subsequently, she comes upon a drunken black man brutally beating his donkey.

The death of the drunken white man is for Rosa a mystery, an event that is not amenable to a political explanation or a rational interpretation:[7]

> What could we have known that would have made it possible to understand how he left us while among us ... I had seen my brother dead and my mother and father; each time the event itself, so close to me, was obscured from me by sorrow and explained by accident, illness, or imprisonment. It was *caused* by the chlorinated water with flecks of his pink breakfast bacon in it that I saw pumped from my

brother's mouth when he was taken from the pool; by that paralysis
that blotted out my mother limb by limb; by the fever that my father
smelled of, dying for his beliefs in a prison hospital.
　　But this death was mystery itself. (78–79)

The tramp's death makes Rosa acknowledge the limits of the materialist analysis and political understanding of South Africa that she gets
from her parents and that enjoins on her the moral responsibility of
ending suffering and injustice: apartheid. For our purposes, this event
is important because the drunken man echoes the drunkenness of Mikolka. By dividing Dostoevsky's drunken, brutal peasant into two figures, one white, the other black, Gordimer forces us to consider race
as it is constituted (constructed) in and by the system of apartheid.[8]
That is, this division places in the foreground both the race and the
brutality of the man who beats his animal and makes us confront his
brutality as an image of apartheid, the product or effect of the specific
political and racial economy of South Africa. But, as we shall see in a
moment, Gordimer does not simply equate this event with apartheid
and thereby sum it up. She neither sacrifices nor subordinates her
sense of the contingent character of events — what, in the case of the
tramp, Rosa calls a mystery — to her political analysis of South Africa
but rather opposes them, puts them in dialogue.

　　As the setting of Raskolnikov's dream, a road that runs past a
tavern and leads away from a village, evokes the Russia of his child-
hood, the scene of the donkey-beating that Rosa witnesses — a road
between Johannesburg and a nameless "place" inhabited illegally by
blacks — belongs specifically to South Africa in the 1970s. That Rosa is
driving on this road at all signifies her difference from most white
South Africans, for she has taken one black woman home from a political meeting to the unnamed "place" and is on her way to a clandestine
visit to another black woman, a banned political activist. As noted earlier, the multi-voiced, third-person narration of *Burger's Daughter* is
played off against the first-person narration of Rosa herself. Some of
the novel's incidents are presented only in the third person, and some
— the death of the tramp, for example — are presented both in the
third-person narration and in the first-person, but the scene in which
Rosa comes upon the man beating his donkey is given only in her first-
person account. Rosa's narration of this incident is *internally* unme-
diated: that is, it is presented without the irony that virtually defines
Gordimer's novelistic style. But it is externally or intertextually double-
voiced, offered with what Bakhtin calls a "sideward glance" (PDP, 199)
at *Crime and Punishment*. I want to suggest that *Burger's Daughter*

reaccentuates *Crime and Punishment* by altering and rearranging its narrative discourse: that, to borrow Bakhtin's terminology, Gordimer dialogizes Dostoevsky's polyphony by rendering it as a kind of interior monologue.

This reaccentuation focuses our attention both on Rosa as narrating self and on the specific historical context of her narration. This context — South Africa in the 1970s — at once necessitates and precludes moral and political choice. In this respect, this episode is a contemporary instance of novelistic pathos as Bakhtin describes it:[9]

> In the novel a discourse of pathos is almost always a surrogate for some other genre that is no longer available to a given time or a given social force — such pathos is the discourse of a preacher who has lost his pulpit, a dreaded judge who no longer has any judicial or punitive powers, the prophet without a mission, the politician without political power, the believer without a church and so forth — everywhere, the discourse of pathos is connected with orientations and positions that are unavailable to the author as authentic expression for the seriousness and determination of his purpose, but which he must, *all the same,* conditionally reproduce by using his own discourse ... In pathos-charged speech one cannot take the first step etc. In this lies the "curse" of novelistic pathos when it is expressed directly. (DN, 394–95)

Rosa, whether or not she speaks for Gordimer, is unable either to assume or not to assume the "power, rank, position" conferred by speaking: in this sense, she suffers the curse of pathos. Neither does she experience nor evoke in the reader the kinds of transgressive, disruptive, or otherwise carnivalesque responses characteristic of Raskolnikov (or Dostoevsky).

As a result, in reading this episode, one is free of the disturbing excitement induced by the description of Raskolnikov's dream: indeed, Gordimer's rewriting of Dostoevsky eliminates what Peter Stallybrass and Allon White identify (19) as a carnivalesque tendency to demonize weaker groups — such as the peasantry in *Crime and Punishment.* Unlike Raskolnikov, who is confused, even unhinged both during the dream and afterwards, Rosa is quite clear about what is happening and fully conscious of her own role, her responsibility in the event. The boy in Raskolnikov's dream asks his father to intervene, but the father either will not or cannot. Rosa, in contrast, sees that she can intervene, but does not, believing that to do so would be to use her white authority and privilege to oppress the poor black man:

I had only to career down on that scene with my car and my white authority. I could have yelled before I even got out, ... and then there I would have been standing, inescapable, fury and right, might, before them, the frightened woman and child and the drunk, brutal man, with my knowledge of how to deliver them over to the police, to have him prosecuted as he deserved and should be, to take away from him the poor suffering possession he maltreated. I could formulate everything they were, as the act I had witnessed; they would have their lives summed up for them officially at last by me, the white woman — the final meaning of a day they had lived I had no knowledge of, a day of other appalling things, violence, disasters, urgencies, deprivations which suddenly would become, was nothing but what it had led up to: the man among them beating their donkey. I could have put a stop to it, the misery; at that point I witnessed. What more can one do? That sort of old man, those people, peasants existing the only way they know how, in the 'place' that isn't on the map, they would have been afraid of me. I could have put a stop to it, with them, at no risk to myself. No one would have taken up a stone. I was safe from the whip. I could have stood between them and suffering — the suffering of the donkey.

As soon as I planted myself in front of them it would have become again just that — the pain of a donkey.

I drove on. I don't know at what point to intercede makes sense for me ... I drove on because the horrible drunk was black, poor and brutalized. If somebody's going to be brought to account, I am accountable for him, to him, as he is for the donkey. Yet the suffering — while I saw it was the sum of suffering to me. I didn't do anything. I let him beat the donkey. The man was a black. So a kind of vanity counted for more than feeling; I couldn't bear to see myself — her — Rosa Burger — as one of those whites who can care more for animals than people. (209 – 210)[10]

In describing the scene of the man beating his donkey, Rosa uses concrete terms *(drunk, brutal)*; a language of morality *(suffering)*; a language of race *(black)*; and a language of class *(peasants)* that may be more appropriate to the world of Karl Marx and Dostoevsky than to her own world. But all of these discourses fall under the rubric of novelistic pathos, since all are identified with "orientations and positions" that do not enable Rosa to act. Like her language, Rosa's predicament in this episode exemplifies the situation of white opponents of apartheid in the early- and mid-1970s: here, she represents her author as well. In addition, Rosa's inaction at once recalls and differs from Raskolnikov's. Like the boy in Raskolnikov's dream, Rosa is in a double bind, unable either to intervene or not to. Like him, she witnesses a scene that is a figure, a metonym, for the social structure of the world she inhabits; but unlike him, she chooses not to act, and the element of conscious choice is underscored by the first-person narration. But if Rosa is less passive than the boy in the dream, the scope of her actions, in this episode at least, is severely limited.

Just how limited is evident if we read this scene intertextually with the incident in *The Story of an African Farm* in which Waldo protests the brutal beating of an animal,[11] for Gordimer's rewriting of Schreiner accentuates the differences between South Africa in the 1880s and the 1970s and points to the very different situations of whites opposed to racism in the two periods. Schreiner's Waldo suggests the failure of self-reliance (Waldo) and the exploitation of the working-class (Farber), and he sympathizes with and stands in for the suffering of South African blacks in the second half of the nineteenth century. Waldo attacks his master on a wagon train when the man whips, then stabs and kills one of his oxen. Waldo cannot remain with the master after he attacks him, so he walks away, virtually penniless because he has not yet been paid for his work (244–45). Rosa's situation is, of course, quite different from Waldo's, since she is, unlike him, "safe from the whip" and since the man beating the animal in *Burger's Daughter* is a poor black not a white boss. But even so, the clear-cut sense of moral outrage that Waldo expresses is not available to Rosa, or rather, it is complicated by her opposition to apartheid. Rosa chooses not to intervene because she refuses to assume the "white authority" that would enable her to "deliver" the man to the police and because, as she puts it, she does not want to be seen or to see herself as caring more for animals than people. Yet this choice means that she runs the risk of not acting at all, of not being "accountable for him, to him, as he is for the donkey" (210), and thus of acquiescing in the misery and suffering that Waldo protests against, however ineffectively. In addition, Rosa's moral actions, unlike those of Waldo, occur entirely within the arena of her own thoughts: the limited scope in which she operates and the displacement of action by thought are manifest in her use of counterfactuals: *could have yelled, could have put a stop, would have stood.* The quoted passage gives Rosa's retrospective report an interior dialogue, but even this dialogue is limited or foreclosed by Rosa's sense of her own situation. Rosa's refusal, both at the time of the event and at the time of narration, to "formulate" or "sum up" or give voice to the lives of the black man and his family and his donkey leads to an impasse both narrative and political, an impasse that Rosa attempts to circumvent by "defecting" from South Africa. Eventually, though, Rosa returns from exile, and the novel ends with the heroine in jail for participating in the movement sparked by the Soweto students.

Gordimer's rewriting of Dostoevsky foregrounds the political and the moral dimension of suffering or misery. As Gordimer presents it, brutality is both universal and historically specific, and the sight (or site) of the black man beating his donkey rehearses the entire history of human cruelty at the same time as it inscribes the political structure of South Africa—apartheid:

> The entire ingenuity from thumbscrew and rack to electric shock, the infinite variety and gradation of suffering, by lash, by fear, by hunger, by solitary confinement — the camps, concentration, labour, resettlement, the Siberias of snow or sun, the lives of Mandela, Sisulu, Mbeki, Kathrada, Kgosana, gull-picked on the Island, Lionel propped wasting to his skull between two warders, the deaths by questioning, bodies fallen from the height of John Vorster Square, deaths by dehydration, babies degutted by enteritis in 'places' of banishment, the lights beating all night on the faces of those in cells.... (208)

If the emphasis on moral and political agency and the rewriting of Mikolka as two characters, one black, the other white, point to the significance of race in the African context, the episode in *Burger's Daughter* also asks us to consider differences of gender. We meet Mikolka outside a tavern in the company of numerous drunken men who urge him on, but in *Burger's Daughter* we encounter the man who beats his donkey with his family, his wife and child who look on, afraid, Gordimer implies, that he might turn his violence on them. Although we first see the group of "donkey, cart, driver, and people behind him" as "a single object" (208), we soon recognize that black women and children are doubly victims of apartheid. In showing that apartheid affects women and men differently and suggesting that for black women sexual oppression reinforces the effects of racism, Gordimer insists on the significance of gender. But at the same time, she eschews an essentialist conception of sex and gender: in this episode, she deconstructs the identification of Woman as victim with inert or subjugated nature. Dostoevsky's horse is female, or perhaps it is more accurate to say that the horse is feminized. In addition, the imaginative logic[12] of *Crime and Punishment* makes this horse — also given in the Coulson translation as *nag, mare* — a figure for Raskolnikov's mother, his landlady (Part II, chap. 2, p. 97), Alyona Ivanovna, and the feminine or masochistic components of Raskolnikov himself. The sex of Gordimer's donkey, however, is not specified. Nor does Schreiner specify the sex of the beast of burden, but despite her subversion of received ideas about sex and gender, she reifies race, for it is through Waldo's identification with the ox that we see him as standing (in) for the exploited blacks that the ox also represents. In obliterating the sex of the beast while insisting on its suffering, *Burger's Daughter,* like *The Story of an African Farm,* dissolves the identification, so important to carnivalesque cultural practices and to patriarchal ideology in all its versions, of woman and (bestial) nature, but unlike Schreiner, Gordimer does not reconstruct sexual difference as racial otherness.[13]

III: Patience on a Monument

If *Burger's Daughter* enacts a dialogue with European literature as it decarnivalizes *Crime and Punishment,* it also interrogates the idea of *dialogue* which, along with *carnival* and *heteroglossia,* is a central organizing concept of Anglo-American literary and cultural criticism that Bakhtin inspired.[14] This interrogation occurs chiefly in Rosa's conversations with Brandt Vermeulen, an Afrikaner with connections in the Ministry of the Interior and elsewhere in the government, whom she asks to help her get the passport which the State would surely deny to Lionel Burger's daughter. In many ways Rosa's opposite number, Vermeulen stands for the ersatz versions of dialogue that Rosa resists. In endorsing Rosa's resistance, Gordimer elaborates her own notion of dialogue as opposition.

In this section of the novel, Gordimer's irony undercuts Vermeulen's coupling of cultural sophistication and commitment to apartheid and its regime. Familiar with both "the" European cultural tradition and with modern art and literature, Vermeulen has, the narrator says, a "sophistry to transform the home-whittled destiny of white to rule over black in terms that the generation of late-twentieth-century oriented, Nationalist intellectuals would advance as the first true social evolution of the century" (175). In other words, he regards Plato, Shakespeare, modern art, and the so-called sexual revolution as part of the same package as apartheid and the Broederbond. Vermeulen signals his "modernity" by displaying in his house such artifacts as drawings and lithographs by Picasso, O'Keefe, and Kandinsky, a print from an African herbalist's shop showing the Royal Zulu lineage, and a sculpture that represents a female torso — no head — as a collection of sexual parts and erogenous zones (181). Similarly, he demonstrates his cultural sophistication by alluding to Shakespeare: he takes a line from *Twelfth Night* out of context when he tells Rosa that she will get her passport but that in order to do so she will have to be "patience on a monument." Here, the narrator observes, "They continued to speak in Afrikaans together, but the tag came in English" (188). The "tag" itself is a veritable touchstone of misogynist misreading, and Vermeulen's allusion accordingly inscribes him in the legions of (male) readers of Shakespeare who misconstrue it as an assertion of women's submissiveness, whether by ignoring or forgetting that Viola uses these words while disguised as Cesario who is describing a sister who does not exist. But Gordimer's revisionary strategy stresses the critical moment of dialogics over the affirmative or "liberatory interest in language" (53) that Yaeger emphasizes.[15] Moreover, gender may be less important as a determinant of Gordimer's critique of Vermeulen, as of her literary production in general, than the politics of race and place. Shakespeare stands, in this episode, for the Humanities and for the *cultural* hegemony of English in South Africa. Gordimer suggests, then, that by self-consciously referring to Shakespeare and by speaking English, Vermeulen announces his cultural literacy, identifies himself with the hegemonic culture (or with cultural hegemony), and attempts to differentiate himself from the old-fashioned, narrow-minded, culturally backward or illiterate Afrikaners who run the government. At the same time, he endorses their politics, both in his publicly held views and actions and in the racist language he uses out of what the narrator describes as an "affection for these old descriptive terms so innocently, artlessly insulting": *coolie-pink,* for example, and *kaffertjie* (189, 181).

In Vermeulen's appropriation of Shakespeare, Gordimer not only shows the dialogic links of one cultural text with another (PT, 105) but, more important, exposes the ways that culture is complicit in, legitimates, and reproduces political hegemony.[16] In other words, she undermines the distinction, so important to Vermeulen and men like him, between politics and culture, and she does so by showing that the privileging of an autonomous cultural or aesthetic realm is itself a strategy that legitimates political hegemony in South Africa as elsewhere in the modern world.[17] Taking Vermeulen's measure, Rosa notes that he is "fascinated" with her and with his sense that what he is doing — helping her to get a passport — is "final proof of his eclecticism" (193). In foregrounding the politics that Vermeulen's smug and sexist "fascination" aestheticizes and therefore attempts to put in the background, Gordimer recalls the views of Walter Benjamin, writing in 1938 on the ways that fascism substitutes aesthetics for politics:

> Fascism attempts to organize the newly created proletarian masses without affecting the property structure which the masses strive to eliminate. Fascism sees its salvation in giving these masses not their right, but instead a chance to express themselves. The masses have a right to change property relations; Fascism seeks to give them an expression while preserving property. The logical result of Fascism is the introduction of aesthetics into political life. (241)

Benjamin offers as an antidote to the fascist aestheticization of politics the Communist response of politicizing art (242). While Gordimer does not explicitly turn to this solution, her treatment of Vermeulen exposes the "eclecticism" that purports to give South African masses a chance to express themselves. But here, as in the donkey-beating episode, Rosa is silent, or more precisely, she says what is on her mind to the novel's readers and to the former lover to whom she addresses this part of the novel, but she does not speak to an interlocutor within the text.

Although the reader may well mark Rosa's silent words as another instance of the curse of pathos, her silence suggests — to the reader, if not to Vermeulen — both her resistance to the order that Vermeulen represents and the limits of that resistance. Like the narrator, who reaccentuates Vermeulen's speechifying to draw attention to his misogynist misreading of Shakespeare, Rosa strains against these limits, repudiating Vermeulen and his politics by superimposing on his words the slogan of the African National Congress (Gordimer uses these same words as the epigraph to Part Three of the novel):

> Peace. Land. Bread. But Brandt knows only the long words — ethnic advancement, separate freedoms, multilateral development, plural democracy. (194)

Rosa cannot speak out: that is, she silences herself, since speaking out would mean that she would effectively be silenced. The novel ends, in fact, with a censor's erasure of part of a letter that Rosa writes from prison. (The vicissitudes of Rosa's words in the novel prefigure the later history of *Burger's Daughter,* which was banned after its publication in South Africa and subsequently unbanned.[18]) In Rosa's inability to speak, Gordimer at once demystifies Vermeulen's pretense of dialogue and puts her own critical version in its place.

Although Vermeulen purports to be engaging Rosa in a dialogue, he actually treats her as a kind of captive audience, object of his rhetoric. As Rosa puts it:

> Brandt was deeply committed to his kind of freedom. He had told me how much importance he placed on the *human scale* of policy action (the succinct phrases are his); that meant that when one has found the Kierkegaardian idea for which one must live or die, one must support its policy passionately in theory and at the same time take on the job of personal, practical, daily responsibility for its interpretation and furtherance. He gave me an informal luncheon-type address on the honourable evolution of Dialogue, beginning with Plato, the dia-

logue with self, and culminating in 'the Vorster initiative,' the dialogue of peoples and nations. With me he was self-engaged in that
responsibility on the human scale; for him, his afternoons with Rosa
were 'Dialogue' in practice. (194)

Vermeulen attempts to legitimate Vorster by linking him with Plato
and, therefore, with "western civilization" and European culture, but
Rosa's, and thus, the novel's double-voiced presentation of Vermeulen's
paternalistic "address" distances the reader from his self-serving mys-
tifications and severs Vorster from Plato, racism from philosophy, torture from freedom. Gordimer reveals that the "Vorster initiative"
conceals racial difference and indeed racism in the jargon of policy
and progress, on the one hand, and in the terminology of nationhood
and nationality, on the other. Gordimer's irony exposes the "Vorster
initiative" as just another name for apartheid in its most recent guise
of settling — the state would say resettling — blacks in so-called national homelands that have no existence except in the official rhetoric
of the South African government, that is to say in language as it con-
figures power.[19] In other words, *Burger's Daughter* insists that the "dialogue of people and nations" of apartheid and the Afrikaner regime is
spurious, in fact, a monologue, and acts as a rejoinder which perforce
renders the monologue a dialogue. In short, *Burger's Daughter* elaborates an analysis of discourse that is, at the same time, an act of
opposition.

Finally, I want to suggest that in its rethinking of *dialogue* as in its
representation of social heteroglossia and its rewriting of European
texts, *Burger's Daughter* suggests the limits of Bakhtinian dialogics and
gives us a model of dialogic critical practice. In self-consciously and
critically reaccentuating the speech genres and dialects of contemporary South Africa and such texts as *Crime and Punishment* and *The Story
of an African Farm*, Gordimer makes visible terms like *race* and *gender*
that are often occluded in Euro- and androcentric discourses and indeed, as Wayne Booth among others reminds us, in the work of Bakhtin himself. In addition, Gordimer repudiates Vermeulen's
(mis)appropriation of European literary culture and speaks out
against the repressive political order that engenders and is in turn le-
gitimated by such (mis)appropriations. But at the same time, she asks
us to confront the limits of *dialogue*. Implicit in Rosa's knowing silence,
both in the donkey-beating episode and with Vermeulen, is an analysis
of and rejoinder to the order of apartheid that inscribes the moment
when Gordimer wrote the novel. But Rosa is not patience on a monument smiling at grief, and her silence also reminds us that the dismantling of apartheid requires a vocal and collective opposition.

Notes

I am grateful to the University of North Carolina Press for permission to publish a part of this essay that appears, in a different form, in "Exiled in and Exiled from: The Poetics and Politics of *Burger's Daughter*," in *Women's Writing in Exile*, ed. Mary Lynn Broe and Angela Ingram.

1. See especially *Rabelais, Problems of Dostoevsky's Poetics*, the essays collected in *The Dialogic Imagination*, and the essay on the *bildungsroman;* on re-accentuation as a "feel" for "distancing" in double-voiced discourse, see DN, 419 – 22 and PSG, passim.

2. See Elizabeth A. Meese, R. Radhakrishnan, and Stephen Clingman on the question of "subject positions" in *Burger's Daughter.*

3. See DN, 290 – 91. Bakhtin defines "speech genre" as "not a typical form of language, but a typical form of utterance" (PSG, 85).

4. Vološinov stresses the relationship of speaker and addressee in the construction of meaning (85, 95, 102).

5. See R. D. Laing for a reading of this episode as a "counterpoint" of dream, phantasy, imagination, and reality. Raskolnikov's dream is reworked in the episode which precipitated Nietzsche's decline into madness: observing a cabman beating his horse, Nietzsche threw his arms around the horse's neck and lost consciousness, awakening, says his biographer, "not himself" (Hollingdale, 289). Thanks to Geoffrey Field for bringing this to my attention.

6. Stephen Clingman points out (178n.) that Gordimer based this episode on an incident that occurred while she was writing the novel. I would argue that Raskolnikov's dream shapes the ways that readers of European fiction understand such incidents. Carl Resek makes a similar point about the reworking of Raskolnikov's dream in such classic American texts as *The Sun Also Rises, Call It Sleep*, and Jane Addams's autobiography.

7. Elizabeth Meese observes that "This anonymous death comes unfiltered through responsibility or explanation; it eludes discursive captivity" (259). But Meese overstates the case, for in describing the death of the tramp both Rosa and the narrator "capture" him, even if in a language that resists reification as "discourse."

8. See Henry Louis Gates, Jr., on race as socially constructed, an effect of inscribed or ascribed rather than biological difference (5).

9. I thank Jane Marcus for bringing this to my attention.

10. Here, Rosa echoes Raskolnikov's dream that he had "almost fallen under the horses' feet, in spite of the coachman's repeated cries" (Part II, ch. 2, p. 96).

11. I thank Alan Scott, a student at SUNY Purchase, for pointing this out to me and Jane Marcus for helping me to think through its significance.

12. For this phrase and much else, I am grateful to my undergraduate teacher, the late Isabel Gamble MacCaffrey.

13. The unravelling of the connection between woman and nature is what feminism has most in common with Derridean deconstruction. See Jane Flax, Sherry Ortner, and Chris Weedon, and the essays by Leslie Wahl Rabine and Mary Poovey in the Spring 1988 issue of *Feminist Studies*. Wayne Booth argues that the carnivalesque thrust of Bakhtin's *Rabelais* (and Bakhtin's Rabelais) excludes or subordinates women. Similarly, Mary Russo notes the "complicitous place" of carnival in "dominant culture" and suggests that there are "especial dangers for women and other excluded or marginalized groups within carnival" (214).

14. As Robert Young points out, *dialogue* is not only a central term but one whose definition is contested. Indeed, a large part of "Bakhtinian criticism" or Bakhtin studies may be defined as the terrain occupied by dialogue about "dialogue." See, for example, Allon White's "Fraternal Reply to Robert Young" and Mary Russo's examination both of theories of carnival and the carnival of theory.

15. Gordimer's strategy is a version of the "defiant negativity" (Theodor Adorno's term) that Neil Lazarus argues is central to the project of oppositional white writers in contemporary South Africa.

16. Thanks to Bob Stein and Morris Kaplan for helping me to see this.

17. See "The Essential Gesture" for Gordimer's views on the relation of politics and art. Gordimer argues that the high modernist project, to "transform the world by style," cannot be the "essential gesture" of writers in contemporary South Africa (296).

18. Gordimer describes this history in a pamphlet entitled *What Happened to Burger's Daughter?* See Clingman, 188–90.

19. Ann McClintock and Rob Nixon discuss the substitution of a rhetoric of nationality for a language of color and race in recent South African history (342–43). The so-called homelands are not so much rhetorical as discursive formations, in the Foucauldian sense of the word.

Works Cited

Bakhtin, Mikhail M. "The *Bildungsroman* and Its Significance in the History of Realism (Toward a Historical Typology of the Novel)." *Speech Genres and Other Late Essays*, 103–31.

————.*The Dialogic Imagination.* Trans. Caryl Emerson and Michael Holquist. Ed. Michael Holquist. Austin: University of Texas Press, 1981.

————."Discourse in the Novel." *The Dialogic Imagination,* 259–422 (DN).

————."From the Prehistory of Novelistic Discourse." *The Dialogic Imagination,* 41–83.

————."The Problem of Speech Genres." *Speech Genres and Other Late Essays,* 60–102 (PSG).

————."The Problem of the Text in Linguistics, Philology, and the Human Sciences: An Experiment in Philosophical Analysis." *Speech Genres and Other Late Essays,* 103–31.

————.*Problems of Dostoevsky's Poetics.* Trans. and Ed. Caryl Emerson. Minneapolis: University of Minnesota Press, 1984 (PDP).

————.*Rabelais and His World.* Trans. Helene Iswolsky. Bloomington: Indiana University Press, 1984.

————.*Speech Genres and Other Late Essays.* Trans. Vern W. McGee. Ed. Caryl Emerson and Michael Holquist. Austin: University of Texas Press, 1986.

Benjamin, Walter. "The Work of Art in the Age of Mechanical Reproduction." *Illuminations.* Ed. Hannah Arendt. Trans. Harry Zohn. New York: Schocken, 1966. 217–52.

Bialostosky, Don H. "Dialogics as an Art of Discourse in Literary Criticism." PMLA, 101 (1986): 788–97.

————."Response to MLA Special Session — Bakhtin in Different Voices: Problems of Theory and Applications."

Booth, Wayne C. "Freedom of Interpretation: Bakhtin and the Challenge of Feminist Criticism." *Bakhtin: Essays and Dialogues on his World.* Ed. Gary Saul Morson. Chicago: University of Chicago Press, 1986: 145–76.

Clingman, Stephen R. *The Novels of Nadine Gordimer: History from the Inside.* London and Boston: Allen and Unwin, 1986.

Dostoevsky, Fyodor. *Crime and Punishment.* Norton Critical Edition. Trans. Jessie Coulson. Ed. George Gibian. New York: Norton, 1975.

DuPlessis, Rachel Blau. *Writing Beyond the Ending: Narrative Strategies of Twentieth-Century Women Writers.* Bloomington: Indiana University Press, 1985.

Flax, Jane. "Postmodernism and Gender Relations in Feminist Theory." *Signs,* 12 (1987): 621–43.

Gates, Henry Louis, Jr. "Introduction: Writing 'Race' and the Difference It Makes." *"Race," Writing, and Difference*, Chicago: University of Chicago Press, 1987: 1–20.

Gordimer, Nadine. *Burger's Daughter*. New York: Penguin, 1979.

———. "The Essential Gesture." *The Essential Gesture: Writing, Politics and Places*. Ed. Stephen Clingman. New York: Knopf, 1988. 285–300.

———. "A Writer in South Africa." *London Magazine*, NS 5 (May 1965): 21–30.

Hollingdale, R. J. *Nietzsche: The Man and His Philosophy*. Baton Rouge: Louisiana State University Press, 1965.

Kauffman, Linda. Ed. *Feminism and Institutions: Dialogues on Feminist Theory*. Cambridge, MA. and Oxford: Basil Blackwell, 1989.

Laing, R. D. "The Counterpoint of Experience." Norton Critical Edition of *Crime and Punishment*: 612–22.

Lazarus, Neil. "Modernism and Modernity: T. W. Adorno and Contemporary White South African Literature." *Cultural Critique* 5 (1986–87): 131–155.

Marcus, Jane. "Laughing at Leviticus: *Nightwood* as Woman's Circus Epic." Forthcoming in *Cultural Critique*.

McClintock, Ann and Rob Nixon. "No Names Apart: The Separation of Word and History in Derrida's 'Le Dernier Mot du Racisme?' " *"Race," Writing, and Difference*: 339–53.

Meese, Elizabeth. "The Political is the Personal: The Construction of Identity in Nadine Gordimer's *Burger's Daughter*." *Feminism and Institutions*: 253–75.

Ortner, Sherry. "Is Female to Male as Nature Is to Culture?" *Women, Culture, and Society*. Ed. Michelle Zimbalist Rosaldo and Louise Lamphere. Stanford: Stanford University Press, 1974. 67–68.

Poovey, Mary. "Feminism and Deconstruction." *Feminist Studies* 14 (1988): 51–65.

Rabine, Leslie Wahl. "A Feminist Politics of Non-Identity." *Feminist Studies* 14 (1988): 11–31.

Radhakrishnan, R. "Negotiating Subject Positions in an Uneven World." *Feminism and Institutions*. Ed. Linda Kauffman. Cambridge, MA: Basil Blackwell, 1989: 276–290.

Russo, Mary. "Female Grotesques: Carnival and Theory." *Feminist Studies/Crit-*

ical Studies. Ed. Teresa de Lauretis. Bloomington: Indiana University Press, 1986. 213–229.

Schreiner, Olive. *The Story of an African Farm.* 1883. Rpt. New York: Schocken, 1976.

Stallybrass, Peter and Allon White. *The Politics and Poetics of Transgression.* Ithaca: Cornell University Press, 1986.

Volovsinov, V. N. *Marxism and the Philosophy of Language.* Trans. Ladislav Matejka and I. R. Titunik. Cambridge: Harvard University Press, 1986 (MPL).

Weedon, Chris. *Feminist Practice and Poststructuralist Theory.* Oxford and New York: Blackwell, 1987.

White, Allon. "The Struggle Over Bakhtin: Fraternal Reply to Robert Young." *Cultural Critique* 8 (1987–88): 217–41.

Yaeger, Patricia. *Honey-Mad Women: Emancipatory Strategies in Women's Writing.* New York: Columbia University Press, 1988.

Yelin, Louise. "Exiled in and Exiled from: The Poetics and Politics of *Burger's Daughter.*" *Women's Writing in Exile.* Ed. Mary Lynn Broe and Angela Ingram. Chapel Hill: University of North Carolina Press, 1989. 395–411.

Young, Robert. "Back to Bakhtin." *Cultural Critique* 2 (1985–86): 71–92.

Afterword

Patricia Yaeger

It's sexy these days to talk about silence. We like to celebrate the unspoken, the unsaid, the unsayable. To cozy up to the abyss, the lacuna, the rupture, the *mise en abyme*. We are in love with the *aporia*, the *differand*, the unknowable, the nonsymbolizable: these phantasms, these negativities, these slim deliriums have become our textual goddesses, our political deities.

In this world brimming with silence, how does a book like *Feminism, Bakhtin, and the Dialogic* fit in? In "Psychoanalysis and the Polis," Julia Kristeva defends the academy's passion for absence. She argues against those who believe in either dialogic or straightforward speech, explaining that post-Freudian knowledge systems must incorporate our dreams and deliriums. The system "Freud calls perception-knowledge ... is always already marked by a *lack:* for it shelters within its very being the nonsignifiable, the nonsymbolized" (Kristeva, 81). The unconscious may be structured like a language, but it nevertheless strains against speech:

> Delirium is a discourse which has ... strayed from a presumed reality. The speaking subject is presumed to have known an object, a relationship, an experience that he is henceforth incapable of reconstituting accurately. Why? Because the knowing subject is also a desiring subject, and the paths of desire snarl the paths of knowledge. (Kristeva, 81)

In redefining the knowing subject as a person whose wisdom is gnarled by her dreams, we have the potential for a new politics. Suddenly, knowledge can be redefined and relocated as "situated" knowledge; the "delirium" of the marginalized becomes a source of information and force for action; the blanks and gaps we used to ig-

239

nore in literary texts become new sites of knowledge — the points where oppressions flare up, where oppressed voices speak.

If the speechless subject is full of political intent, if the silent signatures of the oppressed can be recovered through a study of the dominant culture's split subjectivities, if a real force for social change labors within the ghostly voices of the semiotic, can we find room in these new heterodoxies for the noise and nuisance of the dialogic?

The dialogic stands apart; it refuses to celebrate the arcane and unspeakable. The word's roots make this plain: "dia-" with its connotation of togetherness, and "legesthai," meaning to tell, to talk. To talk with one another, to argue, to exchange information — these activities assume the importance of voice, of presence, of deliberate intersubjectivity, and urge us to re-investigate our commitment to the critically fashionable sounds of silence. As *Feminism, Bakhtin, and the Dialogic* suggests, the intersections of feminist practices and dialogic voices promise a renewed sexual/textual politics in which women's marginal voices must be amplified — that is, made ample. The narratives that we read are filled with power struggles in which some voices rise higher than others. The business of the dialogic imagination is to elicit these forbidden vocalities and show them at work. The business of a feminist dialogics is to gender these voices and unmask the complex, contorted play of hegemonic forms and female speech — to explore the ways in which women from a variety of temporalities, ethnicities, races, and classes initiate dialogues with their oppressions.

The essays in this volume argue convincingly that feminist theory offers exciting and much-needed revisions of Mikhail Bakhtin's mainstream theories. These essays give us stunning examples of a feminist dialogics; they overcome the male-centeredness of Bakhtin criticism and replace its fallacies with new forms of textual and cultural critique — providing the resistance from the margins that Bakhtin applauded but refused to gender.

At the same time, these essays suggest that the dialogic imagination has a great deal to offer feminism. Bakhtin develops a dynamic theory of language that can help us understand the conversations and arguments among feminists; in appropriating and reworking his ideas we counteract a reified, ossified notion of language as phallocracy, as a system too-stultified, too-replete with patriarchal intent. A feminist dialogics can help us pinpoint and describe the dynamic changes within feminism itself.

These changes careen around us; the transformations within feminist theory happen at breakneck speed. To clarify the relationships between feminism and dialogism, we need to examine several of

Bakhtin's terms: first, his notion that language wavers and oscillates — that it is marked by *centrifugal* and *centripetal* forces; second, his description of language's *stratifications* — the ways in which every speech system divides itself into multiple languages that keep our speech alive and developing along its copious fault lines; third, the concept of *heteroglossia* — Bakhtin's insistence that there are forces within language that offer systematic resistance to discursive unities. "Hetero-glossia" suggests that language is clamorously multivocal; our daily speech opens itself to the bray and cackle, the hum and protest, of multiple dissents. Heteroglossia describes, then, the dynamism among "stratified" languages and the ways in which these languages may work together to explode dominant forms of thought.

Finally, we come to *dialogism* itself — a concept foregrounding those moments when languages square off, when they face one another with appropriative force, and the struggle implicit in heteroglossia and stratification becomes visible. If our normative language is saturated with the forms and desires of a dominant culture, this saturation is met, day after day, with abrupt counter-languages that scorch with their contrary logic. In tracing the struggle among sociolinguistic points of view, Bakhtin draws our attention to the contestatory violence of everyday speech. This violence is heightened in literary texts. In examining Western literature's war of words, Bakhtin finds contestation where others see only system and order. By insisting on the literary word's dynamism — on language as struggle, and literature as the magnification of that struggle — Bakhtin shows us the political consequences of textually antagonist codes.

How do these ideas apply to feminist theory? One of the vital signs of feminism is its voracious desire to multiply practices and theories, to develop new ways of correcting and coping with female voicelessness. And yet, as with any political movement, there is a tendency — even within feminism — to normalize categories, routines, ideologies: to set some standard for politically correct thought and behavior. In light of this conservative/conservationist tendency, I want to suggest that the "dialogic imagination" describes some of the most radical — and necessary — moments within feminist thinking.

To illustrate, let's examine the dialogic roles of two groups of women who have been marginal to mainstream feminist thought: first, the place of transsexual women within feminism, and, second, the relation of women with disabilities to feminist condemnations of heterosexual romance.

During a conference on "Feminism and the Critique of Colonial Discourse" at the University of California, Santa Cruz, Wendy Chapkis described the pandemonium surrounding her book, *Women and the Politics Of Appearance*. Chapkis began with a reference to the contestatory, aggressive nature of language: "Hearing the discussion about the borders of identity really hit me today because of a book I wrote about a year ago ... One of the things that [my] book tried to do was to bring in all the differences in the category 'woman' — raising experiences of women in other cultures as well as in Europe and America and other non-European American cultures" (99).

Chapkis attempted to capture the stratifications and multi-voicedness, the heteroglossia of women's parti-cultured speech. Her book enacts what Bakhtin describes as the centrifugal tendency of language: words spin outward, multiply, refuse to mesh with a hegemonic center. But her publishers were obsessed with this center — with words' centripetal or unifying properties: "All of that was very enthusiastically received by the British publisher," Chapkis said. "Those were all differences that made us one; we are still all women" (99).

To define "all women" as "one" gives us the centripetal turn within language — an act with dire political consequences. This oneness is imaginary and exclusionary. As Bakhtin suggests, when we conceive of language as a unifying world view, we ask our speech to make us "one" by excluding those who do not fit our social categories. This ensures "a maximum of mutual understanding in all spheres of ideological life" — translated here as a maximization of the publishers' capital. Chapkis reveals just how constrictive this profit motive can be:

> I got a letter today where the differences hit the wall. They asked me to please take out the interview with the transsexual because, after all, this is really not a woman. It's amazing. She said that lesbian feminist bookstores in England would not stock the book if this interview is in it. And that I either have to take it out or I have to make clear that author and publisher do not make the assumption that a transsexual is a woman, that we do not take what he or "she" has to say either at face value or as having the same value as the evidence of a woman. They said there should be quotation marks around the she and that I should make clear that I don't actually think that a transsexual is a woman. And I'm sure you don't says the publisher, but this needs to be said for market. (99 – 100)

Chapkis concludes that even though we are trying to "include our differences within racial groups and within national groups and within classes ... everybody hits the wall at some point" (100).

This recurring metaphor of being "hit" by language, or of watching one's words "hit" the wall, evokes words' aggressions. To think dialogically means to think about this aggressivity. What happens when ideas "hit" the wall of those centralizing, unifying, institutionalizing tendencies within language that stop our speech? A feminist dialogics insists that the publisher's desire to define all women as "one" will not succeed. Instead of envisioning normative language as monolithic, Bakhtin sees norms as "the generative forces of linguistic life": as forces that struggle to overcome the heteroglossia of language, but also generate this heteroglossia. So, when Chapkis' ideas "hit the wall," this wall falls under siege, becomes embattled by the disunifying force of angry dialogue.

For Chapkis' publisher, the wall is impermeable, the path up or out: political correctness and capital gains go hand in hand. But for Chapkis' listeners, the path must be dialogic. If the definition of "women" is under contestation, then we must foreground the imponderability of our terms and heighten the conflict among world-views. By highlighting a passel of antagonistic voices, Chapkis furthers the dialogic work of feminist inquiry. This is to argue that, despite Bakhtin's interest in public (i.e., dominant) voices, despite his disinterest in the rebellion of a private unconscious, the dialogic is not a force for domestication. Its principles help us define real traumas that scatter and defame the unifying tendencies of patriarchal *and* feminist language systems.

While the role of the transsexual helps to illuminate the conflictual nature of feminist language and to explore Bakhtin's dynamic concepts of centripetal/centrifugal speech, a recent essay about disabled women and romance will help us explore the pressures toward "stratification" and "heteroglossia" in feminist theory. As we will see, the language systems located in disparate socioeconomic, ethnic, and racial, and differently-abled bodies must be "hybridized": organized into a dynamic system that uses and acknowledges our contentious differences. For Bakhtin, "each word tastes of the context and contexts in which it has lived its socially charged life ... Contextual overtones ... are inevitable in the word" (293). The impetus for dialogue changes for disabled and non-disabled women.

In "In Search of a Heroine: Images of Women with Disabilities in Fiction and Drama," Deborah Kent refuses a feminist truism — she suggests that heterosexual romance, with its hierarchical construction of gender relations and its idealization of female passivity, may not be destructive for all its female practitioners as we have imagined.

Kent embarks on this argument by intensifying the feminist critique of heterosexual romance. She speaks out against novels that both enshrine women in the marriage plot and exclude handicapped women from this enshrining: "the smallest flaw — an uneven gait, a malformed hand, a squint — was enough to disqualify a woman from romance, from all hope for happiness. If even a trifling imperfection could loom as such an insurmountable obstacle to fulfillment, what chance was there for a girl who was totally blind, as I was?" (90).

But Kent also reminds us that identification with female characters in books may have a lasting impact upon young women's sense of themselves: "To want to become a heroine ... is to develop the beginnings of a 'raised consciousness.' It liberates a woman from feeling, and therefore perhaps from being, a victim or a dependent or a drudge ... " (Brownstein, xix, quoted in Kent, 91). Kent analyzes fictional stereotypes of disabled women and finds that these stereotypes consign handicapped women to desirelessness and despair.

For Kent, this despair is intolerable. She wants to fill novels and mysteries with a new romance — to portray disabled heroines as vamps, to plunge them into heterosexual love nests and libidinal espionage. Kent argues that non-disabled feminists should reassess their critique of the heterosexual heroine's role and reverse their rejections of the heterosexual love-plot, despite its destructive clichés: "Non-disabled women may, together, be outgrowing the marriage plot; but I, for one, would still warm to the story of a blind woman or a woman with cerebral palsy who falls in love, gets married, and lives happily ever after."

Kent's essay argues that feminist discourse must acknowledge the stratifications, the multivoicedness, and the antagonisms of female speech. A feminist dialogics will insist that our different contexts should merge, but not blur, in our speech. To separate the discourse of heterosexual women with disabilities from the discourse of non-disabled women is to recognize the stratification inherent in different moments of feminist embodiment. The next step is to bring these discourses into dialogic relationship so that neither discourse saturates the other with its ideology — so that neither world view nor mode of embodiment becomes normative. A feminist dialogics does not bear witness to plural speech situations, but to something more difficult than heterogeneity; that is, to the social/ideological contradictions and contradictory goals of diverse feminist speech-worlds.

By outlining the uses of a feminist dialogics among women — its uses for intra-feminist theory and practice — I have suggested that the dialogic imagination can help us to describe and understand women's intertribal conflicts, as well as our hazardous battles with patriarchy. The various chapters in this book take this analysis many steps farther. As the first book-length study of its kind, *Feminism, Bakhtin, and the*

Dialogic is contentious, celebratory, ground-breaking, and contagiously multivoiced.

Both feminist praxis and dialogic thinking emphasize the political struggles of our texts and our lives, insisting that there should be no reign of normative speech without revolt, protest, challenge, invective — in short, without trouble. This volume re-invigorates our quarrels with patriarchy and re-illuminates our debates with one another. These chapters not only work dialogically, but they also challenge and amplify our most cherished feminist assumptions.

Works Cited

Bakhtin, Mikhail M., *The Dialogic Imagination*. Trans. Caryl Emerson and Michael Holquist. Ed. Michael Holquist. Austin: University of Texas Press, 1981.

Brownstein, Rachel. *Becoming a Heroine: Reading about Women in Novels*. New York: Penguin, 1984.

Chapkis, Wendy. "Panel Discussion 2." *Inscriptions* 3/4 (1988): 99–100.

Kent, Deborah. "In Search of a Heroine: Images of Women with Disabilities in Fiction and Drama." *Women with Disabilities: Essays in Psychology, Culture, and Politics*. Ed. Michelle Fine and Adrienne Asch. Philadelphia: Temple University Press, 1988.

Kristeva, Julia. "Psychoanalysis and the Polis." *Critical Inquiry* (1982): 77–92.

Contributors

Dale M. Bauer is associate professor of English and Women's Studies at the University of Wisconsin-Madison. Author of *Feminist Dialogics*, she has also published essays on feminist theory and pedagogy, James, Wharton, and Chopin. Her current work is a book on the connections among reproductive technology, fascism, and Edith Wharton's late novels.

Jaye Berman is assistant professor of English at Villanova University, where she specializes in contemporary American literature. Her essays have appeared in *Contemporary Literature, Dutch Quarterly Review, Perspectives on Contemporary Literature, Midstream, Antithesis*, and a collection on *Joycean Catalogs* edited by Fritz Senn. Her current research is on the Holocaust and parody in popular culture.

Brenda O. Daly, assistant professor of English at Iowa State University, is currently completing a book on the fiction of Joyce Carol Oates for the Ad Feminam series with Southern Illinois University Press. Daly has published additional essays on Oates which have appeared in the University of Minnesota's *Paradigm Exchange* and in *The Journal of Popular Culture*. She is also co-editing a collection, forthcoming from the University of Tennessee Press, called *Novel Mothering*, which includes her essay, "Teaching Alice Walker's *Meridian*." Her essay, "Laughing with, or Laughing at the Young Adult Romance," recently appeared in *The English Journal*.

Josephine Donovan is professor of English at the University of Maine. She is the author of a number of books and articles on feminism and women's literature, the most recent being *After the Fall: The Demeter-Persephone Myth in Wharton, Cather, and Glasgow* (1989).

Diane Price Herndl is assistant professor of English at the University of Vermont. She has published an essay on Charlotte Perkins Gilman, Bertha Pappenheim, and "hysterical" writing and is finishing a book-length study, *Invalid Women: Figuring Feminine Illness in American Fiction and Culture, 1840 – 1940.*

Peter Hitchcock, assistant professor of English, Baruch College, CUNY, wrote *Working-Class Fiction in Theory and Practice: A Reading of Alan Sillitoe* (Ann Arbor: UMI Research Press, 1989). His fields are twentieth-century cultural studies and literary theory. His book-in-progress is called *The Dialogism of the Oppressed.* He says, "I live in the West Side of Manhattan but my heart is in the East End of London."

Deborah Jacobs is assistant professor of English at Drake University. Her work concerns turn-of-the-century British discourse on science and aesthetics. She has also published on the Modern British writer, Iris Murdoch.

Suzanne Kehde is a graduate student at the University of Southern California. She has published short stories in little magazines and an article on feminist theory. Her play, *Everything You Always Wanted,* won the 1988 International Student Playwriting Competition and was produced at Wichita State University. She is currently writing a dissertation on the image of America as Paradise in contemporary British novels, a topic in which she became interested while studying at the University of London as a Fulbright Scholar in 1985 – 86.

Susan Jaret McKinstry is associate professor of English literature and film at Carleton College. She has published articles on Jane Austen, Toni Morrison, Emily Brontë, T. S. Eliot, Emily Dickinson, and Margaret Atwood, and she is currently working on feminist theories of film adaptation.

Patrick D. Murphy, associate professor of English at Indiana University of Pennsylvania, is editor of *Studies in the Humanities.* He has edited *Critical Essays on Gary Snyder* (GK Hall) and *Staging the Impossible* (Greenwood); has coedited Critical Essays on American Modernism (GK Hall), *The Poetic Fantastic* (Greenwood), *Science Fiction from China: Eight Stories* (Praeger), and *Essentials of the Theory of Fiction* (Duke); and has authored over two dozen essays on modern poetry, the fantastic, and feminist issues, many of them employing Bakhtinian dialogics. He is currently writing *Understanding Gary Snyder.*

Mary O'Connor is an assistant professor in the Department of English at McMaster University, teaching courses in comparative literature, modern critical theory, and feminist theory. She has published and given papers on Alice Munro, Bharati Mukerjee, T. S. Eliot, and the British poets of the 1890s, including a book on John Davidson (Scottish Academic Press).

Gail Schwab is an assistant professor of French at Hofstra University, Hempstead, New York. She has published on Flaubert and Bakhtin, as well as on Luce Irigaray, and is currently collaborating with Irigaray on her ongoing research on gender differences both in language use and in attitudes toward love and sex.

Susan Sipple is a doctoral candidate at Miami University in Oxford, Ohio. She is currently at work on her dissertation dealing with the sociology of motherhood as it is represented in American literature of the 1920s and 1930s.

Sheryl Stevenson is assistant professor of English at the University of Akron. Her publications include essays on gender in *The White Devil* and on the female carnivalesque mode, as exemplified in the work of Djuna Barnes. She has also completed an analysis of Stevie Smith's poetry, highlighting its dialogic character.

Patricia Yaeger, associate professor of English at the University of Michigan, has published *Honey-Mad Women* (1988). She has published essays on Chopin, feminist theory, and Southern fiction. Her current project is a study of the Southern grotesque.

Louise Yelin is an assistant professor at SUNY Purchase, where she teaches courses in the novel, nineteenth- and twentieth-century literature in English, and critical theory. She has published essays on Charles Dickens, Christina Stead, and feminist criticism and is currently working on a book entitled *From the Margins of Empire,* a study of twentieth-century women writers from English colonies and former colonies.

Index

A

Aggression, 127
Always Coming Home (Le Guin), 50
Ambivalence, 166, 175
Analysis
  material, 66, 67, 71*n29*
  textual, 67, 71*n29*
Androcentrism, 39, 220, 233
  romantic, 41
Androgyny, 188, 193
A New Home (Kirkland), 90
Anthropocentrism, 4, 48, 52
Anvil, The, 144–145
Apartheid, 6, 219–233
Auerbach, Erich, 88
Austen, Jane, 7, 12, 21*n5*
Author-function, 13–15
Authority: dialogic, 1–2; discipline, 85–
  86; failure of, 5; ideal, 206;
  institutional, 19, 20; interrogation, 123;
  laughter at, 11, 18; masculine, 17;
  overthrow, 201; patriarchal, 75;
  representation, 107; resistance to, 8, 9,
  10; white, 228
Autonomy, 1, 41, 79

B

Bakhtin, Mikhail, 2, 4, 30, 40, 45, 47, 80,
  85, 98, 99–100, 100, 104, 105, 110, 123,
  132, 149, 181, 182, 191, 201, 220, 221;
  Dialogic Imagination, The, 7, 8, 9, 27, 28,
  29, 82*n5*, 86, 185, 190, 199, 203;

homeostasis, 176, 179*n5*; limits of
  dialogics, 233; linguistic model, 57, 67,
  199; *Marxism and the Philosophy of
  Language*, 57–58, 190, 199; model of
  self, 6; novelistic discourse, 7–8;
  Problems of Dostoevsky's Poetics, 99, 126,
  184, 199; *Rabelais and His World*, 9, 73,
  85, 176, 179*n9*; sociolinguism, 219;
  worldview, 101, 242
Barker, Jane, 87, 88
Barker, Pat, 95–115; radical dialogism, 5
Barthelme, Donald, 5, 123–132
Barthes, Roland, 191
Bauer, Dale, 1–6, 67, 68
Bender, Eileen Teper, 177
Benjamin, Jessica, 1
Benjamin, Walter, 231, 232
Berman, Jaye, 123–132; women in
  parody, 5
Bialostosky, Don, 223
Bisexuality, 195*n8*
"Blind Spot in an Old Dream of
  Symmetry; The"/"La Tache aveugle
  d'un vieux vêve de symétrie"
  (Irigaray), 59, 61, 63
Blow Your House Down (Barker, P.), 104
Bonding, women's, 108
Booth, Wayne, 7, 67, 85, 91*n3*, 202, 233
Boxcar Bertha: An Autobiography
  (Thompson), 137–138, 152*n4*
Brontë, Charlotte, 7, 21*n5*
Brontë, Emily, 7, 21*n5*
Brophy, Brigid, 6, 181-194
Brown, Reva, 106
Burger's Daughter (Gordimer), 6, 219–233
Burney, Fanny, 7

C

Canting, 78
Capitalism, 42, 66, 208; failure, 138; hegemony, 51; inequities, 135
Carnival, 28, 123–132, 194, 215, 219, 223, 224, 226, 235*n13*; elements, 157; laughter, 9; logic, 156; power of, 148; of public discourse, 174; theory, 21*n9*, 201
Carnival and Theory" (Russo), 82*n1*
Carroll, David, 8–9, 19
Cavendish, Margaret, 5, 89
Censorship, 85; of public passion, 173
Center, 51; centrifugal force, 48; erotic, 65; hegemonic, 242; rejection of, 25; relation to margin, 51
Centrifugal: dialogism, 189; force, 40, 47, 48, 99, 185, 241, 242; speech, 243
Centripetal: force, 40, 47, 185, 241, 242; monologism, 189; speech, 243
Century's Daughter (Barker, P.), 95–115
Chapkis, Wendy, 241–242, 243
Chronotope, 45, 105, 110, 113, 119*n24*
Cixous, Hélène, 46, 47
Clark, Katerina, 66–67
Class, 3; authenticity, 97; consciousness, 210; hierarchies, 157; identity, 117*n10*; knowledge, 111; language, 104, 105, 227; oppression, 97; prejudice, 118*n17*; relations, 98; roles, 149; sensitivity, 26; social, 46; struggle, 67, 70*n14*, 150; subjectivity, 95; working, 95, 96–115, 228
Clingman, Stephen, 221
Color Purple, The (Walker), 199, 200, 202, 203, 204, 213
Communication: failure, 113–114; identity relations, 95
Community: action, 149; bonds, 112; de-gendered, 209; experience, 105; identity, 105, 116*n4*, 118*n15*; importance, 146; isolation, 155; knowable, 95, 96, 115, 115*n1*; memory, 97, 108, 114; reality of, 201; relations, 112; shattered, 110; sign, 100; underclass, 149; women's, 131, 140, 148, 150; working-class, 108, 148
Control: bodily, 79, 138, 144, 145; masculine, 1, 31; need to, 35; social, 144
Coward, Rosalind, 189

Crime and Punishment (Dostoevsky), 219, 220, 223, 224, 225, 226, 229, 230, 233
Criticism: cultural, 230; dialogical, 220; feminist, 10, 17, 18, 19, 20, 50, 73, 91*n3*; literary, 13, 25, 53*n4*, 57; masculine, 13
Cross-dressing, 75, 76–81, 82*n4*
"Crossdressing, The Theatre and Gender Struggle in Early Modern England" (Howard), 75
Culture: black, 202; consciousness, 79; differences, 73, 81; dominant, 2, 5, 10, 137, 208, 235*n13*; feminine, 20*n2*; gendered, 81; multilingual, 183; myth, 126; official, 138, 146, 147; patriarchal, 5, 39, 66, 128, 129; transient, 146

D

Daly, Brenda O., 5, 155–178
Davis, Natalie, 128
Dead Father, The (Barthelme), 126
de Beauvoir, Simone, 70*n14*
Deconstruction, 25, 26, 61, 200; Derridean, 235*n13*; gender, 190
"Deep Ecology" (Devall/Sessions), 43, 44, 47, 52
Dekker, Thomas, 73–81
Depersonalization, 2
Derrida, Jacques, 26
Development: deconstruction, 51; novelist's, 8; of revolution, 68
Dialogic: character, 51; contact, 28; ecofeminist, 39–54; feminist, 1, 6, 7–20, 96, 220; imagination, 28; language, 189; limitations, 233; strategies, 99; textuality, 67
Dialogic Imagination (Bakhtin), 7, 8, 9, 27, 28, 29, 86, 185, 199, 203
Dialogism: carnivalesque, 5; closed, 65; Irigarayan, 57–69; many-voiced, 190; open, 65; of oppression, 98–99, 117*n9*
Dialogue: angry, 243; limits, 233; related to knowledge, 59
Díaz-Diocaretz, Myriam, 202
Discourse: alternative, 189; androcentric, 233; authoritative, 5; carnivalesque, 189; competing, 132; counter-

hegemonic, 96; cultural, 39; dominant, 4, 189; double-voiced, 100, 104, 106, 202, 222, 234n1; emancipatory, 204; Eurocentric, 233; extra-literary, 156; feminist, 131, 244; indirect, 87; male, 205; marginalizing, 64; Marxist, 220; "master," 60, 66; multiple, 222; novelistic, 7, 8, 12, 13; objectified, 104, 156; official, 86; parodic, 186; of pathos, 226; patriarchal, 99; phallocentric, 61–65; philosophical, 60, 66; private, 3; public, 3, 5, 174; of resistance, 103; scientific, 63, 64, 65, 66; shared, 181, 188; social, 96, 183, 200; subjective, 156; theoretical, 10; women's exclusion, 86–87

"Discourse in Life and Discourse in Art" (Vološinov), 45

"Discourse in the Novel" (Bakhtin), 203

Dock, Leslie A., 192

Domination, male, 2, 43, 65, 156, 201

Donovan, Josephine, 5, 12, 15, 20n2, 85–90

Dostoevsky, Fyodor, 184, 220, 229; polyphony, 226

Doubiago, Sharon, 41

Driver, Paul, 105

DuBois, W. E. B., 202

E

Eagleton, Terry, 8, 12, 13, 25

Eclecticism, 231, 232

Ecocentrism, 52

Ecofeminism, 4–5, 39–54

Economy: capitalist, 42, 135; crisis, 98; failure, 138, 139

Ecosystem, 40, 42; balanced, 43-44

Eliot, George, 8, 21n5, 95

Ellison, Ralph, 202

Emerson, Caryl, 27, 67, 68

"Emphasis Added: Plots and Plausibilities in Women's Fiction" (Miller), 20n2

Essentialism, 68

Ethics of Sexual Difference, The Ethique de la différence sexuelle (Irigaray), 60–61, 63, 66

Ethnocentricity, 220

Eugenics, 143

"Explanation and Culture: Marginalia" (Spivak), 25

F

Fascism, 231, 232

Faulkner, William, 191

Fear: of observation, 140, 145; in poverty, 137

Female: identified with unconscious, 48; language, 126, 130, 131; parody, 185; self-definition, 6; solidarity, 6; speech, 244; subjectivity, 201; voicelessness, 241

"Female Grotesques: Carnival and Theory" (Russo), 21n7, 148-149

Feminine: culture, 20n2; language, 7, 12; logic, 7; sensibility, 12

Feminism, 53n2; adoption by men, 50; black, 199; cultural differences, 81; essentialism in, 68; Eurocentric, 79; liberal, 44; Marxism, 44; materialist, 20, 83n8; monolithic, 1; political, 65; psychoanalytic, 20; radical, 44, 57; socialist, 44, 119n22; suppression of, 44; as threat, 2; transformative, 44; univocal, 1; violence in, 3

Feminist: criticism, 10, 17, 18, 19, 20, 73; dialogic, 1, 6; dialogism, 220; discourse, 244; gender study, 189; interrogation, 41; language, 6, 243; praxis, 245; theory, 53n2

Feminist Dialogics (Bauer), 67

Fiennes, Celia, 88

Fischer, Bram, 221

Fisher, Philip, 89

for colored girls who have considered suicide (Shange), 200, 213

Formal Method in Literary Scholarship, The (Bakhtin/Medvedev), 199

Foucault, Michel, 13–14, 189

"Freedom of Interpretation: Bakhtin and the Challenge of Feminist Criticism" (Booth), 7, 9n3, 67, 85, 202, 233

Freud, Sigmund, 60, 61; theory of unconscious, 27, 48

Freudianism: A Marxist Critique
(Vološinov), 44, 45–46

G

Gallop, Jane, *n22*, 59, 60, 62, 69*n6*
Gates, Henry Louis, 202, 205
Gender, 3; amnesia, 6, 181, 186, 192;
authenticity, 97; categories, 156; codes,
77; conflict, 126; differences, 229;
discrimination, 70*n14*; division of labor,
103, 107; hierarchical system, 41, 75, 77,
157; identity, 181, 182, 186, 187, 188, 193,
194; interrogation, 41; and language,
66, 181–194; oppression, 43, 97;
parody, 181; polarity, 1; politics, 132,
220; psychological issue, 41; restrictions,
31; roles, 125, 138, 141, 148, 149;
sensitivity, 26; significance, 229; social
construction, 149, 194; struggle, 70*n14*,
79; systems, 81; theory, 186; trait, 17;
transvalued, 82*n1*
Gender and the Politics of History (Scott), 73
Geng, Veronica, 123
Gilbert, Sandra, 181
Gilligan, Carol, 42, 88
Gordimer, Nadine, 6, 219–233
Graff, Gerald, 39
Griffin, Susan, 159
Grotesque, 77–78, 144, 148–151, 176,
179*n9*, 201
Gynocriticism, 53*n2*

H

Haines, John, 49
Hegemony, 117*n10*, 231
Henderson, Hazel, 41–42
Herndl, Diane Price, 4, 7–20
Heterarchy, 41–42, 43, 51
Heterogeneity, 157
Heteroglossia, 9, 28, 29, 36, 178, 182, 185,
230, 241, 242, 243; partial, 221; social,
6, 221, 233; women's, 99
Hierarchy: gender, 77; inverting, 28;
masculine, 30, 33; resistance to, 8, 9, 11,
108; sex-gender system, 75; social

relations, 19; subordination, 87;
subversion, 20; value, 89
Hirschkop, Ken, 64
History of Sexuality (Foucault), 189
Hitchcock, Peter, 5, 95–115
Hogan, Linda, 49
Holquist, Michael, 66–67, 157, 163
Homeostasis, 156, 175, 176; Aristotelian-
Freudian, 177; family, 177; social
aspects, 5, 177; theory, 156; violence in,
177–178
Homophobia, *n21*
Howard, Jean E., 75
Humanism: liberal, 85; Marxist, 222;
pluralistic, 4, 39; secular, 39
Hyatt, Mary, 89
Hypotaxis, 87–88, 89, 90

I

Identity: class, 117*n10*; collective, 105, 144;
community, 105, 116*n4*, 118*n15*; crisis,
181; gender, 181, 182, 186, 187, 188, 193,
194; masculine, 123; middle-class, 74;
organic, 173; politics, 2; suppressed,
124; testing, 124; working-class, 110
Ideology: behavioral, 46, 47; official, 46,
47
Imperialism, critical, 73–81
In A Different Voice (Gilligan), 42
Independence, 79; female, 75
"In Search of a Heroine" (Kent), 243–244
Institutionalization, 142–143, 144
In Transit (Brophy), 6, 181–194
Irigaray, Luce, 5, 57–69, 100; pluralism,
11; use of Marxist theory, 62
Irony, 230, 233; critical, 86; novel's use, 86

J

Jacobs, Deborah, 5, 73–81
James, Henry, 4, 29
Jaret McKinstry, Susan, 1–6
Jeffers, Robinson, 49
Johnson, Barbara, 41
Journeys (Fiennes), 88
Joyce, James, 187

K

Kamuf, Peggy, 17
Kaplan, Cora, 107, 201
Kehde, Suzanne, 4, 25–37
Keller, Evelyn Fox, 177
Kent, Deborah, 243–244
Kermode, Frank, 191, 192–193
King, Ynestra, 43
Kirkland, Carolyn, 90
Kolodny, Annette, 14
Kristeva, Julia, 155, 159, 239

L

Labor: hierarchical division, 88;
  intellectual, 88; manual, 88; sexist
  division, 103, 107
Lacan, Jacques, 16, 62, 67; unconscious,
  46
Lafayette, Mme. de, 7
Laing, R. D., 177
Language: acquisition, 27; antisystematic,
  185, 190; awareness, 203; changes, 67;
  class, 98, 104, 105, 227; conventional,
  126; depersonalized, 11; dialogic, 11,
  189; differences, 146; disruptive, 189,
  193–194; "dreck," 124; feminine, 6, 7, 8,
  10, 12, 16–17, 126, 130, 131, 243;
  fictional, 16; gendered, 66, 181–194;
  ideologically charged, 189; internally
  persuasive, 2, 5, 132; literary, 9; "living,"
  191; male, 126, 130; mutilation, 182;
  novelistic, 15–17, 18; official, 11, 86;
  other, 16; patriarchal, 62, 243;
  phallocentric, 68, 99; pluralized, 11;
  poetic, 9; polyphonic, 11; problems, 176;
  public, 2; racial, 227; racist, 231;
  represented, 221; resistance in, 3;
  scientific, 64; shared, 131; social, 58,
  219; stratification, 185, 221, 241; as
  struggle, 241; theory, 183; transient,
  185; unitary, 86, 91$n5$; unofficial, 9;
  usurped, 10
"Laugh of the Medusa, The" (Cixous), 46,
  47
Laughter: ambivalent, 9; at authority, 11,
  18; carnival, 9

Le Guin, Ursula K., 49, 50
Le Sueur, Meridel, 5, 135–151
Limited Inc: a b c (Derrida), 26
Literary Theory: An Introduction (Eagleton),
  25
Literary Women (Moers), 90
Lodge, David, 188
Logic: epic, 159–160; feminine, 7

M

Manipulation, 40
Marginalization, 4, 19, 25–37, 57, 67, 73,
  74, 90, 91$n5$, 96, 117$n9$, 151$n2$, 215,
  235$n13$, 239; of discourse, 64; of
  women, 87
Marriage: as primary institution, 32;
  social emphasis, 36
Marriages and Infidelities (Oates), 157
Marxism, 26, 52, 62, 70$n14$; dialectics, 40;
  humanist, 222
Marxism and the Philosophy of Language
  (Volosinov/Bakhtin), 57–58, 190, 199
Masculine: bias, 2; control, 1, 31;
  hierarchies, 30
Masquerade: women in, 123–132
"Mechanics of Fluids, The"/"Le
  Mécanique des fluides" (Irigaray), 61
Memory, 105, 108, 119$n24$, 156;
  chronotopic, 113; community, 108, 114;
  historical, 115; problems, 116$n2$; use of,
  112
Middleton, Thomas, 73–81
Miller, Nancy, 14, 15, 20$n2$
Mimicry, $n17$, 61, 62
Moers, Ellen, 90
Moi, Toril, 60, 61, 65, 66; essentialism, 68
Monologism, 6, 28, 63, 64, 65, 100, 155,
  163; epic, 157; scientific, 157
Monologue, 129–130, 131
Morality, conventional, 138
Morphology, female, 65
Morrison, Toni, 201
Motherhood: controlled, 143; in poverty,
  151; as weapon, 147
Multivocality, 4
Murphy, Patrick D., 4, 39–54
Mythology, 129; Christian, 30; cultural,
  126

N

Narrative: autobiographical, 90; historical, 116n2; inter-generational, 105; multi-voiced, 4, 224; official mode, 90; point-of-view, 101; polyphonic, 224; working-class, 105
Naylor, Gloria, 6, 200, 201, 210
Nostalgia, 52, 112, 119n25
"Notes from Underground" (Dostoevsky), 184
Novel: bourgeois, 104, 118n18; classic form, 13; experimental, 191; as feminine genre, 13–15, 18; parody, 123–132; postmodern, 188; realistic, 97; sentimentalist, 89; transitional, 156; working-class, 95, 96–115, 105

O

Oates, Joyce Carol, 5, 155–178; dialogism, 156
Observation, fear of, 140, 145
O'Connor, Mary, 6, 199–215
Ohmann, Richard, 50
Oliver, Mary, 49
Ong, Walter J., 87
Opposition: binary, 41; collective, 233; deconstruction, 25; vocal, 233
Oppression: class, 97; dialogism of, 117n9; disruption; gender, 43, 97; internalized, 139; of nature, 53; political, 90; polyphony of, 19; sexual, 229; silence in, 240; violence in, 102; of women, 41, 53, 65, 67, 171; women vs. class, 42–43
Orlando (Woolf), 188, 195n9
"Other," 2, 74; denial of voice, 48; formation, 45; nonhuman, 50; poetics of, 202; related to "one," 58; self-existent entity, 41

P

Paradise (Barthelme), 129
Parataxis, 87, 88
Parodic-travestying forms, 29

Parodies: An Anthology from Chaucer to Beerbohm (Geng), 123
Parody, 28, 123–132, 182, 187, 189, 191, 219; in Bakhtin, 4, 29, 30; context, 29, 36; in discourse, 186; and gender, 181; of revolution, 210; targets, 31; women in, 5
Parole, 45; historicity, 46, 47
Passivity, 126, 141
Patch-work Screen for the Ladies, A (Barker, J.), 87
Pathos, 226, 232
Patriarchal: authority, 2, 75, 156, 201; closure, 155; control, 138; culture, 5, 39, 66, 128, 129; discourse, 99, 205; dualism, 53; hegemony, 47; ideology, 117n6; image of women, 50, 200; instability, 152n4; language, 62, 126, 130, 243; oppression, 171; perceptions, 43; power, 199; society, 126; standards, 148; structure, 41, 68; textuality, 68; voice, 4, 131, 132
Phallocentrism, 41, 58, 61–65, 68, 69
Phallogocentric thought, 12, 14, 15
Phallophor, 31
Piaget, Jean, 27
Pleasure of the Text (Barthes), 191
Pluralism, 39, 41-42, 53n1, 85
Politics: cultural, 149, gender, 220, racial, 220, sexual/textual, 240
Politics and Poetics of Transgression, The (Stallybrass/White), 74
Polylogue, 5, 129
Polyphony, 36, 223, 224, 226, of oppression, 19
Polysyndeton, 89
Polyvocality, 4
Portrait of a Lady (James), 36
Poverty, 135–151
Power: capitalist, 66; of carnival, 148; controlling, 136; development, 147; differentials, 85; disruptive, 139; gender-based, 128; of grotesque, 148–151, 151; institutional, 19; lack of, 139, 141; maintaining, 25; monotonous, 104; of the oppressed, 20; patriarchal, 199; personal, 127; of rage, 138; relinquishing, 19; and style, 85–90; threatened, 144; through dialogue, 126; white, 199

Praxis: affirmative, 39; feminist, 245; fictional, 5; multivoiced, 65; political, 5; use-value, 90
Pride and Prejudice (Austen), 12
Problems of Dostoevsky's Poetics (Bakhtin), 99, 184, 199
Psychoanalysis, n17, 26, 45, 62
"Psychoanalysis and the Polis" (Kristeva), 239
Pykett, Lyn, 106

Q

Questions" (Irigaray), 59

R

Rabelais and His World (Bakhtin), 9, 73, 176, 179n9
Race, 3; language, 227; sensitivity, 26; significance, 229
Racism, 210; and sexual oppression, 229; white opposition, 228
Radcliffe, Ann, 7
Rationality: neutral, 2; overcoming emotion, 48; public, 1
"Reading Women Writing" (Kamuf), 17
Relationship: chronotopic, 110; environmental, 40; gendered, 3; spatial, 110; temporal, 110; time/space, 112; transforming, 67; women and language, 158
Reproduction: choice, 144; control, 14, 138, 143, 144, 146, 147; exploitation, 43
Resistance, 226, 232; to authority, 8, 9, 10; carnivalesque, 176, 179n11; cultural, 3, 4; discourse, 103; hierarchical, 8, 9, 11, 33, 108; models, 73, 74; multivoiced, 8; to official disciplines, 88; organized, 146; polyphonic, 8; by positionality, 3; to subordination, 5, 86, 90; to unifying disciplines, 86; working-class, 96
Reuther, Rosemary, 42
Revolution, 210; development, 68
Rich, Adrienne, 41
Rise of the Novel, The (Watt), 11, 90
Riviere, Joan, 124

Roaring Girl, The (Dekker/Middleton), 5, 73–81
Robinson, Lillian, 73
Rochefort, Christiane, 15–16
Rose, Mary Beth, 75
Rowe, John Carlos, 32
Russo, Mary, 148; on carnival, 21n7; grotesque, 82n1

S

Salleh, Ariel Kay, 44, 47
"Salvation Home" (Le Sueur), 138, 146, 147, 148
Sand, George, 8, 21n5
Scholes, Isabel, 105
Scholes, Robert, 12
Schreiner, Olive, 223
Schwab, Gail M., 5, 57–69
Scott, Joan W., 73
Scudery, Mme. de, 7
Sea Changes (Kaplan), 107
Self: awareness, 208; concept, 155; definition, 6, 187, 188, 219; fictitious, 193; formation, 45; multiple, 193; reliance, 228; unified, 201
Sensational Designs (Tompkins), 20n2
"Sequel to Love" (Le Sueur), 138, 142
Sex, Class, and Culture (Robinson), 73
Sexegesis, 194
Sexism, 135
Sex-typing, 53n1
Sexual: abuse, 172; ambivalence, 188; conduct dictated, 142; ideology, 187; interpretation, 188; jealousy, 101; oppression, 229; promiscuity, 79, 141; transgression, 135–151
Sexuality: discouraging, 138; in poverty, 151
Sexual/Textual Politics (Moi), 60, 66
Shakespeare, William, 77
Shange, Ntozake, 6, 200, 213
Sign: community, 100; ownership, 100
Silence, 13, 20, 50, 136, 149, 156, 171, 209, 226, 232, 239; before authority, 108; contexts, 3; in feminine language, 10
"Silence is Broken, The" (Donovan), 12
Sipple, Susan, 5, 135–151
Smith-Rosenberg, Carroll, 189

Snow White (Barthelme), 123–124
Snyder, Gary, 49, 50
Social: agencies, 137; awareness, 108; class, 46; conflict, 181; control, 138, 144; expectations, 35; heteroglossia, 221, 233; hierarchy, 107; interaction, 40, 47, 67; language, 219; order, 81; relations, hierarchical, 19; revolt, 149; stasis, 155; topography, 76
Society, women's place, 20*n*2
Sociological stylistics, 10
Solidarity, 132, 139; empowerment, 210; female, 6; inter-generational, 98
Souls of Black Folk (DuBois), 202
Speaking subject: instinct, 48; nature, 48–49; nonhuman, 49, 50; women, 50
Speculum of Other Women, 59, 60, 62, 66
Speech: inner, 27, 46, 47, 68, 184; outer, 46, 47, 68; reported, 205, 221
Spivak, Gayatri Chakravorty, 25, 26, 27, 29, 40; zone of deconstruction, 29
Stallybrass, Peter, 74, 226
Standpoint theory, 2
Status quo: altering, 67; perpetuating, 78
Stein, Gertrude, 89
Steiner, George, 183
Stereotyping, 123, 200, 244; sex-role, 42
Sterilization, 138, 143, 144, 146, 147
Stevenson, Sheryl, 6, 181-194
Stewart, Susan, 185
Story of an African Farm, The (Schreiner), 219, 220, 223, 228, 230, 233
Style: "dashaway," 90; devices, 90; "gossiping," 90; paratactic, 88, 89, 92*n*10; plain, 87, 89; and power, 85–90; unofficial, 88; women's, 87
Subordination: hierarchical, 87; resistance, 5; women, 31
Subversion, 78, 79; in cross-dressing, 75; of hierarchies, 20; models, 74; of patriarchy, 76; of power structure, 36
Superego, 48
Survival, 139; species, 44; trangressive behavior, 141

T

Tempest, The (Shakespeare), 77
Textuality: monologistic, 69; patriarchal, 68

"They Follow Us Girls" (Le Sueur), 138, 144–147, 146
This Sex Which is Not One (Irigaray), 61
Thompson, Bertha, 137–138, 152*n*4
Tompkins, Jane, 20*n*2
To Speak is Never Neutral/Parler n'est jamais neutre (Irigaray), 58, 64, 65, 66
Totalization, 40; opposition, 51
"Toward a Women's Poetics" (Donovan), 20*n*2
Transgression: carnivalesque, 223; sexual, 135–151
Transsexuality, 6, 241, 243
Transvestitism, 124
Turner, Victor, 132

U

Ukhtomsky, Aleksky Alekseevich, 176
Ulysses (Joyce), 187
Unconscious: articulation, 40, 46, 47; identified with female, 48; recognition by Freud, 48
Union Street (Barker), 97–115

V

Value: ecological, 42; egalitarian, 2; exchange, 42; female, 16; hierarchical, 89; male, 16, 33; of manhood, 31; power structure, 36; sexual, 75; social, 75; surplus, 103, 107; use, 42, 90
Ventriloquy, 99
Violence: familial, 137, 177; in feminism, 3; in homeostasis, 177–178; in oppression, 102; universal, 229
Voice: authorial, 28; authoritative, 2, 115, 132; of black women, 199–215; communal, 204; competing, 6; denial, 159; dissenting, 19, 32; dominant, 4, 7, 215; double, 9; female, 96, 103, 159, 171, 173, 207; gendered; marginal, 4, 19, 25–37, 240; monologic, 28; multiple, 9, 11, 17, 29, 101, 214; of "other," 48; patriarchal, 4, 131, 132, 207; of the poor, 171; private, 2; public, 243; rebellious, 146; silenced, 11; unitary, 156

Vološinov, V. N., 44, 199; reported speech, 221
Vygotsky, Lev, 27, 36

W

Walker, Alice, 6, 199, 200, 202, 203
Warren, Karen J., 44
Watt, Ian, 11, 12, 15, 90
Wegelin, Christof, 30
White, Allon, 74, 226
Williams, Raymond, 95, 99
Willis, Susan, 200, 201
Wings of the Dove, The (James), 29–37
Wollstonecraft, Mary, 89
"Womanliness as Masquerade" (Riviere), 124
Women: disabled, 243–244; and exclusion, 10; function, 171; patriarchal image, 200; sexual love, 208; struggles, 150; subordination, 31, 235*n13*; transient, 135–151; unemployed, 135–151; working-class, 95–115, 96–115, 116*n4*
Women and the Politics of Appearance (Chapkis), 242

"Women in Men's Clothing" (Rose), 75
Women of Brewster Place, The (Naylor), 200, 201, 210, 213
Women on the Breadlines (Le Sueur), 135–151
"Women on the Market"/"Le Marché des femmes" (Irigaray), 61, 62
"Women on Top" (Davis), 128
Wonderland (Oates), 5–6, 155–178
Woolf, Virginia, 89, 188, 195*n9*
Wordsworth, Dorothy, 49
Working-class: exploitation, 228; identity, 110

Y

Yaeger, Patricia, 6, 99, 239–245
Yelin, Louise, 6, 219–233
Young, Robert, 100

Z

Zone: of contact, 86, 87, 89; of deconstruction, 29; unofficial, 90